Henry Marshall Tory

Henry Marshall Tory in 1925. University of Alberta Archives.

Henry Marshall Tory

A Biography

E.A. Corbett

With a New Introduction by

Doug Owram

Foreword by

Chancellor Sandy A. Mactaggart

The University of Alberta Press

This edition published by
The University of Alberta Press
Athabasca Hall
Edmonton, Alberta
Canada T6G 2E8

Originally published as *Henry Marshall Tory: Beloved Canadian* in 1954 by The Ryerson Press, Toronto, Ontario. Reissued by permission of Paul D. Corbett and Joan Corbett Fairfield.

ISBN 0-88864-250-4

Canadian Cataloguing in Publication Data

Corbett, E.A. (Edward Annand), 1884-1964.
Henry Marshall Tory: a biography

Originally published: Toronto: Ryerson Press, 1954
Included bibliographical references
ISBN 0-88864-254-0

1. Tory, H.M. (Henry Marshall), 1864-1947.
2. Educators—Canada—Biography. 3. Education, Higher—Canada—History. I. Title.
LA2325.T6C67 1992 378.71'092 C92-091395-4

The portrait of Henry Marshall Tory by F. Varley used on the cover hangs in the Senate Chamber in the Arts Building. It is from the University of Alberta Permanent Collection and is reproduced by permission of University Collections.

Printed by Hignell Printing Ltd., Winnipeg, Manitoba, Canada
Printed on acid-free paper. ∞

Contents

FOREWORD

Dr. Henry Marshall Tory was instrumental in the creation and development of several major educational and research institutions in Canada. In 1905, he wrote a report that resulted in the creation of the University of British Columbia. He was the founding President of Canada's second largest university, the University of Alberta, and he guided it through its first twenty formative years. Most men would then retire, but he had already been appointed as first Chairman of the National Research Council of Canada. He subsequently became its President, and continued on to become the founding (unpaid) President of Carleton University in Ottawa. It is hard to imagine that a single man could accomplish so much in one lifetime.

Those who admire and love these remarkable institutions will learn new insights from E.A. Corbett's biography of Henry Marshall Tory. Those who have no connections with them will find this a simple story of an unusually capable man who deserves to be better known to all of us who, with smaller shoes, attempt to follow in his pioneering footsteps.

It is a nostalgic biography that is contained within these pages. We no longer believe in heros as we used to, and in this work of the 1950s, the author's admiration of his subject has a different quality than that of a contemporary writer. It is perhaps, less scholarly than we would expect today, but it is filled with the zest of the times, a flavour you may find enjoyable.

It is through the efforts and generosity of The Friends of The University of Alberta that this biography of Henry Marshall Tory has been reissued. The Friends' sole object is to support the University by donations of their time and their finances. The first organization of its kind open to the general public, they were officially established by the Board of Governors in 1943 and have been responsible for many useful projects ever since.

Dr. Harvey Hebb, an old friend, who for many years presided over the meetings of the Friends, approached me last year in my position as fourteenth Chancellor of the University, and described how the only biography of our founding President had been out of print for so long that no copies were currently available. He had approached the University of Alberta Press to request that they issue a reprint, but its mandate requires it to publish contemporary scholarly works. Dr. Hebb advised me that the University Press Committee had regretfully concluded that a reissue of Tory's biography did not fall within these guidelines.

But Dr. Hebb did not give up easily. After quantifying thc financial risks, he persuaded, first myself, subsequently the publisher and the committee of the University Press, and finally the current executive of the Friends that the original biography of such an original man deserved our support. Dr. Doug Owram of the Department of History was then approached to write a new Introduction to set Corbett's biography of Henry Marshall Tory in its historical context.

It is an honour and a privilege to acknowledge the contributions of those whose perseverance and generosity have made the reissue of this biography possible.

Chancellor Sandy A. Mactaggart
March 1992

ACKNOWLEDGEMENTS

THE UNIVERSITY OF ALBERTA PRESS would like to thank Paul D. Corbett and Joan Corbett Fairfield, the copyright holders, for permission to reissue their father's biography, *Henry Marshall Tory: Beloved Canadian.* Mr. Corbett also kindly lent the Press his personal copy of the original book.

Dr. Harvey Hebb, an active member of The Friends of The University of Alberta, wanted Tory's biography back in print because of Tory's contribution to higher education in Canada and, especially important to The University of Alberta, as the history of the first President of the University. He originally proposed the project to the Press in 1988 and, resolutely, over the next four years, made his proposal a reality. His dedication to this project is appreciated. The Friends of The University of Alberta and Chancellor Sandy A. Mactaggart were convinced by Dr. Hebb to provide the necessary funding to reissue the book. The Alberta Foundation for the Arts also provided funds towards publication.

The Press would like to acknowledge Dr. Doug Owram of the Department of History for preparing a new Introduction to this new edition of Corbett's *Henry Marshall Tory* and Chancellor Sandy A. Mactaggart for writing a new Foreword. David Norwood, as Chairman of The Friends of The University of Alberta, and Mary Totman of the Senate Office also have been extremely helpful in seeing this project to fruition. Finally, Dr. Owram and the Press would especially like to thank Trude McLaren of the University Archives for all her help.

Henry Marshall Tory in 1908. University of Alberta Archives.

INTRODUCTION

Doug Owram

E.A. CORBETT'S BIOGRAPHY of Henry Marshall Tory, first published in 1954, is reissued here with the original text. It is a well-written, thoughtful biography of one of Canada's leading educators by a person who knew and admired him. The subtitle of Corbett's original work, "Beloved Canadian," reflects the author's admiration for Tory and something of the nationalist sense of the post-war period. It is not really very descriptive however. More meaningful perhaps is a sentence used in the original Foreword by Tory's successor as President of the University of Alberta, Robert Wallace. To Wallace, Tory was "essentially a builder." Undoubtedly his role as "builder" is what most stands out about Tory, for he was a unique Canadian university president. Though he was a competent administrator of established bodies, he made his mark by establishing new institutions and giving them life. The McGill-affiliated predecessor to the University of British Columbia, the University of Alberta, the Alberta Research Council, the National Research Council and Carleton University all look to Henry Marshall Tory as their founder. This is a pattern of accomplishment (and restlessness) unmatched in the history of Canadian education.

Tory's remarkable career began in very unremarkable conditions. He was born in Guysborough, Nova Scotia, shortly before Confederation. His roots were Scottish but both sides of his family had lived in Nova Scotia for several generations. Tory's family were farmers and he grew up in the comfortable poverty that characterized many rural Maritime families in the later nineteenth century. Religion and education were both important to his family and his community. From early boyhood Tory was exposed to intellectual issues, whether listening to debates about the nature of baptism or reading whatever books came to hand. While Tory was still a youth it seems that he and his family had decided that he would go on to an educated position. Nothing in his own diaries or in Corbett's biography indicates that Tory ever intended to continue the family farming tradition.

Tory found his career in education. He began as a teacher in the local school but, as with many other individuals in this era, school teaching was not seen as a long-term career for the truly ambitious and intelligent male. It was a jumping-off place and as soon as he had saved sufficient funds Tory headed off to McGill with the intention of obtaining a university education and assuming a position in the Methodist ministry. Hard working and intelligent, he was tremendously successful. Undergraduate education was followed by graduate work and eventually a faculty position at McGill. His religious commitment was more ambivalent though. He did do some pastoral work but science took over as his field of study and ministerial activities dwindled.

As Corbett's biography clearly demonstrates, Tory's attachment to building and to the West came as much by accident as anything. In the West of Canada there was, as of 1900, only one significant institution of higher learning—the multi-college University of Manitoba. Yet from the late 1890s through World War I the region grew tremendously. The vast moving frontier of North America had at last reached the Canadian West. Propelled by declining freight rates, high wheat prices, and tremendous investment from overseas the West filled in during these decades. Two new provinces were created. Prairie wheat and lumber from British Columbia became major Canadian exports. From other parts of Canada, the United States, Europe and elsewhere immigrants flowed to the "last best West," as the area was popularly known. Population increased from an 1891 figure of fewer than 350,000 to 1,735,000 twenty years later.

Such growth created tremendous need and tremendous opportunity. A rudimentary social infrastructure had to be transformed rapidly to deal with the tremendous growth that was taking place. The specific purposes of roads, bridges, schools, churches, prisons and hospitals are obviously quite different. The history of their development all shows the same pattern however. In every case the growing population made existing facilities totally inadequate. No sooner were newer, larger facilities built than even larger and better ones were demanded. In the meantime those responsible desperately sought to keep up. Funds were always in short supply but even more important was the need for capable individuals to plan and develop the new facilities. In this formative stage well-laid plans could, after all, benefit the region for a long time to come. Bad ones could force expensive changes in the future. The challenge was to find the people who could build with one eye on the pressures of the moment and another on the long term.

Higher education was no different than other areas. On the frontier education was an extremely practical matter and often viewed akin to roads, hospitals and prisons! An attractive educational system was yet another of those inducements that a region could offer incoming settlers. A university was, however small or new, the crown to that educational system and "proof" that the new community was not a backwater. In other words, the development of new universities was a part of the "booster" spirit which characterized much of western development. Only a small percentage of westerners expected their children to attend university. For a much larger percentage, however, the university was an important part of the movement from frontier to metropolis. There was no desire for an ivory tower institution—an Oxford in the wilderness. Rather, the university was supported by government and business because it was seen as an integral part of making a new community. It was an educational, political, social and business investment all in one.

This was not the tradition in Canada. Though universities had always been seen as a part of the progress of a community, nineteenth century Canadian universities had (McGill partly excepted) been created for primarily religious reasons. The core of the colonial universities had been small theological schools created to prepare students in the Ministry. The colonial universities were thus built around church support and officially tied to a single denomination. Presbyterian universities like Queen's, Baptist ones like McMaster, or Catholic ones like Laval sought to preserve and extend the faith. There were some exceptions. After much controversy the University of Toronto was established as a nondenominational institution. Even there, however, the heart of the university were the various religious colleges: Anglican Trinity, Methodist Victoria, Catholic St. Michaels.[1] Curriculum soon expanded, of course, as universities sought to meet the needs of diverse student populations and a rapidly growing country. Nevertheless, the heart and soul of the earlier university system was religious.

By the time of the western boom, however, the values upon which institutions had developed, were changing. Narrow protestant denominationalism was receding in the face of a new ecumenical spirit. Religion as a whole seemed threatened by new currents of thought that emphasized empirical testing over faith. Secularism was abroad in the land and many of the old wars over dogma seemed increasingly petty and irrelevant in the face of such a momentous change. As one intellectual of the time commented "Men simply do not believe, and it is not true, that the parish priest and the church of to-day are still the focus or centre of illumination, or civilization, or inspiration that they used to be."[2]

Nowhere was the sense of change more profound than in the university. In the decades surrounding World War I the nature of the curriculum, the training of the typical professor, and the very way in which knowledge was approached changed. To put it briefly, the traditional system assumed religious affiliation and common theological beliefs created the guiding spirit of the university. The newer approach emphasized the notion of the secular university resting not on faith but on a spirit of critical inquiry. As the new values took hold the older denominationalism became a liability. Denominationalism became an embarrassment to the forward-looking, self-satisfied age of the early twentieth-century Canada. Thus the new universities of Saskatchewan, Alberta and British Columbia were founded on the new state model rather than on the old denominational one.

Amidst all the change on the frontier and in the university Tory was comfortably situated at McGill and seems never to have travelled to the West. It is therefore unlikely that he had thought much of either the West or its educational needs. Yet both McGill University and Henry Marshall Tory were in many ways well suited to the new spirit of education that was emerging in the West. McGill was situated in Canada's most national city—where the Canadian Pacific Railway had its headquarters and where the fur trade had earlier dominated the vast continental hinterland. It was still, in the early twentieth century, the centre of Canadian business and its hinterland stretched to the Pacific Ocean. Moreover, as the voice of English Protestantism in a French-Catholic province, McGill was not affiliated closely either with the provincial government or with a particular religious denomination. It was, in that sense, a much more independent university than most in Canada. This meant that it was not tied down by narrow particularisms or traditions that would have made it inappropriate as a model for the new booster universities of the West.[3]

What is striking about Tory is the way his own career and views mirrored the larger tendencies in religious and educational thought. Here was a man brought up in a strict denominational tradition, educated for the ministry and profoundly religious in his youth. Yet as time went on he became a tireless opponent of denominationalism, a mathematician and physicist, and thereby an embodiment of the new empirical university. He was, by the early 1900s, also well-suited to the emerging values of the West. Henry Marshall Tory seems to have absorbed a strong dose of that loose middle-class reformist ideology known as progressivism. Progressivism included many things and over the years headed off in pursuit of many causes. In general, though, it was characterized by an attachment to the employment of modern scientific and social scientific means in order to encourage reform. The educated individual, attached to modern ideas and values, had the capacity and the duty to improve society. Phrases like "social engineering," "the search for order," "uplift and efficiency" have been used over the years to capture the spirit of this reformist age.[4] Tory was no radical but he was a dedicated believer in the sorts of values progressivism espoused.

When the opportunity came Tory did not hesitate. He cut his teeth as a builder fighting some very vicious political battles over the establishment of a McGill affiliated institution in British Columbia in 1905. Three years later, fellow McGill graduate A.L. Rutherford, first Premier of Alberta, invited Tory to head the newly legislated provincial university. Before long Tory was once again immersed in political and tactical battles. He did not seem to mind, however. He had a strong political knack and an eye for what it required to create a university. He made some excellent choices in early faculty appointments, asserted the importance of high standards and worked feverishly to turn the paper university into one that had a real existence. Corbett details the early shaky years but these were to be expected. What is revealing is that the University was, within just a few years, well-established in many areas. By the autumn of 1908 the university was functioning in temporary quarters. Within a few more years it had its own buildings, a fairly well developed curriculum and had asserted its control over the field of higher education in the Province.

Tory's progressivism quickly came to the fore in his new administrative and building role. His vision of the new western university was not a colonial one in which he would recreate the glories of Oxford or Cambridge. Instead he gloried in the newness of the institution. As he later argued, western universities had an unparalleled opportunity to develop "unhampered by fixed traditions." The modern university, he continued, was the product of public demand and "such institutions must be conducted in such a way as to relate them as closely as possible to the life of the people." Tory's vision of the university was a practical place, designed not to preserve ancient traditions but to "reach directly or indirectly the mass of the people" (100). At his first convocation address he repeated the theme with blunt succinctness. "The modern state university is a people's institution" (122).

Tory's self-conscious rejection of tradition and isolation in favour of an active, involved, even populist university was one of the great reasons for his success in the West. His ideas fit the values of the booster community who saw the university as an instrument for growth rather than as a guardian of culture. It fit the pragmatic political circumstances of the region where an unrooted population and lack of tradition meant that the new institution had to sell itself to the public. Tory never forgot this and his efforts to establish and expand the University over the years were based on the belief that the university had continually to prove its usefulness.

Nowhere was this more apparent than in the extramural activities of the new university. From the beginning one of the highest priorities Tory had was for the university to reach beyond its normal constituents. Tory travelled thousands of miles and visited most of the towns and villages of the province. His staff logged even more miles. This was an age before radio and a visit from a "distinguished" university professor (they were all assumed to be distinguished) attracted a large and attentive audience. Lectures were offered on physics, history, literature and whatever else a professor might feel competent to speak on. These occasions gave isolated communities a chance for self-improvement and, not incidentally, a social get-together. Corbett's recounting of one poster nicely sums up the nature of the occasion. "Come and hear Dr Broadus lecture on Shakespeare and enjoy yourselves afterwards at a dance" (124).

This element of frontier outreach is also evident in the way in which the university developed. The Arts and Science Faculty came first of course. Thereafter, however, Tory spent a great deal of effort establishing areas of study that would have a direct resonance with a frontier population. The Department of Extension was created in 1912 as a means of coordinating and formalizing all those travelling lectures. The early years, once characterized as the "magic lantern" era for the slide shows that accompanied so many of the talks, were a combination of chaos and tremendous energy.[5] Corbett's account captures this spirit well. It also demonstrates just how important Tory believed the public lectures were to the university. Equally illustrative of Tory's vision was the establishment in 1918 of the Department of Household Economics. The establishment of such a faculty before many that, in older universities would have claimed pride of place, once again reveals Tory's orientation toward the public and practical. In the West, however, the idea of scientific home management seemed an important goal. It accorded with the progressive notion that all modern life could be made more efficient and thereby more comfortable through the application of scientific techniques. It also appealed to various rural and farm movements which wanted to see home life on the farm improved lest families be tempted away by the lure of city comforts. Finally, it was very much in line with Tory's desire to show that the university was concerned with the issues of the day and with the lives of the average Albertan.[6]

Tory's efforts to reach out to the public were not without political purpose. Tory also believed that in a small frontier province like Alberta, it was crucial that the meagre resources available to higher education be concentrated on one institution. Not surprisingly he believed that the appropriate institution was the University of Alberta. Through his years as President he fought a tenacious, consistent and largely successful battle with those elements which sought to set up alternative institutions. Medicine, law and other professional standards were brought under University control. Tory was also able to maintain a strong university presence in Agriculture although he was not able to overcome the desire for parallel technical colleges. Much was at stake in these battles: metropolitan ambition (Calgary was furious at the government's decision to concentrate everything in the capital), the direction of professional licensing and the prestige of the university itself. That Tory was largely successful in the face of such diverse interests says much about his political as well as managerial skills. His continued demonstration that the university could reach out to the people of the province proved invaluable in his search for public support for his institution.

The belief that education was a populist matter led Tory to leave the University of Alberta, albeit temporarily, to head the Khaki University. This was a thoroughly idealistic institution, dedicated to improving the life of the mind of soldiers on active duty. Behind it lay the grim dedication of Canadians to the increasingly vicious First World War. From the beginning the problem of maintaining high democratic and personal ideals while engaged in a modern industrial total war troubled Canadians at home. As one chaplain recounted on his return from the front, the war severely tested humanity's ability to hang on to higher values. "Do you wonder that the hardest fight for these men is not to hold their trenches but their visions?.... It is difficult for idealism to survive in wallow and slaughter and vermin, and stable floors for beds and crouching dugouts for billets."[7]

The Khaki University was intended to offer soldiers a distraction from day-to-day army routine; a distraction that would help encourage a sense of improvement among young men cut off from their normal lives. As Corbett discusses in detail, the movement began sporadically under the YMCA. Then, in 1917, Tory was asked to take the bits and pieces and put them together into some sort of coherent organization. The War was the great moral obsession of the age and there was never any doubt that Tory would accept a chance to play his part—especially when that part involved educational building.

Corbett portrays the accomplishments of the Khaki University in positive terms, referring to the 50,000 men who enrolled in classes either in the scattered lecture theatres or at the centralized institution at Ripon. No doubt the Khaki University did do much good but its significance was not as great as its supporters had hoped. Tory and his supporters overcame a myriad of obstacles in accomplishing what they did but two problems could not be resolved. The first had to do with the attitude to the war itself. The

Canadian government went into the war in 1914 without any plans for handling the social disruptions of modern warfare. There were none of the planning committees, programs or benefits packages provided in the World War II for example. Such efforts as existed were voluntary. The lecture series of the YMCA, which preceded the Khaki University, was typical of this sort of effort.

As the war dragged on and the number of casualties mounted the government realized that this was not like the more limited wars of the past. Total war meant involvement in nonmilitary aspects of the conflict. By 1917 everything from veterans' pensions to post-war land settlement schemes were being discussed. Citizen volunteerism was being transformed into government policy.[8] The consolidation of the Khaki University was thus part of a much larger shift in assumptions about the nature of the war. The trouble was that by 1917 there was too little time for the new attitude to be fully effective. The war ended in 1918 just as Tory's efforts were beginning to bear fruit.

The end of the war brought the second unresolvable problem. Military and government planners presumed that there would be a long transition period between the end of conflict and the demobilization of the army in Europe. This was partly due to transport problems and partly to the desire to ensure that the allied army did not melt away before final peace terms were settled. This raised the possibility of several hundred thousand soldiers free from active duty but a long way from home. The Khaki University seemed an ideal means of ensuring that the soldiers were doing something useful in the interval. For those who did enrol the University was a way of passing the time, learning something and perhaps gaining credits for further study when they returned to Canada. Even the best intentioned efforts, however, could not alter the overwhelming desire on the part of most soldiers to get home as quickly as possible. Morale plummeted and riots broke out.[9] Mobilization plans had to be stepped up and the Khaki University soon found itself with a dwindling clientele. By 1920 Tory was back in Canada, his wartime idealism unshaken.

Tory returned to the University of Alberta after the war and he remained there until 1928. Corbett's biography deals only briefly with these post-war years. Other sources indicate that Tory continued to run the institution energetically along the lines he had established in the first few years. Once it got through the immediate post-war economic turbulence, the province of Alberta grew steadily through the decade. The University grew along with it. Indeed, there was a sharp increase in Canadian university enrolment generally in the 1920s and between 1918 and 1929 Alberta expanded considerably. Aside from the creation of Household Economics, there was the beginning of a full-degree program in Medicine, a Bachelor of Commerce program and the expansion of Pharmacy from a one-year diploma to a full-degree program. Buildings delayed by the war were completed though Tory found his earlier ambitious plans could not be realized. Tory managed the University competently. Now that it was on a firm footing, however, Tory's role as builder was somewhat muted. It was characteristic that he began to turn his attention elsewhere, for in Ottawa a new challenge was developing.

Science was an increasingly important public issue in the first decades of the twentieth century. Industrialization created demands for newer and more effective production techniques. Success stories like Ontario Hydro demonstrated the impact that scientific change could have. The emphasis of the progressive era on the necessity for expertise and professionalism related closely to the emphasis on science. The war itself—the first great modern industrial war—demonstrated just how important technology had become. Scientific education, research and application of new ideas seemed the only way that Canada could take its rightful place in the world.

Several initiatives developed out of this complex of forces. Some of the most important involved Tory. As a scientist and a progressive, Tory very much believed in the importance of scientific development to society. He also recognized that it was yet another area where university could widen its public role. Thus, when he returned to Alberta after the war he became actively involved in pursuing the ideas of a group of businessmen on the need for a provincial research facility. With his usual enthusiasm, Tory travelled around the continent seeking appropriate models for the institution, while, at the same time, lobbying the provincial government to provide funding. By 1921 he had built yet another new institution. Alberta was the first province to establish a provincially funded research council—the Scientific and Industrial Research Council of Alberta.[10] It is the direct forerunner of the present-day Alberta Research Council.

The same scientific enthusiasm of the age also created initiatives at the federal level. One of the most important was the creation and development of the National Research Council in Ottawa. Created shortly after the war, the NRC was initially only an administrative organization handing out research fellowships. By 1923 when Tory was appointed president it had neither land, research staff nor laboratories. This was not what its proponents had envisaged. Even though the presidency of the organization was a part-time position Tory, not surprisingly, set out to achieve the goal of a fully-funded national centre of scientific research. To do so he used the same techniques applied in Alberta. The NRC under Tory sought to show the public its usefulness. Emphasis was put on the practical side of scientific research. Great publicity was given to funds given out that promised immediate economic benefit. Practical projects and maximum publicity were employed by Tory in order to make the politicians and public want to fund the new institution. By 1928 he had succeeded and the NRC developed its own laboratories and research projects. The Presidency had been consuming more and more of Tory's time even before this. Now it was a full-time job and Tory left the University of Alberta to become the first full-time head of the NRC.

Tory's years at the NRC were successful and those around him might have expected this position to serve as a graceful exit from public life. He was 63-years old when he moved from the University of Alberta to Ottawa and the seven-year appointment as

President put him well past retirement age. Nonetheless, as Corbett recounts, Tory's departure from the NRC was tinged by bitterness. R.B. Bennett was Prime Minister at the end of Tory's term and Bennett well-remembered Tory's long-time Liberal connections. As Corbett recounts neither individual was exactly gracious at the end. Tory was bitter but, to be fair, his earlier efforts to consolidate higher education in Edmonton, in supporting the efforts of Liberal premiers like Rutherford and Sifton, indicate he had done little to deserve any particular magnanimity from the former Calgary Conservative MLA.

Tory was one of those people for whom retirement is not a natural state. Though well into his seventies by the time World War II broke out he undertook one final act of educational development. He was instrumental in establishing Carleton College in order to meet the growing demands of the Ottawa area for adult education. Very quickly the system expanded into a regular degree granting institution and would, in later years, expand into the present-day Carleton University. Tory did not live to see that day but his death in early 1947 was, appropriately enough, while he was still active as Chairman of Board and President of Carleton. Somehow it is hard to imagine Tory as an inactive pensioner.

E.A. Corbett's biography of Tory is intelligent, well-written and perceptive. It also comes from the heart. Corbett was a fellow Nova Scotian, McGill graduate and teacher at the Khaki University. When he joined the University of Alberta after the war he began a career as a builder in his own right. His accomplishments include the Banff Centre of Fine Arts and the Canadian Association of Adult Education. Even more than Tory, Corbett saw education in terms of its ability to reach out and touch the lives of average Canadians. Both Tory's philosophy and career, therefore, were something Corbett readily understood.

It is hardly surprising, then, that Corbett's biography of Tory is not a distant impersonal analysis of the individual. It is a successful attempt by a personal friend and admirer to record the life of a man that Corbett saw as a great Canadian. This gives the volume that follows both strengths and weaknesses. The strength comes in the confident familiarity and the honest praise for a man who, undoubtedly, deserves much praise for a remarkable life. The disadvantage is the lack of distance. Corbett is not uncritical of Tory but the perspective from which his biography is written makes criticism incidental in the study of a great man. There are thus times when the reader might want to know more. At one point, for example, Corbett refers to Tory's "many enemies" (199). Why? Was there an element of ruthlessness in Tory's determination and an element of scheming in his manipulation of events? To what degree was his success as a builder dependent upon a hard determination that is glossed over? These and other questions are not answered nor could one expect a volume with this purpose to do so.

There are other gaps in the Corbett biography. In the tradition of both the genre of biography as tribute and the age in which it was written, Tory's public and private lives are kept distinct. Once he passes his "formative years" his private life all but disappears. We know little of his hobbies or leisure activities, if he had any. Most notable, however, is the absence of any discussion of his wife. We are told that Annie Frost was a well-educated woman whose home, near McGill, was opened to students by her parents. Once they are married, however, she plays practically no part in the biography except to note her death after more than forty years of marriage. Obituaries praise her "warm hospitality," "womanliness" and notes that they had no children.[11] Other than that there is little known about her. Her role in supporting Tory, his sense of family and family life all remain obscure. Yet recent biographies have indicated just how important the marital relationship can be to public figures.[12]

The unwillingness of Corbett to enter the private world of Henry Marshall Tory also inhibits discussion in another important area. Tory was raised, as has been mentioned, in a very religious atmosphere. In nineteenth century Guysborough religion was extremely important and Tory seems to have undergone a personal conversion during his youth. His decision to join the Methodist ministry certainly indicates a commitment that went far beyond the ordinary, even for the religious age in which he was brought up. He attended Theological College at McGill, gave sermons regularly in local churches and was ordained by the Methodist Church as a young adult. Yet thereafter his religion faded away. It seems to have played consistently less of a role, at least in his public life, as the years went on. His views on education became strongly anti-denominational. He ceased at some relatively early point to take an active part as a preacher. Then, in 1906 at the age forty he resigned his ministry in the Methodist Church. Thereafter religion plays little part in Corbett's biography of Tory.

Yet religion may be the most important single ingredient in understanding Tory. Philosophically Tory was a Christian idealist.[13] This broad philosophical creed emphasized the sense of community and the individual's responsibility to behave in a committed and moral way toward that community. It was a crucial element in much of the reformism of the early twentieth century and captured the minds and emotions of people like William Lyon Mackenzie King.[14] Like many of his generation Tory never fully incorporated or cared about the finer points of theology. "I had never been able to find enough material on a religious theme to enable me to speak for more than fifteen minutes," Tory once wrote (41). At the same time, however, that he found theology abstruse, he fully absorbed the sense of duty and seriousness of purpose which underlay religious teaching. His sense of mission as a builder of educational institutions, his certainty about his purpose and his commitment to projects underway were all partly complimentary to and partly substitutes for that religious spirit which had been instilled into him as a youth.

In this light many of the contradictions in Tory's life becomes more understandable. In his move from religion to science to education; in his aversion to denominational institutions; in his movement from the Maritimes to Montreal, to the West; in his idealistic efforts with the Khaki University, Tory was following a strong sense of duty given to him by his upbringing and education. Most of all, in his commitment that education must be practical and serve the wider public he was treating education parallel to the way he would treat religion. Like religion itself, it should not be cloistered and removed. The greatest moral good it could serve was to reach the people. In this fashion Henry Marshall Tory carried his sense of duty and his nineteenth century Maritime upbringing to the twentieth century and to the development of Canadian education.

NOTES

1. Michael Gavreau, *The Evangelical Century. College and Creed in English Canada from the Great Revival to the Great Depression* (Toronto: University of Toronto Press, 1991); Robin S. Harris, *A History of Higher Education in Canada 1663-1960* (Toronto: University of Toronto Press, 1976) for a general overview of institutional development.
2. William Caldwell, "The Place of the Church in Modern Life," *University Magazine* 7, no. 4 (December, 1908): 663.
3. On McGill, see Stanley Brice Frost, *McGill University: For the Advancement of Learning* (Montreal: McGill-Queen's University Press, 1980).
4. Robert Wiebe, *The Search for Order 1877-1920* (New York, 1967).
5. Barbara Villy Cormack, *Beyond the Classroom. The First 60 Years of the University of Alberta Department of Extension* (Edmonton: University of Alberta Extension, 1981), p. 1.
6. On the early history of the University of Alberta see Walter Johns, *A History of the University of Alberta 1908-1969* (Edmonton: University of Alberta Press, 1981); Maureen Aytenfisu, "The University of Alberta: Objectives, Structure and Role in the Community, 1908-1928," M.A. thesis, University of Alberta, 1982.
7. John MacNeill, "The Higher Patriotism," *Proceedings of the Canadian Club, Toronto, 1918-1919*, pp. 3-4.
8. R.C. Brown and G.R. Cook, *Canada 1896-1921: A Nation Transformed* (Toronto: McClelland and Stewart, 1974), Chapters 11-12.
9. Desmond Morton, "'Kicking and Complaining:' Demobilization Riots in the Canadian Expeditionary Force," *Canadian Historical Review* LXI, no. 3 (September, 1980): 334-60.
10. Aytenfisu, "The University of Alberta," pp. 264-72.
11. University of Alberta Archives, "Biography Files on Mrs. Annie Tory."
12. See, for example, John English, *Shadow of Heaven. The Biography of L.B. Pearson*, Vol. 1 (Toronto: Lester, Orpen, Denys, 1989).
13. Aytenfisu, "The University of Alberta," pp. 60-63, 69-73.
14. Ramsay Cook, *The Regenerators. Social Criticism in Late Victorian Canada* (Toronto: University of Toronto Press, 1985); Paul Craven, *"An Impartial Umpire," Industrial Relations and the Canadian State 1900-1911* (Toronto: University of Toronto Press, 1980).

HENRY MARSHALL TORY

Beloved Canadian

From a painting by Lilias Torrance Newton.

HENRY MARSHALL TORY

HENRY MARSHALL TORY
Beloved Canadian

E. A. CORBETT, M.A., LL.D.
Former Director of the Canadian Association for Adult Education

With an Introduction by

ROBERT C. WALLACE, C.M.G., LL.D., F.R.S.C.
Former Principal, Queen's University, Kingston, Ontario

THE RYERSON PRESS ~ TORONTO

Published, March, 1954

PRINTED AND BOUND IN CANADA
BY THE RYERSON PRESS, TORONTO

PREFACE

THIS BOOK IS BASED almost entirely upon the personal memoirs, reports and records kept by Dr. Tory himself. I am indebted to his nephews, J. S. D. Tory, Q.C., of Toronto, and J. M. Tory of the Sun Life Assurance Company, Toronto, for making available to me the complete files kept by Dr. Tory covering his work in the establishment of McGill in British Columbia; the University of Alberta; the Khaki University; the National Research Council; Carleton College; as well as a large collection of private papers, correspondence, public addresses and commission reports.

I am also indebted to the large number of people whose letters are quoted in the text; to Dr. J. Roby Kidd for the use of his M.A. thesis entitled, "A Study of the Influence of Dr. H. M. Tory on Educational Policy in Canada"; to Walter Herbert, Director of the Canada Foundation; Dr. John E. Robbins, Editor of the *Encyclopedia of Canada*; Dr. Frank Lathe of the National Research Council; Dr. Robert Newton, Vancouver; Dr. John MacEachran, Edmonton; Dr. W. H. Alexander, Berkeley, California; Dean Geoffrey C. Andrew and Professor F. Soward, both of the University of British Columbia, Dr. A. N. Shaw of McGill and Dr. Lorne Pierce of The Ryerson Press, for their help in assembling additional material and for corrections and suggestions in preparing the manuscript for publication.

The writing and publication of the book was made possible through the generosity of J. S. D. Tory, Q.C. and Dr. N. A. M. MacKenzie, President of the University of British Columbia; Dr. Andrew Stewart, President of the University of Alberta; Dr. M. M. MacOdrum, President of Carleton College, Dr. F. Cyril James, Principal of McGill University and the Boards of Governors of those institutions.

E. A. C.

FOREWORD

My particular relationships to Dr. Tory were in three capacities. I succeeded him in the University of Alberta. I served with him for many years on the National Research Council. I saw him in action in the international organizations of the League of Nations Society and the Institute for Intellectual Cooperation. There are certain facts that stand out in my memory. He won great affection from his staff, and from those who co-operated with him in his farseeing projects. The tone of the book which Dr. Corbett has written is convincing evidence of that fact. He was in himself a truly modest man, but in his ideas and his purposes he encompassed the world. He was essentially a builder—of institutions, of the spread of scientific knowledge, of international goodwill. He delighted in seeing things grow. He was less interested if for any reason growth could not be continued. His lifework was accomplished at a time when Canada needed forward-looking builders, and he stands alone among his contemporaries for constructive accomplishment. He was a truly great man—great in heart and great in deed.

The author has given us a definitive Canadian biography. Dr. Corbett was closely associated with Dr. Tory in one of the most significant periods—the time between the first World War and the sad years of the depression. Together, in an outstanding way, they made the University the servant of the people. They worked as one. Thus it has come about that we have been given not only the man in what he did, but, more significantly, the man in what he dreamed and planned. The monuments are around us for us to see. But the real monument is in the inner life that provided the dynamic. That life is revealed in the pages before us in words of insight and rare understanding.

Robert C. Wallace.

CONTENTS

LIST OF ILLUSTRATIONS

Chapter I

HENRY MARSHALL TORY BELOVED CANADIAN

In July, 1953, I was trying to find Port Shoreham where Henry Marshall Tory was born. I was directed to follow a little-used road that leads from the highway down through heavily-wooded hills to the wide reaches of Chedabucto Bay. There is nothing there now but a gravel beach, the wreckage of an ancient wharf and a few dilapidated fisherman's shacks. Near one of these an old, old man was kneeling on the ground cleaning codfish. When I told him I was looking for some of the landmarks of the Tory family, he pointed with his cleaning knife and said "Up there on that hill is the old Tory homestead, and not far away is the site of the old school which I attended with the Tory children eighty years ago. That was a clever family. The Tory boys all made a place for themselves in the world, but the smartest of them all was young 'Marsh.' Everywhere that man went he made things grow."

From just such beginnings many of Canada's greatest men have gone forth to shape her history, but it is doubtful if any one of them left as many lasting monuments to his memory as Henry Marshall Tory. Certainly few men in Canadian history have done so much to help establish those standards of scholarship which have given Canadian universities and research laboratories a high place among the world's great institutions of advanced learning.

From that pioneer farm in Guysborough County, Nova Scotia, he had worked his way through such local schools as were available, and by private study prepared himself to enter McGill University in his twenty-second year. That was in October, 1886. He won almost every academic honour, including his M.A., B.D., and Doctorate in Science and spent twenty-two years at McGill, first as student and lecturer, then as Professor of Mathematics and Physics. It was not his destiny, however, to continue as a teacher, much as he loved that profession; and his talents as an organizer and administrator called him to a wider field. He became successively (from 1905 on), founder of McGill College in British Columbia, later to become the University of British Columbia; founder and first President of the University of Alberta; founder and President of Khaki University during World War I; President of the National Research Council; and at his death was President of Carleton College, Ottawa, an institution he had been largely instrumental in establishing a few years earlier. He had served on eight national and international Royal Commissions and had been honoured by nine Canadian universities. He had been president of the Association of Canadian Clubs, the League of Nations Society in Canada, the Royal Society of Canada, and many other voluntary organizations.

To a greater degree than most men of his time he had been a maker of history and a builder of bridges between the old world and the new. In spite of the fact that he was warm-hearted and humble, with a gift for friendship, he was in a sense a lonely man, because to many of his friends and associates his dreams seemed unrealistic and the projects to which he gave his life appeared premature.

When he left the University of Alberta, in 1928, to take up his new duties as President of the National Research Council, Professor W. H. Alexander, in an article in the student paper *The Gateway* said:

> The University of Alberta has in these past twenty years grown in a way which the President then foresaw but which we used to regard as the hallucinations of an amiable mind gone wrong on one tack. As a matter of fact what we thought were hallucinations were really visions.

I first met Dr. Tory in January, 1918, when he came to England to take over direction of the educational work already established in a number of the military camps in Britain and France. The late Major R. W. Brock (who later became Dean of Science at the University of British Columbia) and I were in charge of the Khaki College at Seaford in Sussex. Out of some 30,000 Canadian soldiers in the area we had about 2,000 students registered in classes in a wide variety of subjects. It had been our custom to hold a rally every Saturday night in order to whip up interest in the work of the College and to provide a sense of community among the students. For these occasions we usually had either a concert-party or a speaker, and up to that time we had not been very happy in our choice of speakers. Most of them had been dull and heavy-witted, with the result that often only a corporal's guard remained in the hall at the end of the address.

When we learned that Dr. Tory had arrived in London, Major Brock wrote inviting him to meet the officials of the College and address the students. He accepted our invitation and, with the help of the headquarters staff, we made arrangements for a mass meeting not only of the registered students, but of any officers and other ranks who wished to hear him.

When we met Dr. Tory at the station he was wearing the uniform of a Colonel in the Canadian army, and unlike most civilians in uniform for the first time, he looked smart and at ease. He was then fifty-four years of age but appeared ten years younger, and his thick, wavy brown hair was untouched with grey. He was a striking, distinguished-looking man, about five foot ten, stockily built, who gave the impression of intense intellectual and physical energy. He had regular features, a generous mouth and blue-grey eyes which seemed always to be examining you, but had a perpetual twinkle in them. He wore a small moustache, neatly trimmed and angling down sharply to the corners of his mouth, giving it a quality of sternness. But it was always Dr. Tory's head one noticed—big, strong and beautifully shaped, like that of one of Michelangelo's prophets.

He told us he was going to speak on "Science and Education" and I shuddered at the thought of what might happen to him. But my fears were needless, because to the more than two thousand officers and other ranks in the Machine Gun depot gymnasium that January night the man on the platform was superb. He talked in terms of devotion and inspiration about Canada from sea to sea and of the pioneers who had made it great; about its vast natural wealth, waiting for men of training and high adventure. He spoke of the place of education in the making of the kind of citizen Canada's potential future needed. He gave specific examples of what science had accomplished in the development of Canada's mines, fisheries and agriculture. The war was yet to be won, but in the meantime he urged his listeners to take advantage of every opportunity to fit themselves, by education and training, for life in Canada after the war. He closed his remarks by reading a poem I had not heard before, Colonel John McCrae's "In Flanders Fields." This was the man at his warm and moving best, and the men loved it. He did not pretend to be a great orator, but his commanding presence, his electric personality, and the solid core of knowledge and good sense at the heart of his public utterances always compelled the attention of his audiences.

I was to meet Dr. Tory many times after that during the winter of 1918, but it was not until I joined the staff of the University of Alberta in the fall of 1920 that I came to know him intimately. From that time until he left Alberta I saw and talked with him regularly, and came to respect and admire him as one of the greatest human beings I had ever known.

Like all men of great gifts he had his weaknesses. He was impulsive, headstrong, and sometimes so set on obtaining his ends that his opponents considered him ruthless. He had his temper well under control most of the time, and presented to the world an aspect of such warmth and graciousness that it came as a surprise to discover that he could blaze with fury when confronted with dishonesty or injustice. His Scottish temperament made it difficult for him to forgive or forget a deliberate betrayal or a personal affront. At the same time he was readily moved to tears by human suffering and misfortune.

Early in his youth Henry Marshall Tory had a religious experience which turned his thoughts to the ministry of the Methodist Church. He graduated in Theology, was ordained, and did a good deal of preaching. The fact that he had devoted himself to science did not in any way change his basic religious beliefs, and to the end of his days he remained a devout practising Christian whose life was committed to what he believed to be the will of God. He was a man in whom pride of position had no place whatever. On one occasion a neighbour's small son, of whom Dr. Tory was very fond, started calling him "Marsh," which was his wife's name for him. The boy's father was shocked when he heard his child addressing the President of the University of Alberta in such a familiar way and rebuked him for it, but Dr. Tory said he was flattered that a child should feel so much his friend.

Dr. Malcolm Wallace, of the University of Toronto, when visiting the University of Alberta, was taken to the Edmonton Rotary Club by Dr. Tory, who was then a member. Before they entered the dining-room, Dr. Tory said: "They all call me Marsh; I wonder how Sir Robert (Falconer) would like being called Bob?"

Early in the First World War he took his preliminary military training in the C.O.T.C. of the University of Alberta, of which he was President, and sloshed about the campus as vigorously as any undergraduate.

Writing of this period in his booklet *The University of Alberta: A Retrospect 1908-1929* Professor W. H. Alexander says:

> All during the winter of 1915-16 under the command of (Professor) H. J. MacLeod, the C.O.T.C. went steadily on with its task of preparing college men in Alberta for what now seemed their inevitable duty. A platoon of professors was organized, conspicuous among them being Privates Tory, Kerr, MacEachran and such. The instructing officer was the late and much lamented Lieutenant S. D. Killam. On one occasion he had just finished delivering in his best style, plus some of the rhetorical gems in which the Infantry Training 1914, abounded, an explanation of let us say, "Advance in fours to the left," when suddenly from the ranks Private H. M. Tory piped up, "Lieutenant Killam, there's a bad draught through the Convocation Hall. Would you mind shutting the East door?" The foundations of the Empire and every last sacred tradition of the British Army rocked violently to and fro—but Professor Killam shut the door as required and then Lieutenant Killam resumed the drill.

At one time in his youth Dr. Tory had learned to knit, and during the early war years he taught many of the professors' wives to knit socks and caps for the students overseas. Miss Mamie Simpson, now Dean of Women at the University of Alberta, writes:

> During the war at the conversaziones, Dr. and Mrs. Tory did not dance, so the faculty women used to bring their knitting and hand it to Dr. Tory to have him turn the heel properly. By the end of the evening he would always have the job done.

But no introduction to Dr. Tory would be complete without some reference to his sense of humour. I have referred to the constant twinkle in his eyes. This was the expression of an innate love of laughter and a quiet appreciation of the fact that fooling can be a glorious thing.

In Dr. R. W. Boyle's fine tribute to Dr. Tory, prepared for The Royal Society of Canada in 1947, he said:

> No one who knew H. M. Tory could ever forget his sense of humour, his great capacity for amusement and enjoyment, and his innate kindness. Because of this humour and kindness he was all the wiser in his judgment of people and affairs. A sense of humour is a sense of proportion, and being a keen scientific analyst, he was no dogmatist, but saw into men and events with understanding sympathy. Very human himself, he loved human companionship. It is said of some men that they grow old gracefully; Tory hardly grew old at all.

He was full of earthy stories of his youth and amusing people he had met in his life-time. When telling a story that might have an occasional cuss-word in it, it was his custom to close the door to the office of his secretary; then he would walk around the room, his face beaming as he acted out the gestures and mimicked the dialect of his yarn.

I recently recovered from among Dr. Tory's files the programme of a play written and produced by Professor Douglas Killam on December 23, 1920, at the University of Alberta. It is called "The Professor's Dilemma or Fifi from Paris, a Tragi-Comedy in Three Parts, and Several Interludes" and was said to be under the patronage of Johnny Walker of Kilmarnock. Among the *dramatis personae* are Dr. Notorious,

President of the University of Altoota, Hobbies—Stamp-Collecting and No Trump; and Professor of Philosophy John McCracken, a Scotch Gentleman of the Old School, who Kant and Wundt Behave. Dr. Tory's delight in this sort of good-natured spoofing endeared him to everyone. One of the stories he liked best to tell was of the cold winter's night when Professor Killam, dressed in the rags of a woman of the streets and carrying a huge doll, rang Professor E. W. Sheldon's door-bell and when the door opened, threw himself into Sheldon's arms crying: "You are the father of my child!"

Among the qualities that made Dr. Tory one of the most effective speakers of his day on scientific questions was his gift for apt and humourous illustration. Addressing a public meeting in Vancouver at a time when he was head of one of the many Royal Commissions on which he served, Dr. Tory began by saying:

> I heard a distinguished American clergyman, English-born, define the difference between the Englishman and the American in terms of a creed. The Englishman's creed would be "As it was in the beginning, is now and ever shall be, world without end, Amen." The American creed would be, "As it was in the beginning, is now, and by gosh its got to stop." The Canadian creed would go something like this: "As it was in the beginning, is now, and, ladies and gentlemen if we are going to do anything about it, we better appoint a Royal Commission."

Once when he was asked why he so seldom used notes of any kind when making an important public address he said:

> I am like the negro lad who enlisted in the cavalry and then applied to be transferred to the infantry. When asked why he wished to leave the cavalry, he said: "When the time comes to retreat, I don't want to be handicapped by no horse."

Because he was apt to become engrossed in the promotion of the projects to which he devoted himself, many people considered Dr. Tory an impatient man. It is true he was a person of strong opinions and, like most men whose minds move quickly, he found it difficult to suffer gladly the delays imposed by men of more ponderous patterns of thought and action. His successes were achieved mostly by long thought and careful planning, but also by a kind of inspired intuition. He was highly sensitive to atmosphere, and it was necessary for him to be surrounded by friends, warmth, sympathy. In his younger days he was often incautious in his utterances and exposed himself to attack, but in maturity he displayed an uncanny understanding of others, an instinct which told him how to approach a difficult person and win him to his side. To a greater degree than most men he had the gift to "look into the seeds of time and see which seeds would grow and which would not."

In a small book published in 1890, Woodrow Wilson called attention to the social waste of the thinker who cannot lead, and the danger to society of the leader who cannot think. "Our slow world," he says, "spends its time catching up with the ideas of its best minds." Effective leadership, therefore, includes as essential ingredients sympathy, insight and interpretation. Dr. Tory was a thinker who could lead, and his leadership was based upon a profound understanding of human needs and a remarkable capacity for interpreting them.

In a sense he had only one orthodoxy and that was his belief in the freedom of the human soul and his conviction that only the truth can make men free. Hence the motto which he carried like a banner all his life and which he and Professor W. H. Alexander selected for the University of Alberta crest: *Quaecumque Vera*—Whatsoever things are true: Philippians 4: 8.

CHAPTER II

FAMILY BACKGROUND

THE COUNTY OF GUYSBOROUGH, NOVA SCOTIA, the birthplace of Henry Marshall Tory, was largely settled by United Empire Loyalists and disbanded soldiers following the American Revolution. The county is separated from Cape Breton Island by the Straits of Canso. From the southern end of the Straits, Chedabucto Bay sweeps inland like the long curve of a gull's flight, thirty miles almost due west from the ocean. Two rivers flow into the Bay at its headwaters; the Salmon River from the west and the Milford Haven from the north. The former flows through a series of inland lakes and is a tidal stream, navigable for fishing boats for a portion of its length. The Milford Haven is really an arm of the sea into which a few small streams enter. It forms a natural harbour of entrancing beauty and one long famous for shipping. During the French régime, a fort was built on the north shore of the Bay and some farming carried on in the surrounding country. After the expulsion of the Acadians from the Nova Scotia peninsula, in 1755, a number of families from the American colonies settled in the County, especially along the shores of the harbour. But it was not until 1783 and the years immediately following, that the country began to fill up with small settlements along the river valleys and wherever land suitable for cultivation could be found.

On the west side of the harbour near the mouth of the Milford Haven River a town site was laid out, a part of which is now occupied by the town of Guysborough, the county seat. From the hills behind the town, looking eastward to the sea, the scene is one of rare beauty, even in a Province noted for the magnificence of its scenery. The racial affiliations of the people who settled here one hundred and seventy years ago are indicated at once by their names: Aikens, Brown, Bruce, Campbell, Cunningham, Cummings, Ferguson, Hadley, Hughes, Lipsett, Keay, MacDonald, MacIntosh, MacKay, MacMaster, Morris, Nash, O'Gorman, Sullivan, Tory. There are also some names of German origin: Myers and Deckoff will serve as examples.

Of the names mentioned above two are of special interest to us: Tory and Ferguson, since Henry Marshall Tory was directly descended from the pioneers of both these families.

The Tory family of Nova Scotia is descended from a well-known Scottish lowland family which has been associated with the Shires of Elgin and Aberdeen for centuries. The name is spelled in a variety of ways: Tory and Torry in the South of England, where a branch of the family has lived since the early 17th century; Tory, Torry and Torrie in Scotland, where the family history dates back to the 14th century. In the United States the name is generally spelled Torrey. The Nova Scotia family has always used the spelling Tory. The name appears occasionally in Scottish history. During the year 1424 Adam Torry, the Provost of Elgin, was the leader of a delegation of ten who carried to England the one hundred thousand pounds ransom demanded by Henry VI, King of England, for the release of James the First of Scotland, who had been a prisoner at the English Court for nineteen years. During the reign of Alexander III of Scotland, one George Torry was beheaded and his estates were confiscated for joining a rebellion against his sovereign.

The village of Torrey, now a part of the city of Aberdeen, was once the property of a branch of the Torry family. The first immediate ancestor of the Nova Scotia Torys was William Torry who lived in Aberdeenshire on the border of Elginshire on a property known as Garneston. William Torry was the father of five sons and from one of these, James, all of the Nova Scotia Torys are descended. James Torry, great-great-grandfather of Henry Marshall Tory, was an ardent Jacobite and one of those unfortunate men who joined the Rebellion of 1745 in an effort to place Prince Charlie upon the throne of England. He was a cloth manufacturer and a staunch Episcopalian in a family whose tradition was entirely Presbyterian. After the

Rebellion he was reported as "loitering," which means he was not captured and shot as so many of his fellow rebels were.

After the amnesty in 1749 he returned home, and having lost his business started a private school at a place called "Craig of Garneston." His most notable student was his nephew, Patrick Torry, the son of his younger brother Thomas. Although he had neither the sympathy nor support of his immediate family, James Torry must have maintained his religious and political opinions and taught them in his school. He inspired his nephew with such zeal for his views that he became not only a distinguished theologian, but one of the chief proponents of the Episcopal Church of Scotland, an establishment with ancient litany and service distinct from the Church of England. He later became Bishop of St. Andrew's, Dunkeld, and Dunblane and was for years one of the most important figures in the Episcopal Church of Scotland. He was responsible for the building of the Cathedral Church in Perth, where his body lies buried.

James Torry, great-grandfather of Henry Marshall Tory, like many other followers of Bonnie Prince Charlie, came to America and fought on the British side during the American War of Independence. At the end of the war he was for some time a prisoner of war in New York. Later, in 1783, he joined the ranks of those who in leaving the United States were given the choice of going to "Hell, Hull, or Halifax." He received a grant of land from the British Crown in the Guysborough Intervale near the headwaters of the Milford Haven River, with certain allotments in the townsite of Guysborough. A few months after his arrival he was married to Elizabeth Kirk of Stirling, who came out from Scotland to join him. Two sons were born of this union, James and Henry. James Tory remained on the old homestead, married, and had a large family. Henry Tory, grandfather of Henry Marshall Tory, purchased a large tract of land in what is now known as Port Shoreham, married and had a family of five sons and five daughters.

One of the sons, Robert Kirk Tory, although the fourth in line, was apparently a favourite of his father, for he was selected by him to remain at home and inherit the homestead.

This arrangement was made after he had settled James and Henry on parts of his original purchase and John in a neighbouring district. Robert Kirk was the father of H. M. Tory. The mother was Norah Ferguson. The Ferguson family had made their way to Guysborough County by the same route followed by James Tory. Alexander Ferguson of Perthshire had taken part in the Rebellion of '45, had settled in America, joined the British forces in the American Revolution and after the war was given a grant of land close to the Tory homestead in the Guysborough Intervale. The Fergusons are one of the oldest of the Highland clans of Scotland. The name has been current in Scottish history since the first settlement of the Scots from Ireland in the fourth century of our era. The invasion, tradition has it, was headed by one Fergus, King of the Scots, whose descendants and followers, known as the Clan Ferguson, have been prominent in Scottish history ever since.

Alexander Ferguson was the father of a large family of which one son, James, was the father of Norah Ferguson, who was the oldest of a family of five sons and two daughters. These two families living side by side had much in common. They had the same tradition of public service: their forefathers had suffered in common causes—on the battlefield and in the political life of their country. Intellectually and temperamentally, however, the two families were very different. For a number of years after the two families settled in the Guysborough Intervale they were not on intimate terms because of political and religious divergence.

The Tory family remained true to the Episcopal form of Church organization and worship. The first and only Episcopal Church erected in the Guysborough Intervale was built upon property given by James Tory, the founder of the Nova Scotia family. In politics the Torys remained eager supporters of the Conservative party in the county. Speaking of this period of his life in a speech which the writer heard him give in 1930, Dr. Tory said in part:

> The leading members of the senior branch of my family when I was a boy were so fixed in their opinions as to be wholly incapable of responding to any emotional, social, religious or political appeal.

When on the occasion of the second Dominion election after Confederation, a Liberal candidate had the audacity to contest the Guysborough constituency, my grandfather indignantly declared that he should be horsewhipped out of the county.

The Fergusons on the other hand were Low Church and Liberals and equally strong in their religious and political opinions. When the Wesleyan ministers entered the Guysborough district and arranged for continuity of service and worship, the whole Ferguson Clan joined the movement and became permanent supporters of that denomination. In the movement for responsible government under the leadership of Joseph Howe in the early years of the 19th Century they enthusiastically supported the cause of reform. They became then and have remained ardent Liberals. In fact Dr. Tory used to tell of the indignation of his mother when, after forty years in office, the Nova Scotia Liberals were swept out of power in the election of 1925. She refused at first to believe the reports, and when she finally had to recognize the truth it seemed to her that the whole world had gone wrong.

In this atmosphere of political and religious intensity young Henry Marshall Tory grew up. The whole countryside enjoyed the hospitality of a home which was always open to friends and strangers alike. The political discussions centred around Joseph Howe on the one side and Sir Charles Tupper on the other, and were thrashed out in the presence of the young family. Here undoubtedly was awakened the interest which the family has always shown in politics and in questions of public interest.

So these two families—the steady, stubborn, Conservative Torys, and the emotional, ardent, Liberal Fergusons—were the soil out of which grew the personal attitudes of Henry Marshall Tory. Due to these early influences, he was able in later life to adapt himself to conflicting points of view, and to exercise at times remarkable patience with those who were disposed to be unreasonable or hostile to projects upon which he had set his whole heart.

Chapter III

THE COMMUNITY

In Marsh[1] Tory's boyhood the Guysborough community was already moving away from its original state of pioneering self-sufficiency into a new period, when commercial relations with the outside world were beginning to play a much more important part in its economic and social life. The spread of new ideas and new methods as a result of easier and more frequent communication with other parts of the country began to stimulate new activities, and the sensitive and observant youngster had the opportunity of sharing in the old era as well as the new. Substantial material progress had been made in the settlement. The stump-filled clearings, hewn with enormous labour from the heavily wooded land, had become green and lovely rolling farm lands, with white painted frame buildings perched high on the hills overlooking the bay taking the place of the old log houses and barns. Farming continued to be the chief community occupation, and it was based on the fundamentally sound idea that the land, if properly cultivated, could and would supply all that a family needed in food, clothing and shelter and enough cash to provide for emergencies. Want, in the sense of being without the necessities of life, was unknown. If these people were poor they didn't know it, and they never talked about it.

Those living within convenient distance of the sea combined fishing and farming, as thousands of Maritimers still do. A major difficulty in this situation was that both operations to be successful had to be worked on at the same time, in the spring and summer, and since the sea is a part of the blood and bones of a Nova Scotian, farming was bound to be the neglected occupation. Later, when fishing became less profit-

[1]This was the name he was called throughout his lifetime by his family and intimate friends.

able, the neglected farms proved incapable of supporting large families, and the young people of the county in Marsh Tory's day were already moving away from the land and the small communities to find places for themselves elsewhere.

The major part of the population of the County of Guysborough devoted itself wholly to making a living from the land and the sea; cash crops were cattle, fish and forest products. Practically everything needed in the way of food was produced, processed and consumed in the home. On every farm a small acreage was devoted to wheat; not for sale, just enough to supply bread for the family. Oats, barley, buckwheat, potatoes and turnips were produced for human and animal consumption. There were flocks of geese, ducks and hens everywhere, and hogs, milk cows, beef cattle and sheep roamed over the rolling pastures during the summer and fattened themselves on aftercrops in the autumn. There was such an abundance of wild life in the forests that hunting and trapping in the fall and winter was a part of every farmer's programme.

Small orchards had been planted by the early settlers and there was an abundance of apples, plums, cherries and small fruits for family use. Berry picking was a major summertime occupation for women and children, and every cellar was a storehouse of hundreds of jars of blueberries, wild strawberries, raspberries and cranberries, packed on shelves beside the bins of vegetables and the barrels of salt herring, codfish, oysters and clams. Winter held no terrors for these people. There was fuel for the taking and no one need suffer want.

But the winter was just as busy a time as summer. Enough logs for building had to be cut and hauled from the woods. Material for making barrels to pack fish and apples was also a source of income. Fishermen made and mended their own nets. Only twine and rope were purchased. Farm power, both in summer and winter, was supplied by oxen. Only the very prosperous members of the community, of whom there were few, could afford the luxury of a carriage or saddle horse.

Sheep supplied all the wool needed for clothing. Every home had its spinning wheel and many were equipped with homemade looms for weaving. Blankets, quilts, rugs, featherbeds, heavy boots and moccasins were manufactured in the home, in some cases by the members of the family, sometimes by travelling shoemakers and tailors who lived in the home until the work was completed. Much of the news from other parts of the country and gossip from nearby villages was carried by these itinerant craftsmen. Some of them were like a weekly newspaper in the home and as eagerly awaited.

To give full scope for the self-sufficiency of the community, special industries were developed. These were nearly always of family origin and associated with farming or fishing but intended for the whole community. These centres of home industry were usually promoted by men who brought with them from the old country special knowledge of the operations involved, or the native-born with special aptitudes and ambitions.

In most communities there were grist-mills for grinding grain, a fuller's mill for dressing cloth, tanneries for preparing leather from hides, shoemaking establishments for making and mending shoes, although in many cases this work was done in the home. There were, of course, blacksmith shops where horses and oxen were shod, carriages and carts rimmed, ploughshares and coulters repaired or sharpened and other work done which involved the use of iron and steel. There were small wood-working establishments where windows and doors and other specialties were made.

The town of Guysborough in Marsh Tory's boyhood was the chief trading centre for a whole group of districts of which Port Shoreham was one. Trade was conducted mainly by barter of the surplus products of the farm. These consisted mainly of home-made woollen goods, knitted stockings, socks and mittens; beef, mutton, pork, eggs and butter and cheese. Fish were usually disposed of in the same way by fishermen-farmers who sold to fish merchants who were also general merchants. The supplies received in return were material for the better class of clothing for men and women, although most men were content with clothes made from home-made cloth dressed at the fuller's mill. Coffee, tea, sugar, molasses, cotton goods, linen, household furniture, axes, saws were paid for by barter.

Trading with the outer world was conducted by means of sailing vessels or horse-drawn vehicles. The railway did not reach Guysborough County until 1875 when Marsh Tory was eleven years of age. It has not yet reached the town of Guysborough.

The situation with regard to religion was as complicated as it is in many communities today. Originally most of the settlers belonged either to the Church of England or the Roman Catholic Church, with a sprinkling of Presbyterians and Baptists. The Catholic Church was well established, but the Presbyterians soon withdrew from the community for want of sufficient adherents to support a clergyman. The Church of England and the Baptists struggled along, each in splendid isolation. The entry of Methodist missionaries into the field during the early years of the 19th century, with their absence of formalism, their evangelical fervour, their doctrine of "free grace" for all believers, their readiness to preach in the homes of the people or in the open air if buildings were not available, had greatly stimulated interest in religion.

Many to whom the Church of England had ceased to appeal were at once attracted by the gospel preached by itinerant Methodists. The establishment of Sunday Schools in homes and country schoolhouses brought Methodism into the lives of the people more intimately than was the case with other Protestant denominations.

The chief competitors in the Protestant field in Guysborough were the Methodists and Baptists. The writer heard Dr. Tory, in his later years, tell a story which illustrates the sharp divisions of belief and doctrine which separated the two. One Sunday when the lad was about fifteen years of age, powerful expositions of church doctrine had been given to their people by the ministers of the Methodist and Baptist Churches. The Baptist minister had declared with great conviction that the ceremony of baptism could mean only one thing, and that was complete immersion. The Methodist minister had not only quoted extensively from the Bible in favour of sprinkling but had gone further, and quoted a reference from a classical Greek authority to prove that sprinkling was the historic and universal method of baptism. The argument was continued with great excitement in the general store the next Saturday night and produced the following dialogue:

MR. HULL *(Baptist)*: Mr. Hadley, my Methodist friend, let me inform you once and for all that the word baptize means to dip and nothing but to dip.

MR. HADLEY *(Methodist)*: Mr. Hull, you talk nonsense, and you know it. Read your Bible, man and if you don't believe that, read from the classics. Did not an ancient Greek writer speak of "baptising the sea with blood"?

MR. HULL *(Obviously stumped)*: Mr. Hadley, the trouble with you is you don't know the alphabet of religion.

MR. HADLEY *(Insulted and very angry)*: Mr. Hull, the trouble with you is you're a damn liar.

At that time for a church member, particularly a Methodist, to say "damn" in public was almost enough to drive him out of the Church, and Dr. Tory used to tell the story to illustrate the tension often existing between the two denominations. Perhaps, too, it might have been a secret consolation to him in later years when he occasionally permitted a tense or angry "damn" to pass his own lips.

Robert Kirk Tory, the father, was an ardent Methodist, but he also had a keen sense of humour and he loved to tell stories poking fun at what he called the "hardshell" Baptists. One of these stories the writer heard Dr. Tory tell among friends many years later in Alberta:

A well-known Baptist evangelist from a neighbouring town was conducting a series of revival meetings (camp meetings they were called) near the town of Guysborough, and on Sunday crowds of people thronged the banks of the Milford Haven River to witness the immersion of the converts. One of the penitents who presented himself for baptism was an enormous Negro who was noted in the community as a fighter and general roustabout. In lowering him into the water the minister let the Negro slip from his hands. Not being able to get hold of him again, the evangelist stood up straight and cried out: "The Lord giveth and the Lord taketh away. In the name of the Lord send along another one." In the meantime the huge, gasping convert scrambled to his feet and shouted, "If this damn nonsense don't stop, somebody sho' as hell is goin' to get drownded!"

Illiteracy in the sense of being unable to read or write was almost unknown in Guysborough County. The Scottish tradition of education had been firmly established by the original settlers and when Marsh Tory was growing up there were schools of a sort in every community. Books were not plentiful. It was long before the day of the public library, but almost every home had a large ornate, brass bound family Bible in which the names of the children and the dates of their births were carefully entered. This Bible nearly always occupied a place on a small table in the centre of the parlour, and was in most cases seldom opened. There was usually another one—dog-eared, thumbed and underlined—which was used for reading. I can remember my father, who was a Presbyterian minister in the Maritimes, telling of a visit he made to a widow in his congregation who told him with great solemnity of the wonderful comfort she got from her daily reading of the Scriptures. When father opened the Bible to read to her as was his custom, a key fell to the floor, and the woman exclaimed, "You know, I've been looking for that door-key for months!" Other books commonly read were Bunyan's *Pilgrim's Progress* and Foxe's *Book of Martyrs.*

In those early days, also, colporteurs (they were called coalporters in the Maritimes) travelled through the rural districts selling religious books and Bibles. The *Family Herald and Weekly Star* of Montreal and John Dougal's *Witness*, also of Montreal, later came to many homes. But it was the regular reading of the Bible at family worship, and privately, which gave to those early communities whatever flavour of culture they had, and accustomed the ears of young Nova Scotians to the sound of good English.

Whatever social life the community enjoyed centred around the Churches' Boards of management, and school trusteeships provided about the only opportunities open to those who had a gift for administration and local politics. Families became known for their attachment to the church of their choice. Integrity and kindliness rather than possessions were the badges of merit. The only aristocracy recognized was that of intellect and character. Business was organized and conducted on religious and political lines, and it was accepted as a matter of course that families traded with those of like religious and political faith. But on the other hand neighbourliness and a sense of community were always uppermost, and the whole district would turn out to aid anyone in distress or in need of comfort or physical help.

By the time Marsh Tory left Guysborough to make his way in the world much of this had changed. The exodus of young people had speeded up because of lack of opportunity at home. The products of the factories were beginning to replace the products of home industry. Purchasing power declined and the sheer need of cash hastened the collapse of a thriving and self-sufficient economy. Only the ancient beauty of the sea and the tree-clad hills which nature gave to Guysborough were unchanged.

MR. AND MRS. H. M. TORY

Taken in Montreal shortly after the wedding.

H. M. TORY JAMES C. TORY

JOHN A. TORY

Chapter IV

HOME AND SCHOOL

The record of the Tory family in the old family Bible shows that Robert Kirk Tory and Norah Ferguson were married at Port Shoreham in 1861, and that there was born to them a family of six children. In order of age they were James Cranswick (late Lieutenant-Governor of Nova Scotia), Henry Marshall, Martha Ellen (Mrs. John Henderson), Sarah Jane (Mrs. William Bruce), the late John Alexander (a prominent executive of the Sun Life Assurance Company of Canada) and Elizabeth Ann. Henry Marshall Tory was born on January 11, 1864. They are all deceased now (1953) except Sarah.

Robert Kirk Tory was not a strong man physically and apparently not overly ambitious, but he was greatly beloved in the community because of his warm, kindly personality, his pawky wit and love of fun. The mother on the other hand was a woman of superb physical stature and health. In all her ninety-four years of life she never saw a doctor except at times of childbirth. She was a deeply religious woman, who devoted herself to her family and to every activity which promoted the religious, educational and social welfare of the community. She had a firm hand with her children, and while other young people were scattering to the United States to work in factories she kept her family together and at school. The result was that all her daughters became school teachers and her sons laid the foundations for prominent and useful careers in Canadian life. When she considered punishment necessary, she did not spare the rod. She demanded and received complete obedience from her children. But her great kindness and solicitude for other people made her beloved by everyone.

As long as she lived it was the custom of her distinguished

sons to spend some time together with her every year. In December, 1934, Dr. Tory wrote to her from Ottawa regretting the fact that, owing to illness, he would not be able to be with her on Christmas Day, her birthday, and congratulating her on reaching the age of ninety-two. The letter is full of tender references to her continued inspiration to himself and all her family, and assures her that there is no reason why she should not achieve the century mark if she would just be careful of her health.

The homestead at Port Shoreham where Marsh Tory was born had been occupied for fifty years before he and his brothers and sisters appeared on the scene. The grandfather had been one of the most prosperous men in the district, but he had taught his sons the use of every tool and instrument on the farm. The house they lived in (and almost everything in it) was the product of their skill as carpenters and mechanics.

The big comfortable frame house in which Marsh Tory was born and brought up had been built throughout by the Tory men. After a full cellar had been excavated they built a great stone chimney twenty feet in height and six feet wide. The house was actually erected around that chimney. It had large fireplaces on the north, east and west sides. The result was a solid imposing structure immune to the whipping gales of the fall and the heavy winter storms. It stood four square to all the winds that blew and was in that respect typical of the men that built it. The framework was hewn timber brought from the woods in winter. The boards to cover the framework had been sawn by hand, even the shingles were split from green cedar and cured and dressed in the farm workshop. Stoves were not available when the house was first put up, and hardwood logs burned in the three fireplaces all day long. It was an open house to the whole community, where in many a discussion political and religious questions were thrashed out in the long winter evenings while the children listened and learned the early wisdom of country youngsters.

The school which Marsh Tory attended was an elementary county school about three-quarters of a mile from the home. The public school system of Nova Scotia had been established in 1864, the year of his birth. Previous to that the schools were of an exceedingly primitive type, maintained by the community. The teachers were wholly untrained; many of them were old soldiers with little education, but a tradition of stern discipline. It was the custom for a group of families to get together and employ a teacher, agreeing in advance on the salary to be paid, usually from one hundred to one hundred and fifty dollars a year and "found," which meant that the teacher was boarded free of charge for definite periods by the contracting families.

By the time young Marsh Tory was ready for school the Old Red School House had disappeared from the district and the newer type, encouraged by the public school system, had taken its place. In his diary Dr. Tory has given a detailed description of the school he first attended:

> The school-house was not a pretentious affair, but it was a great improvement on that which preceded it. There was a separate entrance for boys and girls. The teacher's desk was in the middle at the entrance end on a raised platform. Over it was a plaster blackboard for the use of the teacher and on the side walls similar blackboards for the use of the pupils. Over the teacher's blackboard, when not in use, hung a large map of Nova Scotia, the only decorative object in the room. The school room was divided into two equal sections, the front half being kept on the floor level, the rear half rising from the floor level to about three feet elevation at the back. There were three rows of desks with attached seats on the front half; the front row stood back about four feet from the teacher's desk to make room for classes to stand for reading and instruction. In the middle of the room was a large wood-burning stove. The seating capacity was from forty-eight to fifty-four. In my day the school was crowded in the winter time. Today (1945) I am informed there are less than a dozen. . . .
>
> I distinctly remember my first day in school. I was five years old at the time, and was taken there by my cousin, who lived with us. The same day another new pupil, Will Bruce by name, arrived, and to whom I was introduced. We were seated together. For the ten years that I attended that school we were constant companions, always seated together, one or the other of us always leading in the school examinations. We always managed to get on the same

side in competitive games. Morning and evening, during the fishing season, we went fishing together for trout in the streams and lakes and for cod and haddock in the bay. During those ten years we only had one quarrel which lasted only for a few minutes. We drifted apart, but the memory of those days of constant friendship, without care, free from enmity, I have always rejoiced to recall.

The teachers in the county schools were for the most part young women, who had about the equivalent of a Grade X standing of today. There were, however, a considerable number of young men who were making a few years of teaching a stepping stone to a profession, generally in law or theology.

There were certain prescribed texts for reading, history, geography, arithmetic, grammar, composition and copybook writing. There were seven grades of reading books and, so far as the parents and general public was concerned, reading ability was the major consideration in promotion. It was a very great distinction indeed to advance to the use of the seventh reader which was the top grade of the small country school. Generally speaking each subject stood by itself, and it was entirely possible to be in Grade VI in reading and at the same time battling it out with arithmetic at the Grade III level.

The greatest drawback in these small schools was that the teachers were constantly changing. The school year was divided into two terms, one beginning in November and the other in May. Teachers were usually engaged for six months—one term—very seldom for a whole year.

The result was a great variation in the quality and standard of the work done. Teachers' salaries were exceedingly small, usually from $150 to $200 a year from local sources and a government grant graded according to the academic standing of the teacher. Ratepayers meetings were very often the most exciting episodes in the life of the community. There was a constant battle between those who wanted a high grade teacher and those who wanted the cheapest they could get. The appointment of the trustees, the voting of the money for the school, and the choice of a secretary-treasurer who was also tax-collector were political struggles of first-rate importance in the district.

At the time when young Marsh Tory was beginning his education a vigorous effort was being made by the educational authorities to popularize the new public school system. Established in 1864, it was still regarded with some suspicion by the older members of the community. References glorifying the new scheme were scattered here and there throughout the pages of the school readers, and were injected cunningly into the prescribed songs used in the opening ceremonies of the school every morning. In the notes he kept covering this period of his life Dr. Tory says:

> I remember a verse of one of these songs, the authorship of which I do not know, but which had a very definite tinge of politics in it. Without mentioning him by name, it called down a blessing on the head of the late Sir Charles Tupper under whose administration as Premier of Nova Scotia the new education act was passed. The song, which is no tribute to the poetic instincts of its author, ran as follows:
>
> Now three cheers all together,
> Shout for common schools forever,
> Shout for blessings on the founder
> Till we make the air resound!
> And for those who labour for us,
> And whose guardian call is on us,
> We will shout the grateful chorus
> Till the echoes back resound!

Before he was ten years old young Marsh Tory's preferences in study began to appear. There were three arithmetics prescribed in the schools, one elementary, and two more advanced, suitable for high school grades. By the time he was twelve years of age he had worked his way through every problem in the three books.

Fortunately about this time a young male teacher with a first class certificate was employed by the school board. His name was Dougall Campbell and he had attended Pictou Academy where he specialized in algebra, trigonometry and geometry. Campbell remained three years in the Port

Shoreham school and played a large part in shaping the direction of young Tory's education. Of this period Dr. Tory later wrote:

> Finding my interests were similar to his own, Campbell encouraged me to start geometry and algebra and later trigonometry. This was a new world for me in which I delighted. By the time I was fifteen I had gone through the standard text-books of the day in these subjects. Then I soon acquired a love of books and reading from which I have never recovered. To this day I am wholly unable to resist the desire to accumulate books and now that I have quiet leisure for the first time in my life I have ceased resisting. (This was written after his retirement from the National Research Council in 1935.) The period about which I am writing was before the days of public libraries and not many books were available. The school readers especially in the higher grades containing as they did choice selections in both prose and poetry were such as to stimulate reading and I quickly memorized all the poetry for school recitations. Many of the prose selections were from Burke and Pitt and other political leaders, the content of which fitted into the atmosphere of my home, where politics and British greatness were constant themes of discussion. All such quotations I almost unconsciously committed to memory. Just a few years ago in an address to students I quoted a passage on the American Revolution from one of Pitt's speeches, and when asked where I got the quotation, I suddenly remembered that I had been quoting from the old text reader of my school days and I had not seen the passage since. Next to mathematics I found my greatest delight in reading such books on British history as were available.
>
> The school texts in history were Collier's *British History* and Collier's *Great Events.* Collier's *British History* I committed completely to memory from the Norman conquest to the end. This was due, I think to the poetic rhythm of the writing as much as to the delight in the record of events. The story of Magna Carta is always associated in my mind with "Of John we can say nothing good. He was a mean coward, a shameless liar, the most profligate of a profligate age, the most faithless of a faithless race." His vivid description of battles was perhaps his greatest appeal to boys. The opening sentence in the description of the battle of Waterloo, "It is said that Wellington wept, etc." are typical examples of statements not easily forgotten.

It was from Collier's *History* also that Marsh Tory got his first idea of attending a university, a far cry indeed from his pioneer surroundings. In a passage describing Cardinal

Wolsey, Collier tells of his receiving his B.A. degree at Oxford when he was only fourteen years of age. After reading that passage young Marsh Tory made up his mind that some day, somehow, he would get a college education.

By the time he was fifteen he had read every book he could get his hands on, including those of the small library Campbell, the school teacher, carried about with him. He had received all the public school could give him, and as his parents could not afford to send him to the county academy it became clear that if he was to have further education he would have to find a way to manage it himself.

Meanwhile he had shared in all the work on the farm. Ploughing, seeding, haymaking in the summer and wood-hauling in the winter helped to give him that rugged constitution he enjoyed through life.

In the notes he later jotted down covering his boyhood experiences, he says:

> Apart from farm work and the necessary chores, we had ample time for play and recreation. Toys could not be purchased as today, so we made our own. Our hand sleds were fashioned like the larger wood sleds for winter use. For fishing purposes rods and lines had to be prepared. Our rods we made ourselves from small trees cut in the forest and dressed down to proper size. Lines and hooks, of course, had to be purchased. Swimming in lakes and rivers and in the open sea after school hours were among the greater joys of summer, with skating and snowshoeing in winter. Our snowshoes we made ourselves from sawed lumber and our skates had runners made by the local blacksmith, the tops being made of wood fastened on by rivets. Swimming and skating were competitive games in which boys of the whole community participated. We were a healthy, happy community of young people.

CHAPTER V

OUT IN THE WORLD

IN HIS SIXTEENTH YEAR MARSH TORY was offered a job as a clerk in a general store in Guysborough which was owned and operated by James Buckley. He was to be paid four dollars per month, plus board and lodging with the Buckley family. When the offer was made there were long consultations between young Tory's father and mother and the grandfather who was nearly ninety years of age but still a force to be reckoned with in family affairs. The grandfather insisted that Marshall be kept at school, since James the older brother had gone to sea as first officer on a ship sailing between Halifax and Montreal.

But young Tory saw in this opportunity a chance to save money for his college education and at the same time learn something about business and the world of trade. He persuaded the family to allow him to accept the position.

The town of Guysborough was at this time (1879) a fairly important seaport. Coastal fishing was carried on from April to November, and many of the schooners used Guysborough as a home port and were fitted out here for the season's work. Scores of fishermen from both sides of Chedabucto Bay bought all their summer and winter supplies at the Buckley store. This meant accounts and credits on a considerable scale. Shortly after Marsh Tory reported for work James Buckley left on his regular autumn buying trip to Halifax, and the young apprentice was given the responsibility of looking after the book-keeping during his absence. This was a great adventure for Marsh Tory. He knew nothing about book-keeping but his mathematical gifts made it easy for him to catch on quickly, and in his diary he writes:

I shall never forget the thrill I got when in my second year Mr. Buckley handed over to me the keys of the safe and gave me full responsibility for the cash and the books. The whole system of merchandising at this time was one of credits and barter. The Merchants bought from the wholesaler on credit. The farmers and fishermen bought from the merchant on credit except in the case of the farmers, many of whom exchanged farm products for store goods. Everybody in the community had a certain well-known credit standing and growing accounts had to be kept carefully. Two prices existed in all retail houses; one was a credit price, the other a price for cash. The credit price, which was generally ten to fifteen per cent higher than the cash price, also applied to the farm products exchanged for merchandise. It was an expensive way of doing business from the point of view of the purchaser and a hazardous one for the merchant.

Years later (1934) when he was Chairman of a Royal Commission investigating the apple industry in Nova Scotia Dr. Tory was surprised to find that this procedure still existed in some parts of the Annapolis Valley. In his report on that occasion he says:

The coming of the banks into the small towns has gradually eliminated that method, but the great apple merchants still keep it alive as a means of maintaining a claim on the growing fruit. As a method of extending credit, it approaches close to usury.

As in most seaport towns there was a considerable amount of drunkenness among the younger men of Guysborough, especially those who went to sea during the summer and returned home for the winter. But young Marsh Tory was not intrigued by the seamy side of life in Guysborough. He and his brothers had for years practised boxing and wrestling on the farm and when occasion arose, as it apparently sometimes did, he could look after himself. One night he fought his way back to the store through a mob of young toughs who had waylaid him on the wharf. On that occasion he gave such a good account of himself that he was left severely alone thereafter.

His religious training stood him in good stead and he promptly associated himself with the church and the Sunday School. During his second year with the Buckley family,

Marsh Tory passed through a definite religious experience. This was brought about by a combination of circumstances: his early training, the influence of his mother, and his close association with the Guysborough Methodist Church and its minister, the Reverend James Tweedy. Writing of this period, he says:

> Mr. Tweedy was a rough and ready preacher, a profoundly sincere man who exerted a wholesome influence upon the young people of the community. The old-fashioned evangelical preaching of the time, however unphilosophical it may have appeared to those who disliked its methods, had one redeeming feature. It presented a concise plan for making one conscious of God as a fact of human experience. To me the great message of Christianity was the assurance which became a conviction with me, that God could have a place in one's personal life and that all of life's activities could be directed under that conviction. It meant to me that in deciding on a goal in life to which one could give complete devotion, the idea of the will of God should direct choices and action. The effect on me of this change of outlook was at once to force me to a decision as to the purpose to which my life should be devoted. Three courses seemed open to me at the time. First to continue in business as my employer wished me to do; second, the life of a lawyer; and third, the ministry of the church, which was the prayerful wish of my mother. I deliberately decided to study for the ministry. At the same time I determined not to do as so many others were doing—take a selected course in theology—but at whatever cost of time and energy to go through a university arts course as preliminary preparation.

Marsh Tory's sights were now set for the future, and he began by private study and reading to prepare himself for the long struggle ahead of him. Guysborough Academy had by this time become a flourishing institution. The principal was a man of university education and a born teacher. Young Tory made arrangements with him for private study and tuition. He began to study Latin and advanced mathematics. Business hours were from 7 a.m. to 9 p.m. so that there was not much time for study. He arranged, however, with some cousins who were attending the Academy to bring him the prescribed school work for each day. These assignments he worked out at night and his cousins called for the solutions to be presented to the Principal each morning. During the school term Marsh

Tory had kept up with the regular school work and had made a good start on the matriculation requirements in Latin.

He was now eighteen years of age, and it was becoming clearer to him every day that if he was ever to reach the goal of his dreams he would have to find a more remunerative job. During the two years and eight months he had worked in the Buckley store his salary had been $48.00 for the first year, $72.00 for the second, and for the eight months of the third year, $72.00. He had saved of this amount only a little over $100, as in addition to small personal expenses he had sent home to his parents each month nearly 50 per cent of his income. Since $100 would be ample money for a term at the Academy, young Tory entered school again in January, 1882, a week before his eighteenth birthday, and after six months of desperate study (the only high school training he ever received) he succeeded in securing a teacher's diploma from the Provincial Department of Education. That year two hundred and fifty students from the various Nova Scotia Academies succeeded in passing, and Marsh Tory stood fifteenth on the list.

After a summer spent on the farm he received a teaching appointment for the term commencing in November in a school only three miles from home, and by walking the six miles each day he was able to live at home. Thus began an educational career that was to continue without a break for sixty-five years, and was to make the name of Henry Marshall Tory known to scientists and educators throughout the English-speaking world and beyond.

His first teaching job was not easy for the first few months.

The school had been in the hands of a young woman and was in a state of utter indiscipline. Attending the school was a young man of unsavory reputation, much older than the other pupils, who had become the leader of a group of unruly boys. They were aided and abetted by two young women who should have been in high school and had probably ceased to benefit by the teaching they had received. This was not an uncommon condition in the schools of that time; male teachers were scarce. I have no doubt I was employed because of the state of the school. My first problem was to restore discipline. I began with firm but kind treatment. This, I soon saw was being interpreted as weakness and I quickly saw that other methods would be necessary. I decided to wait until the case for punishment became so clear that everyone in the school and community would say I was right in what I did. The test came quickly.

One day I was standing with my back to the school demonstrating on the blackboard when I heard a sharp sob from a pupil behind me. I turned quickly and enquired what was the matter. Between sobs a little red-headed chap told me that the young man referred to had hurt him, and called him a vile name. Turning to the young man, I said: "Is that true?" "Yes," he said, "what are you going to do about it?" I decided to make a rough and tumble job of it once and for all. To his great surprise I seized him by the coat collar, pulled him out of his seat, shook him until he began to howl with fear and then, after a few well-directed open-hand blows, threw him back into his seat. That ended the matter of discipline so far as the boys were concerned. The question of what to do with the young women remained. They would talk out loud and leave their seats to sit in conversation with other pupils. They were determined to put me to the test, believing I would not dare to punish them.

One afternoon I called the school together and said: "There are a couple of young women in the school who think they are privileged because of their families and the fact that they are of the female sex. I am going to dismiss the school for the day. Tomorrow I will bring a strap with me, and I will use it without mercy and without fear or favour." Someone shouted out a loud "Amen!" The statement was so unexpected that I burst out laughing; the whole school followed my example. Then I said, "All right, Amen it is!" The next morning I arrived with my strap but I never had to use it. That was the end of my trouble.

Marsh Tory soon discovered that he not only had a gift for teaching but that he loved it as well. His salary at this time was $250.00 a year, out of which he paid his board and bought whatever he needed in the way of clothing. At the end of three years' teaching he had saved $200, enough to start his university career.

It had been his intention to enter Mount Allison University, Sackville, N.B., in the autumn of 1886 and all his plans had been completed. During the summer, however, an event occurred which changed the major current of young Marsh Tory's life and incidentally that of his two brothers as well. It happened that a small Congregational church, built in the days of Grandfather Henry Tory and closed for many years, had been reopened for summer services in 1884. In the summer of 1886 a young student from the Congregational College in Montreal—whose name is not mentioned in Dr. Tory's notes—arrived in Port Shoreham to conduct summer services in the little church. Marsh Tory met the young missionary and they became fast friends. He told young Tory of McGill University and its advantages. The cost of attending McGill was not more than at Mount Allison and the possibility of summer employment was much greater. There were also a number of bursaries and scholarships available at McGill which were not open to students at Mount Allison. He immediately applied for admission to Wesleyan Theological College, Montreal, an affiliate of McGill, and was accepted. During the summer vacation at home before entering McGill an incident occurred which Dr. Tory recalls with great delight.

The regular minister of the church we attended was absent attending a church conference and the church was closed for the period of his absence. My mother, who was a leader in all such matters, was exceedingly anxious to have the church services continued and persuaded me to undertake the minister's duties for one Sunday. I was exceedingly loath to do so but was finally persuaded, and notice was sent out that I would conduct the services on the coming Sunday afternoon. We had a neighbour named MacIntosh whose character presented great contrasts. When he was friendly he could not do too much for you, but when he was in a bad mood he was a very troublesome person. At this time he was in a rage with my father and the whole Tory family. He came to the church on this occasion and brought with him another neighbour, George MacMaster. When I saw them enter the church I knew they were not there for any good purpose.

I laboured through the service as best I could, the sermon being only about fifteen minutes in length. It was, I fear, a most commonplace address, as I had little background of knowledge from which to draw material. After dismissing the congregation I walked down the aisle and noticed that MacIntosh and MacMaster were waiting for me. Just as I passed them MacIntosh turned to MacMaster and in a hoarse whisper intended for my ears said: "George, wasn't that a hell of a sermon?" The humour of the situation caught me and turning, to his great surprise, I said laughingly: "You are perfectly right." A short time before leaving for Montreal, my Mother persuaded me to call on Mr. MacIntosh to say good-bye. I did so and found him out cutting wood at his door. I said to him: "Mr. MacIntosh, I am going away and may not be back for some years, so I have come to say good-bye." He looked at me for a moment, then reaching out his hand, he said: "Well, good-bye and let me give you some advice. Never walk when you can ride, and remember God never blesses anything which has not a head and a tail." The latter statement, of course, referred to my sermon. I never saw him again but I always remembered that closing bit of wisdom.

CHAPTER VI

LIFE AT McGILL

MARSH TORY'S TEACHING CONTRACT did not end until the last of October, and it was the first week in November, 1886, when he finally arrived in Montreal to register as a freshman at McGill. A room had been reserved for him at Wesleyan Theological College so that he did not have to search for a place to live, but it was his first time away from home and his first experience in a big city. He was a month late in registering, which was in itself a handicap, not only so far as classwork was concerned, but because class friendships had been formed and he was an outsider. For several weeks he was a confused and very lonely young man. At that time students were permitted to enter the university without examination, and if the Christmas tests were passed successfully full standing as an undergraduate was granted until the final examinations in the spring confirmed the standing. As a result of this arrangement young Tory was able to start to work at once, attending lectures and accommodating himself to college life.

The total number of students attending McGill at that time was less than a thousand, including those in Normal School and in the affiliated theological colleges. The only buildings on the campus were the Arts Building and the Redpath Museum. The east wing of the Arts Building was used for administrative purposes and for the new faculty of Applied Science. It contained a couple of lecture rooms and a small museum. There was some very elementary laboratory equipment in the central section of the Arts Building, used mainly for demonstrations in chemistry. The west end of the Arts Building, built with gifts from the Molson family, was called Molson's Hall, and in addition to its classrooms served as the University Convocation Hall. The Redpath Museum was at that time entirely given up to geology and paleontology; it had been built by Peter Redpath, Chancellor of the University; and was the pride and joy of the Principal, Sir William Dawson. These were the buildings in which Marshall Tory did all of his undergraduate work. It was not until 1893 that the first engineering building (later burned) was erected, and shortly after that the physics building was built. These were the gifts of Sir William Macdonald.

In addition to the handicap of late registration young Tory soon found that his knowledge of languages was entirely inadequate. He had made a fair start in Latin, but his knowledge of Greek consisted only of the alphabet. In mathematics he had already done work equivalent to that of the first year. But from the beginning he was fortunate in his friends. He was twenty-two years of age and his working experience had given him a maturity of outlook beyond his years. For this reason most of the friendships he formed were among upper classmen. His most intimate friend in his first year was a theological student by the name of Samuel Brown. Brown, who later became one of the most distinguished preachers of the Methodist Church, was a brilliant student and he and other fourth year men gave generously of their time in helping Marsh Tory to overcome his language difficulties and catch up with the classroom work he had missed.

It was a fortunate thing for him that his early training had given him a tough and enduring health of mind and body, for up until the Christmas examinations he worked fourteen hours a day. But it was well worth it, for when the results were announced Christmas week he had first class standing in all subjects except Greek, and in that subject he was in the second division. All through the winter of 1886-1887 Marsh Tory continued his exhausting daily regimen of fourteen hours study, seven hours of sleep and three hours for meals and exercise.

In those days it was the custom to read out the results of the final spring examinations at a special assembly of the

Faculty of Arts in Molson's Hall. It was an exciting and colourful occasion, as the members of the Faculty, including the Principal, attended in all their splendour of gown and hood. The results were read from the platform by the Dean of Arts, and the whole student body waited in tense anticipation to learn how they had fared in the year's work. At this assembly in the spring of 1887 Marshall Tory waited in fear and trembling for the sound of his name, and undoubtedly his thoughts went back to his home in Port Shoreham and the hopes and prayers of his people. The Dean began with the fourth year, and after what seemed an eternity of waiting he came at last to the first year. Dr. Tory used to say in later life that he had many pleasant memories of work undertaken and brought to a successful conclusion, but none that recalled such suspense, surprise and pleasure as that day when he heard his name read out as first in his year, and with first-class standing in all subjects.

When Marsh Tory entered McGill he had scarcely enough money to carry him through his first year. It was therefore imperative that he should find some sort of summer employment. Many of the students who were registered as theological students spent their summers on mission fields, but he felt that he had neither the experience nor the knowledge to undertake such work. The long journey home was expensive and there was little chance of any worthwhile employment in Guysborough County. In May, 1887, through the good offices of a Montreal friend, Marsh Tory obtained a position as checker with the shipping firm of Robert Reford and Company. His job was to check cargoes from the ships of the firm unloading in the harbour against the bills of lading and to see that the goods were delivered to their rightful owners. The work was not difficult but required great care, and the hours were from 7 a.m. to 6 p.m. The boats were unloaded on a day and night two-shift basis. One week the checkers were on day shift and the following week on the graveyard shift.

It was an irregular and upsetting kind of existence, but the harbour at night, the dark streets, the waterfront saloons where he sometimes enjoyed a bowl of pea soup, and the roustabout character of his associates fascinated the young student. That year brought one of the worst of the periodic spring floods on the St. Lawrence river. It was in the days before the present embankments were built, and the dock and streets were flooded as far back as St. James and Notre Dame Streets. In fact even Craig Street had to be crossed in boats. The result was confusion and disruption of services everywhere in the lower part of the city. During this time young Tory's cool head and accounting and business experience proved extremely useful. He worked overtime long hours to help bring order out of chaos.

Before the summer was over the firm recognized his ability, and he was kept on the job when work slackened and other men were being laid off. At the end of the season he was offered a permanent position with the company. But his first year at McGill had strengthened his ambition and inspired confidence in his own capacity as a student.

That fall Marsh Tory entered the university with enough money to complete his second year. He continued his general course and took the honours course in mathematics as well. But this second year he did more than work at his studies. He took an active part in student activities. The student body had not at that time been fully organized but there were active literary and debating societies. Debates on political and religious subjects were not allowed on the campus, and as a result public discussions were of the conventional literary, historical and social type. At one of the student debates widely attended by staff and students Marsh Tory made a name for himself by his brilliant defence of the beheading of Charles the First. Immediately after this he was elected orator of his class and chosen to represent the student body at an extremely important meeting. In January, 1888, the first of the now well-known McGill reunions was held in the Windsor Hotel. It was followed by a banquet at which Sir Wilfrid Laurier, who was a graduate in law of McGill and then Leader of the Opposition in the House of Commons, was the speaker. On the elaborate programme a place was reserved for a speech by a representative of the student body. On that great occasion the young man from a pioneer farm in Guysborough County sat at the head table beside the guest speaker and made a speech which received high praise from Sir William Dawson and Sir Wilfrid. He had won a firm place for himself on the campus and in the classroom. He finished his second year with first rank honours in mathematics, first-class general standing, and as prizeman in chemistry.

It was now eighteen months since young Marsh Tory had been home or had seen any of his people. There was a generous scholarship in mathematics and physics available for third year students. That summer was spent at home in hard study, and the scholarship he won at the September examinations was good for two years and made the remainder of his under-graduate term financially secure. In the fall of 1888 he returned to McGill and was elected president of his class.

In his diary, written at various times during the closing years of his life, Dr. Tory has little to say about his third and fourth years as an undergraduate, but of his graduation in the spring of 1890, he writes:

> I came out physically fit with first rank honours in mathematics and the Anne Molson Gold Medal for highest standing in the final year. I took the money option, intending to redeem the medal which I had the right to do. In the labour of a workaday world the little glamour of the hour soon passed, and I must record that the medal was never redeemed. The experience of graduation from the point of view of personal pleasure did not give the supreme satisfaction I had on completing my freshman year. On that occasion I had proved my right to go on. It was different with graduation. It was as if a whole period of life had closed. I realized I was now expected to make use of what I had acquired.

Before entering College Marsh Tory had been admitted as a candidate for the ministry of the Methodist Church in the Nova Scotia Conference. As soon as he graduated in Arts he was notified that he had been appointed as assistant to the Rev. William Ainly of Truro, N.S. He had had very little preparation in theology because of the nature of the courses he had taken in the university. The first-class general standing he had received shows that he had done brilliant work in philosophy, history, and the general Arts requirements. He had also done some preaching in the small mission churches around Montreal. One of these experiences he mentions:

Some of these occasions had amusing features connected with them. There was a little Negro church in Montreal at the time which had a self-appointed Negro preacher, and the students of the various colleges used to assist in conducting services there. The preacher had as a regular occupation the calling of trains in the C.P.R. station. In those days a rather ceremonious performance. He had a voice like the wild bull of Bashan and when he started calling trains, everyone paid attention sometimes for the sheer joy of listening to his voice. On one occasion when I was expected to be the speaker at his church, I must have been a few minutes late, and when I arrived, the pulpit was already occupied. Leaning over to me he said, "What hymn would the young brother like me to announce?" and so on for each item of the service. After I had made my little address he kindly commented on what I had said, and then informed the congregation that "the mission board was sending these young brothers here to practise on us" and forthwith proceeded to give a most elaborate discourse. On another occasion he turned up at a great Easter "love feast," a religious exercise beloved by the earlier Methodists but now abandoned. It was representative of all the Methodist churches in the city and was held in the great St. James Church Hall. A group of prominent ministers were on the platform, and Mr. Brown promptly took his seat among them, dressed in the most severe clerical attire. We could all see that the old man was ready for action. After the meeting had been formally opened by singing and prayer, Dr. Douglas, Principal of Wesleyan Theological College, gave a short address followed by Dr. Shaw, the professor of Greek. The addresses were more or less of a testimony type. Immediately Brown got to his feet and this was the type of his testimony: "Brethren, I had a vision. I dreamed I had been called to the marriage supper of the lamb. The thing which pleased me most of all was that they wouldn't begin the supper until we all got there." This was almost too much for the group of distinguished preachers and theologians, but its effect upon the congregation and people, and especially upon a group of not too serious-minded students can be imagined.

But to return to my story. I was a very rapid speaker and must confess I was not adept at imaginative presentations unless the material was historical. My tendency was to take an argumentative subject and to go at the pros and cons with great energy. The Rev. Dr. Douglas, himself a great preacher, who heard one of my sermons read to a class of students as a class exercise, commented

"A good study of the subject, but there is a complete absence of imaginative rhetoric. Its evangelical significance is doubtful." As a matter of fact I had never been able to find enough material on a religious theme to enable me to speak for more than fifteen minutes. On the other hand I had been a ready debater and was regarded as one of the best in my university class. My sermons therefore took rather the form of a debate, by presenting both sides but emphasizing the matter in which I was especially interested. I had a sort of motto that some one had given me as a boy—"Create a need and undertake to supply it."

In this same section of his diary Dr. Tory writes of his experiences as assistant to Rev. William Ainly in Truro:

I shall never forget my first appearance in the pulpit of the main church. As I looked into the faces of the large congregation and announced the opening hymn, I became ill and had to retire for a few minutes while the hymn was being sung. I came back, however, and finished what I had to say. I soon became accustomed to the work and enjoyed it. The preparation of addresses, however, was always difficult. I fear they were hardly sermons in any orthodox sense. I was intensely in earnest about it, and I am happy to say that before the end of the year the little church was packed every Sunday night. I can conscientiously say that I studied hard to make my addresses useful and practical.

On the whole it was an exceedingly happy year. Mr. Ainly to whom I was responsible, was a delightful man to be associated with. From my point of view he was a bit too theological as a preacher, and I think that was the judgment of the congregation. We got on well, however, and I still remember him with great pleasure although he has long since passed into the great unknown.

At the Annual Conference I received the appointment for the second year, but I had barely got started when a letter was received from Sir William Dawson, Principal of McGill, asking me to accept a lectureship on the university staff in the department of mathematics. After some discussion with Mr. Ainly and the church authorities, I was allowed to secure a substitute and released from my obligations. The result was, I returned to the university, now to be associated as colleague with the men by whom I had been taught.

CHAPTER VII

LECTURER AND PROFESSOR

WHEN MARSH TORY RETURNED TO MCGILL in the fall of 1891 a new chapter in his life began. The appointment was only for a year. He accepted it mainly because his heart was still set on the ministry, and the lectureship would give him an opportunity to complete his studies in Theology. He soon discovered, however, that his appointment was in the nature of a try-out, to see if he could both teach and keep discipline in the large classes of freshmen he was assigned to handle. He was actually taking over work previously carried on by Professor George Chandler, head of the Mathematical department in the Faculty of Engineering.

From the beginning young Tory was an outstanding success as a teacher. He had come a long hard road himself, and he had a warm interest in his students as individuals and in their academic and personal problems. Within a few weeks he knew every one of his seventy students by name and was familiar with their qualifications. There were many students, especially from country schools, whose preparation was limited, and for these he established "grind" classes, out of regular hours, which all who desired could attend.

At that time women were not allowed to sit in lecture rooms with men students. This meant that five days a week all lectures had to be repeated at the Royal Victoria College. As the work was very elementary and required little preparation he had plenty of time for personal study. In the next two years he completed the work for the B.D. degree, and also took advanced courses in Philosophy and English. From the time he first began to teach in the little one-room school in Guysborough County discipline had never been a problem for young Marshall Tory. The reason was that he had the rare gift of making his subject so interesting, that students who ordinarily found mathematics a dull and tiresome subject found themselves for the first time able to understand.

During most of his years at McGill H. M. Tory taught the freshman classes in Mathematics, and many of his students recall vividly and with affection their memories of him in the classroom. Mrs Walter Vaughan (known to hundreds of McGill students as Susan Cameron, Professor of English) wrote in December, 1952:

> I came to McGill in 1891 full of nervous apprehension. Though I had been prepared for matriculation at the Girls High School of Saint John, N.B., and had passed respectably I was all too well aware of my deficiencies, especially in Mathematics. In fact I had an unhappy conviction that in this subject I was incapable and incurable. Dr. Tory was then a young teacher and in charge of the work of the First Year. He was a remarkable teacher for students of that grade. Absolutely unpretentious, he used to joke about the relative capacities of himself and his associate Dr. Harkness—a Cambridge scholar of very high attainments. Dr. Tory admired and liked him but admitted that he himself was a better choice for First Year Work. "The poor youngsters don't know what Harkness is talking about." His common sense method of dealing with students of my type was miraculously successful. In effect he said: "Look here, you have shown yourself intelligent in other subjects, any student can master First Year Mathematics—so go to it." I can't claim that he made a mathematician of me but he removed a burden of morbid fear, and enabled me to pass decently the tests required.

Dr. Tory's disciplinary technique is well illustrated in a letter from Dr. A. Norman Shaw, now Professor of Physics at McGill, who studied under him during the early 1900's:

> I recall admiring his method of controlling a large class in elementary freshman mathematics—trigonometry it was. No matter how uninterested in mathematics some of his class might be, he seemed to accept it as a challenge to catch their interest and he usually did. I remember that for some weeks a stray dog was repeatedly smuggled into various professor's classes. It was interesting to see the different reactions of the professors. Some with steely countenances saw to it that the animal was ejected promptly and gave the class a scathing criticism. One man laughed and dodged the problem in discipline by taking part in the fun of

catching the dog. When it came to Tory's turn the dog was put under the lift-up cover of the desk which sat on top of the lecture table. Tory was well launched in his lecture when the dog started to whine, but he could not determine at first where the sound came from. Presently he found it and held the rather miserable looking cur in his arms while he rang the bell for the janitor. The strange thing was that he managed to convey the impression, without giving any reproof whatever, that he was rather ashamed that a class of whom he was fond could be so childish—the whole incident wound up, not with an uproar as in some of the other cases, but with everybody feeling actually ashamed. It really meant that he commanded such respect from his class that they were sorry they had annoyed him.

The first summer after his appointment the youthful lecturer had saved enough money out of his salary ($600 a year) to spend five months at Cambridge University in England. He carried with him letters of introduction from Sir William Dawson to Sir Gabriel Stokes, to Professor J. J. Thompson, head of the Cavendish Laboratories at Cambridge (already noted for his foundation work on the Electron) and to Professor Caley, the most distinguished mathematician of his time. Here for the first time young Tory came into contact with scholars of world-wide reputation, and his fresh and vigorous mind was fired with a new desire to excel in his chosen field.

The stimulating effect of association with these great scholars is shown in some of the entries in the memoirs Dr. Tory began a few years before his death. In one entry he says:

I was attending the four o'clock service in King's College Chapel one day and had been given a seat in the Choir. Sitting opposite, facing me across the aisle, was the most distinguished looking person I had ever seen. King's Chapel was a revelation to me—and I have no doubt I was quite emotional about it all. On enquiry I found that this person referred to was Sir Gabriel Stokes and that he always attended the afternoon services. After that I attended regularly, I fear more to see Sir Gabriel than as an act of worship. He had a wonderfully beautiful face. I have never seen another which so impressed me. The features were exceedingly regular, the brow lofty, the appearance intensely intellectual, but these were coupled with such a benign and reverent expression of the face that I can recall the impression upon my imagination to this day.

Young Tory made friends with many of the faculty families at Cambridge and found a particularly warm welcome in the home of Professor Caley. During the next five months he devoted himself to a study of rigid dynamics—and he records that the opportunity of working with Professors Thompson and Caley in the Cavendish Laboratories was one of the greatest experiences in his life.

When he arrived home from England, in the fall of 1892, for his second year of teaching he had barely enough money to hire a cab to his lodgings. In the meantime the MacDonald Physics building was nearing completion. The head of the Physics Department was Professor John Cox, a Cambridge tripos man whose training was in mathematics and mathematical physics but who had had no laboratory experience. When the Physics Building was completed, in the spring of 1893, the problem of setting up the new laboratory equipment and planning the courses of practical instruction, became an urgent matter. Professor Cox approached young Tory and asked him to undertake the responsibility. To do this required additional training in practical physics, and in the summer of 1893 arrangements were made for him to spend another five months in the Cavendish Laboratories.

Early in June of that year, before leaving for England, Henry Marshall Tory married Miss Annie Frost in a quiet ceremony at the home of her parents. She was the third child in a family of six children born to David and Lephtha Shepherd Frost in the tiny village of Frost, not far from the town of Waterloo in the Eastern Townships of Quebec.

When Annie Frost was twelve years of age (in the year 1878) the family moved to Montreal. She was educated in Montreal schools, graduating from Normal School in her twentieth year, with a first-class teacher's certificate. The Frost home was near the University, and apparently a place where McGill students gathered on Sunday evenings to chat and sing and enjoy the hospitality of a home in which they were always warmly welcomed. It was on one of these occasions that Marshall Tory met the woman who was to be his devoted companion and inspiration for forty-five years.

After the wedding the Torys left immediately for England.

The honeymoon was spent in a month's tour of the British Isles before settling down to work at Cambridge, an experience Dr. Tory once referred to in the writer's hearing as, "the happiest period of my whole life."

Henry Marshall Tory's marriage was the best thing that ever happened to him for his beloved Annie gave to her young husband the companionship and devoted care he had long needed, and more than any other factor strengthened his resolve to devote his life to education. On returning to McGill, in the fall of 1893, the Torys set up housekeeping in a small flat on Durocher Street, not far from the University, and for years to come their home was a rendezvous for students and faculty alike.

On taking up his work Dr. Tory found that a new Professor of Physics had been appointed in the person of Professor Callender, also a Cambridge tripos man. The growth of the Engineering Department at McGill, the buildings for which had been provided by Sir William Macdonald, had resulted in a great influx of engineering students for whom Practical Physics was an absolute necessity. Tory was the only person apart from Professor Callender who had any experience in the preparation of laboratory experiments and lectures.

For the next year he lectured in Mathematics on an average of three hours each morning from Monday to Friday, and three afternoons a week were given to demonstrations for student classes of from thirty to sixty students. The other afternoons and three evenings a week were spent in testing and standardizing equipment and setting it up for student use. In addition, manuscripts had to be prepared for student guidance. The teaching work alone took over twenty hours a week, the preparation of experiments and the checking and marking of students' papers was an extra task. At the same time he was carrying on research work, the results of which were published in the Philosophical Magazine and Journal of Physical Chemistry, and in a text-book on practical physics.

That the Governors of the University had not the slightest conception of the work involved in his programme is shown by the fact, that at the end of the year young Tory was voted an advance of $100, bringing his salary up to the magnificent sum of $700 per year. The Board of Governors of McGill at that time was largely dominated by Sir William Macdonald, whose idea of a professor was a man who went to work at eight o'clock in the morning and stayed at his desk until five or six o'clock like a clerk or a bookkeeper. This attitude was shared by some of the Governors, one of whom undertook to report on those who were on hand promptly at nine o'clock and those who were not.

Dr. Tory tells of arriving at the door of the Engineering Building one morning at ten o'clock. He was halted by this gentleman who said: "Aren't you supposed to be at work by nine o'clock?" Tory had been at work the night before until 12 o'clock. This greeting and the thought of his small salary were a little too much, and Tory blurted out: "Why don't you mind your own affairs?" He goes on to say that as far as he knew, that episode ended the spy system at McGill.

Marshall Tory had taken such an active part in campus activities as a student that he was widely known, and now as a teacher he continued to be counsellor and friend to large numbers of undergraduates. His home was constantly filled with students seeking help with their studies and advice about personal problems. Dr. Norman Shaw records an interesting example of Dr. Tory's genius for giving a student common sense advice about his future, and although it has reference to a later date (1904 to be exact) it may be useful at this point as an illustration. Shaw, who was a brilliant student but was uncertain regarding his future, asked Dr. Tory's advice about going on with the honour course in Mathematics and Physics in his third and fourth years. His reply was in effect as follows:

"Look here, Shaw, you can't tell from examination marks whether or not it is advisable to take up a calling in which you will have to work harder and harder through the years, without any hope of material award. If you feel you would be unhappy doing anything else, then take the course. You are probably good enough to get by but you are not likely to be a Rutherford." Then he said: "Look at me. I am forty, my salary is $2,250, and I have forty hours of lectures and auxiliary work every week. Mrs. Tory and I have no children; if we had I don't know how we could bring them up. I seem to have reached the end of my opportunities. My two brothers were below me in school but they are men of considerable means and influence. Nevertheless I am sticking to education. I was not trained soon enough and adequately enough for a career in research, but I want to promote higher education and I'm going to keep on trying—if you can face obstacles and worries like that—then try your luck."

During the closing years of the life of Sir William Dawson, Dr. Tory became a close friend of the great Principal. Two other men had a strong influence in shaping his career and his thinking. These were Dr. Clark Murray, Professor of Philosophy, and Dr. Alexander Johnson, Dean of Arts, a mathematician from Dublin University. His life-long association with Dr. Frank Adams, later Vice-Principal of McGill, began at the same time.

For the next ten years, life at McGill followed a routine pattern about which Dr. Tory has little to say in the notes he has left. But it is apparent that in those years his position at McGill, his continued study and research, and his widening acquaintance with the life of the city, gave him a place of increasing stature in the world in which he lived. A letter from Dr. Charles W. Colby, McGill University, written in May, 1953, states:

> Time makes many ravages and dims many memories, but I have a lively recollection of Henry Marshall Tory, dating from the moment when he started out as a lecturer in mathematics at McGill. That was in 1891—sixty-two years ago—and the date is firmly fixed in my mind because I became a lecturer in English and History at the same moment. Moreover we continued in active service at McGill for almost the same length of time, his exit from curriculum work having taken place in 1908 and mine in 1909.
>
> During these years "the Faculty Room" was a place of meeting for lecturers no less than professors. What it lacked in breadth it made up in length and between lectures it was constantly frequented by all members of the staff. Since the programme of studies had not yet been subjected to proliferation this room afforded space for members of all departments in the Faculty of Arts—though it must be admitted that the margin of space was not considerable. Close quarters made for intimate contacts and gave full opportunity for the development of acquaintance. In many cases friendships ensued and enmities were rare.
>
> Under such circumstances I came to know Tory very well

indeed, though my intellectual interests lay quite outside his special sphere of mathematics. In that field I have always been a total net loss but he was so kind as not to obtrude solid geometry upon me. From the start we found it easy to harmonize. Helped by the perspective of sixty years I would single out indomitable energy as what at first sight appeared to be his chief characteristic. With it was linked a steady cheerfulness which never failed to arrest attention. His grasp of detail was extraordinary and it soon proved that he could lend a hand in many ways. This qualification remained outstanding in all his later occupations.

Among the things to be put in high relief was his solicitude for the religious development of the undergraduates, and the mixture of seriousness with gaiety in his nature. His helpfulness was not capitalized unduly but it was always there, and throughout his years at McGill extra-curricular activities of a devotional character occupied much of his time. In this way his influence extended through the whole student body.

The Professor with whom I had most to do in my undergraduate days was Dean Moyse, and we were close friends during the time I taught at McGill. Through this relationship I came to know how serviceable Tory's industry and talent for organization were to the Dean, and how much reliance came to be placed upon them. As illustrating his ready responsiveness to a friend I feel moved to mention an incident very definitely within my own knowledge which shows how prompt and effective he could be.

For many years I have had close relations with Stanstead College, where my studies started and where during a long period I have served as a trustee. In 1908 this institution was in need of a Principal and at an important moment Tory told me incidentally that he was on the point of making a trip to Nova Scotia. That Province has special qualifications for the production of Principals and Presidents, so as the appointment of a Principal at Stanstead was largely in my hands I asked him to make inquiries during the course of this trip. He co-operated with diligence and success. Thanks to him Stanstead had George Trueman as Principal for twelve years to its very great advantage.

During the long period when Tory and I were brought together at McGill I came to know a great deal about his qualities and can attest that they were no less humane than solid. Of his later efforts which covered such a wide field I am unable to speak at first hand, but there was nothing he achieved that I found surprising. His driving power and his clearheadedness brought very significant results elsewhere but his gifts and his sincerity were fully revealed while he taught at McGill. Looking back to those days I have a mental portrait of him as one who was eager, capable, sympathetic and devoted to high aims.

In 1903 Tory received the D.Sc. degree and was advanced to a full Professorship in Mathematics. During the next two years he was deeply involved in the establishment of a graduate school at McGill. New schools and universities were arising in Canada, and the smaller colleges of the East were already sending graduate students abroad to Europe and the United States because there were no facilities in Canada. A study was made of graduate schools in the United States, but it was not until 1907, a year before Dr. Tory was to become first President of the University of Alberta, that the McGill graduate school was established.

In the meantime he was asked to undertake the first of a long list of difficult assignments which filled his life from this time until his death.

Chapter VIII

McGILL IN BRITISH COLUMBIA

While still on the staff of McGill University, Dr. Tory had an opportunity to share in the founding of a new university in the far West. He was never a member of the faculty of the new institution, nor was it officially a university until almost ten years after he left British Columbia. Yet largely through his efforts so solid a legal, financial and organizational base had been provided for a college that the university followed in due course.

As early as 1877 there had been some demand for a university in British Columbia. In that year, the Provincial Superintendent of Schools, Mr. Jessop, called public attention to the urgent need for providing the youth of the Province with opportunities for higher education.

There was need for a training centre for the education of teachers, clergymen, engineers and doctors, but there was also an urgent reason because of the political situation. British Columbia had for years been seething with all sorts of proposals for secession from Canada, union with the United States, return to a Crown Colony status, and other disturbing ideas. It was held by many people that an institution of higher learning would serve as a unifying force through affiliation with British and eastern Canadian universities.

But at that time British Columbia's sparse population was spread over a vast area in which communications and travel were difficult, and with almost a half of the total centred in the cities of Vancouver and Victoria. Services for the entire Province were costly and administration a continuing problem. There was no strongly unifying educational tradition since the people of the Province were somewhat heterogeneous, although most of them came from England and various parts of Eastern

Canada. Another factor which complicated the situation was the intense rivalry between Vancouver Island and the Mainland. Many worthy projects failed for lack of agreement on the choice of a site for building purposes.

People living in other parts of the Province, under the impression that their particular town would soon become a metropolis, were clamouring for a court house or an educational institution. It is not surprising, therefore, that with scant resources of money and teachers no serious move in the direction of a university was made for several years.

In 1890, however, the legislature did pass "The British Columbia University Act," which proclaimed that all university graduates present in British Columbia at least two months before the Act would constitute the convocation of a University to meet within four months after proclamation.

The Lieutenant-Governor-in-Council was empowered to appoint a Chancellor and Vice-Chancellor. The Senate was to consist of: the Chancellor and Vice-Chancellor; seven members elected by convocation; three by the Lieutenant-Governor-in-Council; one each appointed by the Municipal Councils of Vancouver, Victoria, New Westminster and Nanaimo; the Speaker of the Legislative Assembly; the Superintendent of Education; the staff of the University; and members of Professional societies. There were to be faculties of Arts and Science, Medicine, Law, Applied Science and Engineering. The University was to be non-sectarian and women were to be freely admitted.

This ambitious plan failed. The jealousy between the Island and the Mainland was apparent at the first meeting of Convocation and resulted in a stalemate. A clause which was added as an amendment in 1891 was the direct cause of the final collapse of the project. As amended the Act required that a meeting of the Senate should take place within one month of the election of Senators by Convocation. The Chancellor, Dr. I. W. Powell, called a meeting in Victoria on July 2, 1891, but a quorum failed to attend. It proved impossible to get mainland members to attend in sufficient numbers for a meeting until the month deadline had passed. Powers of the

HENRY MARSHALL TORY [1909]

MRS. H. M. TORY [1926]

Senate thus lapsed and this first attempt to establish a university ended in failure.

Following this discouraging episode, the Chairman of the Vancouver School Board, Mr. A. H. B. MacGowan, went east to consult with the staffs of leading eastern Canadian universities about the possibility of securing some sort of affiliation with one of them.

McGill University showed immediate interest in his proposals, and the reply Mr. MacGowan took back to his board from the McGill authorities was that undoubtedly a suitable plan could be worked out provided two special conditions could be met. In the first place McGill would have to obtain a change in the provincial statute under which it operated and secondly, the Vancouver School Board would have to seek legislative authority for the contemplated enterprise. Special legislation at both Quebec and Victoria fulfilled these conditions. At Victoria an Act was passed, in 1894, which empowered the affiliation of high schools in the Province with any recognized Canadian university. This was supplemented in 1896 by Section 63 of the Public School Act, which provided that any Collegiate Institute Board might enter into affiliation with any one or more of the recognized universities of the Dominion of Canada, subject to the sanction of the Council of Public Instruction, which might by its Charter and regulations be authorized to admit such boards to affiliation.

Under this arrangement it was permitted to substitute for the Intermediate and Senior Academic Grades the courses for matriculation, and the first and second years in Arts respectively. With these provisions secured, Dr. William Peterson, Principal of McGill, visited British Columbia and formal affiliation was completed. Vancouver High School became Vancouver College, began university work for the first year in Arts in 1899, and added a second year in 1902.

During the latter year, Victoria College (Victoria High School) also became affiliated with McGill and began first year work in Arts.

In granting affiliation McGill was acting in harmony with her avowed policy of assisting in every way possible the general cause of education throughout Canada, and was but extending beyond the Province of Quebec the privileges already extended to Stanstead Wesleyan College, St. Francis College, Richmond, Quebec, and Morrin College, Quebec.

For some years Dr. Tory had been urging upon McGill authorities the desirability of extending affiliation to institutions outside Quebec Province. Acadia, Mount Allison, and King's College, among others, were finding themselves badly handicapped for want of equipment in teaching the Senior courses in Engineering. Dr. Tory suggested to the McGill corporation of which he was a member (as a Governor's Fellow), that arrangements be made with them to co-ordinate their Junior courses so as to fit into the third and fourth years at McGill. Under this arrangement, in 1904, Mount Allison, Acadia and King's College were admitted to affiliation with McGill.

In the fall of 1904, Mr. Lemuel Robertson, a graduate of McGill, then a teacher of Classics at Vancouver High School (later Professor at U.B.C.), came to McGill to do post-graduate work and at the invitation of Dr. Peterson to serve as Instructor in Classics. Shortly after his arrival he discussed with Dr. Tory —a fellow Maritimer—a plan he had in mind to have McGill take over work of university grade in Vancouver. He was definitely of the opinion that if McGill would do so, and was prepared to provide money enough to place the enterprise on a proper footing, the whole Province would welcome such a plan. The matter was further discussed with Principal William Peterson, Dr. Charles Moyse, Dean of Arts, and others, and Robertson was asked to write to the Vancouver authorities asking for assurances that such a move would be acceptable to the Vancouver people. The answer was that a conference had been held with Dr. Alexander Robinson, Superintendent of Education for the Province, who summed up his opinion by saying: "There is the University of British Columbia on a sound educational basis."

In the meantime Lemuel Robertson was asked to prepare a statement setting forth his ideas. He immediately proceeded to draw up a paper outlining in considerable detail his plan for a McGill in British Columbia. The main burden of his argument was, that the Provincial control of education in Canada had originated not in any special belief that education was a matter for the Provinces, but in the fact that it had been impossible for Quebec and the other Provinces to agree on a national system. He further pointed out, that in the sphere of higher education, a virgin field existed from the Great Lakes to the Pacific Ocean, and that the Universities of Eastern Canada might well take a lead in shaping the course of higher education in the West. McGill, as a privately endowed institution and free of denominational or political control, might very well lead such a movement. The report pointed out that a unique opportunity now presented itself in British Columbia, that the financial obligation at the beginning would not be large, and that McGill had here an opportunity to unify and strengthen the whole cause of higher education in Canada by establishing herself in British Columbia.

This report received wide publicity at McGill and in the Montreal papers, as a statesmanlike treatment of an important national issue. The outcome was that Dr. Tory, largely because of his work in furthering the affiliation of the eastern institutions already referred to, was instructed to proceed to Vancouver in the spring of 1905, taking Mr. Robertson with him because of his interest in the project and his knowledge of the local problems involved in its promotion. As matters turned out Robertson was not able to leave until some weeks later, and Dr. Tory proceeded to British Columbia in April, 1905, without him.

Within a few weeks Dr. Tory had visited most of the secondary schools in the Province, had interviewed the government, the Department of Education, the Vancouver School Board, and representatives of various other School Boards of the Province, and on May 15, 1905, he sent the following report to McGill from Nelson, B.C.:

Dear Dr. Peterson:

I think I have talked school and college matters with every man in British Columbia whose knowledge would help me to gauge opinion on such subjects, and as a result have now a fairly clear view of the whole situation. I have had two sessions with the Executive Council of the Government, and I see great difficulty in extending the work of Vancouver College on any other basis than control through a specially appointed Board of Management.

There are the local jealousies always present in a new country between the various educational centres, Victoria, Vancouver, New Westminster, even Nelson being in the contest for any advanced step the government may take. If the Government gives consent to one High School to extend its affiliation it cannot refuse it to another—on the other hand the Government does not feel that the demand warrants them in establishing anything corresponding to a University at this time. They have only a majority of three in the House and deciding on a place for a University might mean defeat under conditions here. They frankly state that they would be glad if we would take the initiative and that they would help, at least to the extent of $460.00 per year to each member of the teaching staff.

Dr. A. Robinson, the Superintendent of Education, said to me: "If you will take the initiative and the responsibility of saying when, where, and how an institution is to be undertaken you will have the whole Province in your hands, and give a most satisfactory solution to what promises to become a most difficult problem for the Province." Such a step would take the higher education of the country out of politics—a most desirable thing.

There is another thing which helps to complicate the situation. They have here National schools and are determined to maintain them. No clergyman of any denomination is allowed to teach in any school, to be a School Inspector, to be a member of a School Board, or Superintendent of Education. The Non-Anglican clergy have consented to this, although they do not like it, in order to make Government-supported church schools impossible. This was brought about in the early days when free schools were first established, because when the Act was being prepared, influences were set in motion to secure the appointment of an Anglican clergyman as Superintendent of Education. Then the Methodists and Presbyterians took a hand in the affair with the above result.

Now the time for the establishment of denominational colleges as in the East is coming. The Methodist Church has established a College (Columbian College) at New Westminster and it is affiliated to Toronto University. It is a weak, struggling Institution with ambitions far beyond its strength. The development of such institutions in this country instead of a strong properly governed one means withholding for years to come the benefits of education in a large and generous sense, from the people. Of course such institutions would be supported largely by Eastern money.

A strong step taken now would in all probability settle this question for all time, not only by making such institutions unnecessary but by making competition impossible.

With these facts before me I have taken a step of which I hope you will approve. I frankly told the Government that I had no authority to spend money but that if reasonable assistance would be given I would report in favour of our assuming the parentage of a College for British Columbia. At their request I have prepared for the Council a tentative memorandum as a basis for discussion, indicating the lines upon which we might be willing to operate.

The memorandum is as follows:

To The Hon., The Minister of Education.

Sir:

As suggested by your Council today I would respectfully submit the following as a tentative proposal for increasing the work of higher education in your province:

(1) That there should be established in connection with Vancouver College, a College incorporated with McGill University offering courses for three years in Arts. Namely, one year in Matriculation, and the first and second years in the Arts Course leading to the B.A. degree; the First Two years in Applied Science, the courses to include Biology and Chemistry.

Students from British Columbia would then be able to take the B.A. degree in two years, the B.Sc., in Arts and Applied Science in two years, and the B.A. and M.D. together in four years. Such an arrangement would give all candidates for higher study an opportunity to complete their courses in Arts and Applied Science and Medicine at McGill where they would have the advantage of the best scientific equipment on the continent, and at the same time secure Degrees and Certificates that would have recognition anywhere in the English-speaking world—I might add that the Scientific Course leads to Degrees in (a) Architecture, (b) Chemistry, (c) Civil Engineering and Surveying, (d) Metallurgy, (e) Mining Engineering, (f) Transportation, (g) Electrical Engineering.

(2) As the academic work of the first two years in Arts meets all the requirements of your Department of Education, the College could be so constituted as to include the Principal of the Normal School as a member of the teaching staff. The College would then do the educational part of the Normal School Work, providing a special training for persons who intend to teach, but have not so trained previously. The strictly professional work would of course be done by those especially appointed for Normal School Work. A Normal Building might then be planned as a College to house both the College and the Normal School proper when the growth of the work of the High School in Vancouver makes it necessary to move from that building.

(3) In carrying out the work a staff of at least eight men would be required. The Vancouver School Board are now carrying on the work of the first two years in Arts, and are employing four men for this purpose, so that four additional men would be necessary. As a minimum contribution the Government might extend the terms under which the allowance now made to High School teachers, $460.00 a year each, to include members of the College staff, and at the same time freeing them from the necessity of qualifying as certificated teachers, a demand not made anywhere in the Empire upon College professors.

(4) I would suggest that a Governing Board should be so constituted as to give representation to all interested parties, and also free it from merely local control, giving it a more thoroughly British Columbia aspect.

Such a Board might be constituted as follows:

The Hon., The Minister of Education
The Superintendent of Education
The Chairman of the Vancouver School Board
The Superintendent of City Schools
The Principal of the College
The Secretary of the Faculty

– Then, representatives from British Columbia selected by the Board of Governors of McGill University so as to represent the widest possible interest, and after consultation with the Council of Public Instruction.
– The Principal of McGill University.

(5) The Board to have power to impose such fees as might be expedient; to make appointments to the teaching staff and to fix salaries. In no case should fees be imposed on teachers-in-training.

To this as a general outline the Department of Education and the members of the Government have consented. I then opened with them the question of a grant of land. They agree in principle to such an arrangement and will provide a beautiful site for buildings overlooking the sea.

I then opened the matter with the Vancouver School Board at a special private meeting called for the purpose. To them I pointed out such facts as seemed advisable and emphasized the necessity for a change of management before any large scheme could be entered into. They saw the point at once and at a special meeting at which I was not present, passed general resolutions agreeing to:

(1) A new Board
(2) Support at least equivalent to that at present given, namely payment of four salaries

(3) The bearing of incidental running expenses while the College is in the High School
(4) Assistance in obtaining equipment as may be agreed upon.

They were very much pleased at the prospect of Vancouver being made an educational centre, and I am confident, with judicious handling, can be depended upon to deal generously when the time comes for a contract.

I think $4,500 a year from us would start the thing going on a sound basis. This, if possible, should be secured by a special endowment if we go forward and determine to hold the field permanently.

I leave for Calgary and Edmonton today, and expect to be home early in June.

Sincerely yours,
(signed) H. M. Tory.

On his way back to Montreal, Dr. Tory visited the two newly organized Provinces of Alberta and Saskatchewan, and was greatly impressed with the educational activity in both. Elementary and secondary schools were going up by the hundreds. In Alberta, in one year (1903-1904) 270 new school districts had been formed. There were already two colleges in operation in Alberta. Alberta College in Edmonton with its vigorous and far-sighted Principal, Rev. Dr. J. H. Riddell, and Western Canada College in Calgary, the former under the auspices of the Methodist Church. A similar institution was being planned for Regina by the Methodist Church.

Dr. Tory visited these institutions and discussed with their leaders the question of affiliation with McGill. In Calgary he wrote to his wife in Montreal:

This country fascinates me. There is wine in the air; a feeling of excitement; of expectancy. It is difficult to explain. Perhaps it is just that everything is new, the people young and the conviction grows that great things are bound to happen in this rich new country.

While in Edmonton he had called upon Dr. A. C. Rutherford, Premier of the Province and Minister of Education. Neither of them could know at that time how intimately their lives would be inter-woven during the next twenty-five years. These two fine men, so alike and yet so unlike, were attracted to each other at once, and began a friendship on that occasion which never lost its warmth for either of them throughout life.

On his return to McGill, Dr. Tory prepared a full report of his activities which was presented before a special meeting of the Faculty of Arts in November, 1905, where the following resolution was passed:

> The Faculty of Arts views with great favour, the further extension of academic work in British Columbia and the Northwest, in connection with McGill University and expresses the hope that means will be provided to realize it.

The same resolution was unanimously approved by Corporation on December 13th.

Three days later at a meeting of the Board of Governors the following statement was incorporated in the Minutes of that body:

> The Principal submitted a resolution of the Faculty of Arts, and also from Corporation, favouring the further extension of Academic Work in British Columbia and the Northwest, in connection with McGill University and expresses the hope that means will be provided to realize it. The Board expressed the fullest sympathy with the prospect but decided that while it would not discountenance any appeal for assistance, it was not possible for the University to undertake any financial liability in connection therewith out of existing funds.

Sir William Macdonald was appealed to personally by Dr. Peterson but was adamant in his refusal to consider the matter. Although Dr. Tory was at that time not in favour with Sir William because of his religious activities on the campus, he persuaded Dr. Peterson to arrange an appointment to see whether his personal presentation of the situation would be helpful. Dr. Tory was coldly received by Sir William, but he was pleased to discover that Sir William had read his report and approved of it, mainly because of its emphasis upon non-denominational organization of higher education. When Dr. Tory mentioned the trifling sum of $5,000 for three years as the amount required to put the scheme in operation, Sir William said, "Is that a business man's estimate or a professor's?" Dr. Tory replied that he did not know the difference.

"Unfortunately," said Sir William, "I do. When I was erecting certain buildings in McGill I asked a distinguished professor for an estimate of the amount of money I would have to have to provide for equipment. I was told $80,000. When the work was completed and the bills all paid I found I had spent $750,000. Do you now see the distinction?"

Dr. Tory admitted that the point was well taken but went on to say: "I will pledge you, Sir William, that if you will supply the amount I have suggested for three years you will not be asked for another cent during that period. And further, if you will allow me to report progress from time to time, I promise you not to ask for money for any object without first writing you asking for a special interview and stating definitely in my letter the purpose of the interview. You may then, if you desire, refuse without embarrassment to discuss the matter." This was a shrewd move to keep the door open and Sir William agreed on those terms to make the grant asked for.

From that time until he left McGill, Dr. Tory had many interviews with Sir William and in his notes regarding this episode, says:

> I found him, under a cold exterior, warm hearted and possessed of great good-will but with prejudice against all clergymen so deep that it affected all his thinking. He wanted, for example, to compel the University YMCA to drop the word McGill from its title. He wanted to keep education as a means of freeing people from religious superstition as he called it. The real reason he agreed to pay for the Adams Survey of Education in Quebec was the hope that he could do something to lessen the influence of the Churches. This anti-religious mentality coloured his whole relationship with McGill.

When it became clear that the money was available to proceed with the British Columbia project, the necessary legislation was drafted. This consisted of two Bills to be passed into Acts by the British Columbia Legislature. The first: "An Act respecting McGill University," giving McGill power to establish a college in the Province. The second: "An Act to Incorporate the 'Royal Institution for Advancement of Learning in British Columbia'," thus creating a Board of

Management for the College and granting it the necessary powers.

Dr. Tory was then asked by the Board of Governors of McGill to proceed again to British Columbia in order to submit the proposed legislation to the Government. Before leaving for the West, he was heartened to receive two letters, one from Alexander Robinson, Superintendent of Education for British Columbia, and the other from the Hon. F. Carter-Cotton, a member of the Cabinet of the British Columbia Government, assuring him of the continued interest of the Government in the scheme, and urging him to come to Victoria in time for the opening of the Legislature on January 11, 1906. Dr. Tory left for the West early in January, 1906, carrying with him the two Acts drawn up for presentation to the British Columbia Government. These were duly presented on February 1, 1906, and read as follows:

An Act Respecting McGill University

Whereas it is desirable, in the interest of higher education in the Province of British Columbia, that a College or Colleges of McGill College and University be established for the higher education of men and women;

And whereas doubts exist as to the powers of McGill University in that behalf;

Therefore, His Majesty, by and with the advice and consent of the Legislative Assembly of the Province of British Columbia enacts as follows:

The Governors, Principal, and Fellows of McGill College and University, may establish, or cause to be established, or co-operate in the establishment of a University College or Colleges for the higher education of men and women in the Province of British Columbia, and may exercise and enjoy in the said Province all the powers, rights, privileges and functions conferred upon them by the Charter granted to them by His late Majesty, King George IV, in the second year of his reign, and amended by Her late Majesty, Queen Victoria, in the sixteenth year of her reign.

An Act to incorporate the Royal Institution for the Advancement of Learning of British Columbia,

Whereas it is desirable, in the interest of higher education in the Province of British Columbia, that a College or colleges of McGill College and University (hereinafter referred to as McGill

University) be established for the higher education of men and women,

Therefore, His Majesty, by and with the advice and consent of the Legislative Assembly of the Province of British Columbia, enacts as follows:

(1) William Peterson, C.M.G., L.L.D., Principal of McGill University; the Hon. F. Carter-Cotton of Vancouver; A. C. Flumerfelt, Esq., of Victoria; and J. W. Creighton, Esq., of New Westminster; together with such persons as they may associate with them for the purpose, are hereby constituted a body politic and corporate, with perpetual succession and a common seal, under the name of "The Royal Institution for the Advancement of Learning of British Columbia," hereinafter called "The Royal Institution."

(2) The Royal Institution shall have power to acquire, by gift, purchase or otherwise, and to hold, grant, lease, sell or otherwise dispose of real and personal property of every kind whatsoever for the purpose of the Corporation.

(3) The Royal Institution may establish at such place in British Columbia as the said McGill University may designate, a College for the higher education of men and women under the name of "The McGill University College of British Columbia," hereinafter referred to as "The College."

(4) The College shall, in respect of courses of study and examination leading to degrees, be deemed to be a College of McGill University, and shall provide courses of study leading to degrees of McGill University.

(5) The Royal Institution shall consist of not less than eight and not more than fifteen members, one of whom shall be elected President. They shall have power, however, in addition, to give such representation to any school board or other bodies in charge of public education as may be agreed upon. The Minister of Education of the Province of British Columbia, the Superintendent of Education of the said Province, the Principal of McGill University, and the Principal of the College shall be members ex officio.

(6) The Royal Institution shall be the Trustee of the College, and as such shall constitute its Board of Governors, and subject to this Act, shall:

(a) Manage all financial and ordinary business of the College including the investment of its moneys, and the appointing of auditors for the examination of its accounts;

(b) Appoint and remove the Principal, Registrar, Professors, Lecturers and Instructors and all other officers and servants of the College;

(c) Constitute the professors and such other members of the teaching staff as they may from time to time determine into the Faculty or Faculties of the College;

(d) Determine from time to time subject to the approval of the Faculty of the College, the fees to be paid by students;

(e) Make Statutes or By-laws for regulating the selection and appointment of members of the Royal Institution;

(f) Instruction given students of the College preparing for degrees shall be of a similar standard to that given in like subjects at McGill University and as announced from year to year in the Calendar of McGill University;

(g) The Royal Institution may enter into an agreement with any Board of School Trustees or any city council—or any other body in charge of any branch of public education in the Province of British Columbia, whereby the Royal Institution shall undertake the conduct or administration of any part of the higher education work now carried on by any such bodies, and any Board of School Trustees, any City Council and any body in charge of any branch of public education in the said Province, may, notwithstanding anything in the public education laws of the Province, enter into any such an agreement with the Royal Institution and may transfer or pay over to the Royal Institution such equipment or moneys in consideration thereof as may from time to time be agreed upon; provided that no agreement made in pursuance of this section shall be valid until it has been assented to by the Council of Public Instruction.

When these Bills appeared before the Legislature, and were published in the Press of Vancouver and Victoria, a bitter controversy developed which continued for several months.

Chapter IX

OPPOSITION TO THE BILL

Dr. Tory had had no previous experience with legislative bodies, and he was taken completely by surprise by the violence of the reaction to the proposed legislation. The opposition came from three different sources:

(1) Some residents of Victoria and the members of the legislature from that city.

(2) The Columbian Methodist College in New Westminster, backed by the offices of the General Conference of the Methodist Church.

(3) Graduates of the University of Toronto and of Victoria and Trinity Colleges then resident in Victoria and Vancouver, supported by the President of the University of Toronto and the Chancellor of Victoria College of Toronto.

Dr. Tory quite understood the opposition which arose in the city of Victoria. It was the kind of opposition with which he was to become very familiar later on in Alberta. There was doubtless the hope that some day the University of British Columbia would come into being and would be located in Victoria. The *Victoria Times* on February 7, 1906, reported in this manner a meeting held in that City:

A Protest Against the University Bill

On short notice a meeting of the Alumni of the Toronto, Trinity and Victoria Universities met this morning to consider the University Bill now before the Provincial House. After some discussion a committee was appointed to wait upon the Government to enter a protest against the Bill as it now stands. The Committee was composed of Chief Justice Hunter, Dr. Watt, Dr. Anderson, Mrs. Watt, Alexis Martin, A. C. Galt, W. J. Dowler, Dr. Milne, Rev. Joseph McCoy, Rev. Dr. Campbell, W. Moresby and Dr. Gibbs.

The Committee met Premier McBride, Hon. F. J. Fulton, Minister of Education, Hon. R. F. Green, Chief Commissioner of Lands and Works, and Attorney-General Wilson. Certain clauses of the Bill were objected to, particularly where the name given implies that the institution is to be a provincial one. As the Bill stood, the Committee maintained that it excluded the establishment of a British Columbia University in the Province, at some future time. It further discriminated against other universities entering the Province. The Committee further objected to the Government handing over to the institution named in the Bill (McGill University) any school properties, and suggested that the name be changed to read "McGill University of British Columbia." They had no objection to a branch of that University being established in the Province. In fact they thought this should be encouraged. The members of Parliament, admitted that there were some points raised that they had not considered in drafting the Bill, and said they wished to place no barrier in the way of any university entering the Province. The impression of the Committee after the Conference was that the Government would consider the Bill again, but no promises of this or any other kind were held out.

On February 8th, a similar meeting of protest was held in Vancouver, and according to the report in the *Vancouver Province* on the following day three important resolutions were adopted:

I. On motion of Mr. F. C. Wade, K.C., seconded by Dr. T. Procter-Hall, "that in the opinion of this meeting the time has arrived when it is advisable for the Province of British Columbia to set about creating a Provincial University."

II. On motion by Mr. George H. Cowan, K.C., seconded by Mr. F. C. Wade, K.C., "that this meeting disapprove of Bill 23 now before the Legislature, and especially the principle embodied in Section 8 thereof, which empowers an extra-provincial institution not answerable to the people of this Province, to take over the conduct and administrate any part of our educational work and disperse our moneys, which our representatives, without delegation to any institution should disburse."

III. The third resolution appointed Messrs. Argue, Wade, Cowan and Wilson a Committee to wait on the Government at Victoria with the resolutions passed by the meeting.

The following editorial in the *Victoria Colonist* appeared on February 18th, 1906, and indicated the attitude of the people of Victoria as a whole:

EDUCATION AND UNIVERSITIES

The University Bill has created a great deal of interest—the *Colonist* has not heretofore discussed the question because we did not desire to give the situation a sectional aspect—on the face of the Bill, it is one solely designed to give corporate rights to an institution to conduct university work in British Columbia. On those grounds we see no objection. As to the opposition which has arisen from other institutions we do not feel qualified to speak. We should not like to infer that it arises from jealousy of McGill. That might be unfair to the institutions that have raised the objections. They may conscientiously believe that the Bill gives McGill an unfair advantage. For our own part we do not see that an effort to do work of a scientific nature on a better basis than it has been done before should be opposed. If higher education is all that its advocates claim it to be, they should not be at enmity with each other. Toronto is purely a state institution and is unable to find the means to branch out in the direction which is possible for McGill to do, nor has it the authority under its Charter. The *Colonist* believes that University Education should be carried on under private auspices—that the whole of the ratepayers should be taxed for the benefit of the few is not a sound policy.

It was natural that there should be strong objection to the Bill from Columbian College in New Westminster. The Church it represented was traditionally in favour of having degree conferring institutions of its own. Power to confer degrees had been sought in B.C. but had been refused, because of the strong public sentiment against denominational education which has already been referred to.

The Columbian College authorities led by the Principal, Rev. W. J. Sipprell, had hoped that a situation like that in Manitoba could be developed, and they no doubt feared that the McGill plan would interfere. Rev. Mr. Sipprell had the gift of fluency and a biting tongue, and he used both to denounce Dr. Tory and all his works. Public meetings were called, the Government was interviewed, and the opposition press exhorted to defeat the Bill. The most remarkable feature of the opposition was the action of the officers of the General Conference of the Methodist Church in Toronto.

A meeting of the General Committee of the Church was convened and a resolution passed, calling upon the Lieutenant-

Governor of British Columbia to veto the Bills after they had passed the Legislature. This action created a good deal of resentment in British Columbia, which found expression in an editorial in the *News Advertiser* of Vancouver on February 22, 1906, in the following terms:

A REGRETTABLE INCIDENT

In common with many others we are greatly surprised at the action taken by prominent members of the Methodist General Conference at Toronto in reference to the Bill passed last week by the British Columbia Legislature relative to the offer made by McGill University to assist in the work of higher education in this Province. That such a body as the General Conference of the Methodist Church should seriously propose to ask the Lieutenant-Governor to veto a Bill that had been passed by a large majority will be regarded by most people as a most extraordinary thing. The General Conference, comprising as it does among its members fathers of one of the greatest religious bodies in the country, is looked up to and properly so—as a body which by example as well as precept, inculcates moderation in all things. But surely it strayed off the beaten path when it took action which can be regarded as nothing less than an attempt to interfere with constitutional methods; to override the will of the Legislature, and to substitute for the decision of those elected by the people and responsible to them—If there is one thing on which the people of British Columbia are agreed it is, that the Provincial system of education shall be absolutely free from even a suspicion of sectarianism—the University of McGill is of all our institutions of higher learning the one most free from either political or religious influence. There is no doubt that this fact has largely contributed to its progress and usefulness and has induced that liberal financial support—which has made it as regards resources and equipment, the foremost of Canadian Collegiate institutions.

Opposition also appeared on the part of the graduates of the University of Toronto living in British Columbia when a public meeting of protest was called to meet in Vancouver. The chief speaker, Mr. F. C. Wade, K.C., on that occasion stated that he did not consider it at all fair that the Province should give one university "a start in the race."

What reason could there be to compel B.C. students to go to McGill rather than to Toronto, Queen's or Manitoba? Every university man was loyal to his Alma Mater, and it was too much to say to a Toronto man that he could not have his sons prepared for higher education except on lines dictated by McGill. Students in B.C. would have to be prepared for a College three thousand miles away, managed by people whom they did not know, whom they had never seen, and over whom they had no control.

A man might wish to send his sons to Victoria if he was a Methodist, to Trinity if he was an Anglican, or to St. Michael's if he was a Roman Catholic, but he would not find in B.C. courses that would fit him for entrance to these colleges. Another speaker, Dr. Pearson, declared that the present campaign in the House was "nothing but an attempt to make B.C. a feeding ground for McGill."

Mr. George H. Cowan, K.C. declared:

As a British Columbian, I protest against this vicious legislation which proposes to hand over our education to a foreign institution. This Bill, he said, would take our students from our midst and expose them to the vices and prejudices of the effete East—This thing is UnBritish and Vicious.

The authorities of the University of Toronto also entered the fray in support of their beleaguered graduates and friends. The following record of this action is taken from the *Victoria Times* of February 7, 1906:

HEAD OF TORONTO UNIVERSITY AND CHANCELLOR BURWASH OF VICTORIA COLLEGE CONDEMN PRESENT BILL AS UNFAIR

(Special to the *Times*)

Toronto, February 7th

President Loudon of Toronto University when shown a dispatch from Victoria, stating that the second reading had been given a Bill establishing a University College of British Columbia, under the direct control of McGill University, said to the *Times* representative: "The matter will very probably be considered by the Senate at a meeting on Friday evening. If the Bill goes through it simply means that the College will be a feeder of McGill. I think it quite unfair that they should receive such an advantage over other Eastern universities. I notice that Sir William Macdonald is giving his support and McGill is sending out a number of professors. They can do this being a privately endowed institution while the University of Toronto, which is a provincial institution, cannot spend money outside the Province, although we can hold examinations and affiliate Western Colleges and collect fees. Columbian College at New Westminster is now affiliated with Toronto University directly through Victoria College. We have a large number of very prominent graduates in British Columbia, and they will doubtless do everything possible to prevent McGill gaining such an unfair advantage.

Chancellor Burwash, of Victoria University, said he considered such a Bill a serious injustice to the Methodist Church and to Columbian College at New Westminster.

"Some years ago," he said, "we applied to the province for a Charter granting Columbian College University standing with courses in Arts and Theology. A Charter giving the power to confer degrees in Arts was refused on the ground that a Provincial University had been provided for, and that no other institution should be allowed to pre-empt the prerogatives which belonged to the provincial university. The Methodist Church accepted that decision, and has founded its institution and carried on the work with a view to affiliation with the Provincial University and unity of action as soon as it was established.

Now to grant McGill University the powers refused to the representatives of the Methodist Church will be to do a very serious injustice to the Church and to Columbian College.

If the Legislature has changed its programme, and does not wish to establish a Provincial University, and is going to let Eastern institutions come in permanently, then the Methodist College, which has been doing the work for the past eight years, should have the same opportunity as any other.

We got word that a university Bill was being railroaded through the British Columbia Legislature, and at once telegraphed for a full statement of the matter, and shall consider the best course to adopt."

The Chancellor added, that there was a possibility of the Lieutenant-Governor being asked to disallow the Bill if it were shown that it caused too great a storm of disapproval.

The result of the foregoing was that Principal Peterson decided to take a hand in the discussion. The following report of his statement is taken from the *Vancouver Province,* February 9, 1906.

Principal Peterson's Statement of the Case and Editorial Comment

Principal Peterson of McGill University, speaking in regard to the criticism of Ontario Educationists on McGill's action in getting connection in British Columbia, said McGill's connection with British Columbia was established several years ago and has been attended with the greatest possible success. In seeking to develop that connection McGill has not been actuated by any motive of rivalry with other Universities. Its sole object has been to do what it can to promote the unification of higher education in Canada. It is important that growing communication in the West should be prevented from repeating the mistakes of the East, where there are so many small Colleges, especially in the Maritime Provinces, out of all relation to each other and very often hampered by some denominational connection.

McGill University is the only university in Canada which was reported recently to the Trustees of the new Carnegie Foundation as being neither denominational nor under State control. For these, among other reasons, it cannot be wondered that the movement for Federation in Education which had during recent years been championed by McGill, should have been heartily taken up by friends of education in the West.

Arrangements have now been made to further develop this connection with British Columbia by giving a definite status to the College at Vancouver as an incorporated college of McGill University. The view which has commended itself to friends of education in the West is, that the time is not ripe for the establishment of a Provincial University, and that the college at Vancouver now to be established will probably long be content to remain a component part of one of the leading Canadian Universities, deriving prestige from its connection with McGill, while retaining in all essentials its own autonomy. From this it will be seen that we are not looking at Vancouver College, as President Loudon seems to suppose, to be merely a feeder for McGill. We intend to help the Vancouver people to do good university work, and we hope that the friends of education will agree with us in regarding it as none the less McGill work because it happens to be done in the City of Vancouver. The University will control the curriculum, assist in providing the staff and confer the degrees. The whole project is the best possible illustration that Canada can have co-operation in higher education, and I regret very much that it should appear to be criticized from the point of view of rival commercial concerns.

The following statement from Mr. C. C. Eldridge, as representing the School Board, was published in the *Vancouver Province* February 11, 1906, as a reason for commending the action of the McGill authorities and the Government.

Mr. C. C. Eldridge Throws Some Clear Light On Present Controversy

Mr. C. C. Eldridge, of this City, has taken considerable interest in the discussion relative to the University Bill now before the Legislature, since he was a member of the Board of School Trustees in

Vancouver, when the first steps were taken toward having the Vancouver High School affiliated with a university or universities.

"In reference to the Vancouver High School affiliation," Mr. Eldridge remarked last evening, when asked concerning the matter, "it was taken up about twelve years ago by the Board, of which I was then a member, with the High School staff. The Secretary of the School Board was instructed to write McGill and Toronto Universities for information bearing on the subject. The authorities at McGill replied, stating that they had no power to allow the Vancouver High School to affiliate with that University, but would apply to the Quebec Administration for the necessary legislation. Mr. A. H. B. MacGowan, M.P., who was also a member of the Board at that time, happened to have private business in Montreal, and interviewed the Governors of McGill, and discovered that we had to have legislation here.

"The necessary law was passed, which allowed all High Schools in the Province to affiliate with any university which might be selected, the only conditions being that they should be able to do the work. Toronto University never answered the letter sent by the Secretary of the Board, and consequently we had no choice but to affiliate with McGill. After the affiliation there was some commotion among the graduates from Toronto, because that university was not chosen. They were told that the university authorities had not replied to the letter of inquiry. This led to an inquiry, and it was announced by the University of Toronto that it had no power or any desire to enter into the scheme. At the time of the affiliation, McGill had no influence on the Board, and, so far as I know, none of the High School staff was a graduate of McGill. On the other hand, Toronto was represented. It would seem a very inopportune time for Toronto University and its influence (some of very late date) to step in and declare that this legislation shall not proceed unless it is made to apply to a university of their choice."

The Victoria Colonist, which was friendly from the beginning, had the following comment on February 2, 1906.

Scheme Outlined for a University Bill, Now Before the House

From the Bill of which notice was given in the House and which has since been printed, it will be seen that McGill University proposes to establish a college at the coast and as far as is known at present Vancouver is to be the chosen spot. The scheme has been developed by Professor Tory, who paid a visit to Vancouver and Victoria six months ago, for the purpose of negotiating for a site and ascertaining what local financial aid would be forthcoming. It is understood that his negotiations were satisfactory, hence the measure now before the legislature. In the first instance the college will house a single faculty, science, and mining section of the Dominion, and at present students have to go from here to McGill for their ordinary course and come back every season with the summer school for their mining practice. This will be remedied by the proposed college, which will be affiliated with McGill. It is also understood that the wealthy eastern benefactors of that institution have promised to contribute liberally to the establishment of the new college and as it will form a nucleus of a provincial university, there is no doubt as to its popularity and should be none as to its success.

During all this discussion Dr. Tory kept close to those who were supporting the passage of the Bill through the Legislature, but remained silent publicly. Only on one occasion did he break his silence, and that was in a meeting of School Trustees at which he was asked to speak, and at which a resolution commending his efforts was passed, with one dissenting voice. The opposition in that meeting came from Miss Agnes Deans Cameron, of Victoria. Miss Cameron was a well known writer at that time and later travelled in the North. She had a great gift of invective and she used it on that occasion. Dr. Tory was described as, "The advance agent of a foreign corporation." When he was sure the Bill would pass, Dr. Tory on February 11th published the following letter:

THE UNIVERSITY BILL

To the Editor of the *News Advertiser*.

Sir: With regard to the University Bill now before the local Legislature, over which such agitation has been raised, I have refrained thus far from speaking, for the simple reason that it has been in the hands of the Parliament of the people of British Columbia. Being a "foreigner," I did not feel that I should take part in a public discussion, but should rather wait the judgment of the people's representatives on the subject. Now, however, that the Bill has passed through the Committee stage, I assume I may, without offence to public opinion, in order to remove the tissue of misrepresentation and side issues which have been brought into the case, state my point of view as representing the University.

First let me say that universities are not, as some people seem to suppose, money-making institutions, but great philanthropic institutions, depending upon private benefactors, supported by the State, or by religious denominations. As private institutions they are governed usually by the gentlemen who are public spirited enough to support them, guided always in their work by the educational specialists who are engaged to control them.

To illustrate clearly what I mean, I will take our own institution—McGill University—which has its headquarters at Montreal. The institution comes under the heading of a private corporation. As a philanthropic institution, however, it is subject to the law which controls such institutions. McGill has, as a Governing Board, a body of gentlemen selected with reference to their public spirit and their willingness to assist in the educational advancement of the country. They are working under a charter granted by the Crown in the reign of George IV, with full university powers. Under the Charter, the Governor General of Canada is the official visitor, and to him the annual report of the University is made, through which they become subject to public criticism. The University, as shown in its last report, has invested in educational enterprises about $6,000,000, and has an annual expenditure of between $350,000 and $400,000. Last year the expenditure was $390,000. The full return from fees from students was $86,000. The balance, over $300,000, was made up from the income of private benefactions. In other words it cost the University annually about $300 for each student enrolled, or to graduate a student cost $1,200. When the University graduates a class of 100 men it represents an outlay of $120,000 more than it has received from them. Of course, the statement refers to the average. In Engineering and Medicine the cost is much higher than the average, in Arts much lower. So what is said of McGill in this connection is true also of Toronto approximately, which is an institution supported by the Provincial Government. Last year, I think, the Legislature voted $150,000 for the support of that institution, and any educationist from Ontario will tell you that they could use a much greater sum with advantage. I believe it is the avowed policy of the present Government of Ontario to largely increase that sum. The same statement regarding expenditure applies in a limited sense to the smaller and less expensively equipped institutions.

I sometimes wonder whether the outlay is justified especially when university trained men can be found who make such statements as have been made during the present discussion.

Now, with regard to our relation to British Columbia, I believe it is on record that in the early days of the development of High Schools in this Province, the Vancouver High School made an application to the University in the matter. The Board then wrote to McGill concerning the same subject and we replied, as we have always done in such cases, that if the schools were equipped to do work up to our standard we would gladly assist in every possible way. A member of the School Board visited Montreal and the matter was gone into and the affiliation accomplished. Later on

Victoria applied for the same privilege, and it was accorded the same advantage in a limited way, Vancouver being affiliated for two years in Arts and Victoria for one. As far as McGill is concerned, it is our settled policy to assist in every way smaller institutions if they are making worthy efforts to advance education. To prove this, I have only to point out that in the Eastern Provinces two of the smaller universities were not likely to be very successful if they did the work unaided. They asked us if we would permit them to do two years' work of our course under affiliation, permitting their students to graduate by taking the third and fourth years only. It was represented that this would be in the interest of many deserving students. When we saw that they were equipped to do the work of the first two years, we gladly made the arrangement knowing that it would result in students from these localities going to these institutions for two years instead of coming to us. If further proof were needed to prove what our traditional policy has been, I have only to refer to the fact that Sir William Macdonald, one of our governors, has himself distributed money freely from the Atlantic to the Pacific in developing lines of educational work through other than University agencies, when these agencies were not suitable. Even Toronto has benefited by his magnificent generosity to the extent of $200,000, through the Agricultural College at Guelph.

I have referred to the circumstances which brought us in touch with your educational system. Through Vancouver and Victoria we have been working for a number of years, I believe greatly to the benefit of education in their High Schools. Throughout these years no pressure was ever brought to bear by us in any way to bring students to McGill. I believe, as a matter of fact, that the majority of the men who go East come to us, but that is absolutely of their own free will. May I add, that on matriculation we issue certificates to all students, certificates which will permit them to enter any university on this side of the Atlantic, Toronto included, whose certificate we, in turn, accept.

About a year ago it was suggested to us that there was a class of work much needed in British Columbia, viz., advanced scientific work, for which no provision was being made and that there was an opportunity to take an advanced step in connection with our educational enterprises. Dr. Peterson had already been discussing with me the subject of a visit to our affiliated colleges to enquire into their work. He asked me to go to British Columbia and study the question and report to their Board of Governors. I did so, conferring with gentlemen in Victoria, Vancouver, New Westminster, the Department of Education, and with those interested in education all over the Province, before finally making up my mind on the matter. I then reported to our Board, requesting them in the name of the University to take the step suggested, with a view especially to supplement what was already being done by advanced scientific work. I recommended that it be done by co-operating with one of the school boards and the calling into existence of a corporation of gentlemen who would be interested in the subject, the method of government to be fashioned after the Board at home. I frankly stated, and I state now, that I thought as this larger work would be done in the interest of a larger class, its management should be in the hands of men representative of British Columbia as a whole.

Such being the case, the question of method had to be settled. The way open to me was either to ask the Government to appoint a Board and make a Government controlled institution, or to have a private corporation, like McGill, with Government representation. The latter method was decided on for the simple reason that it appealed to me that as the local Government would not be likely for some time to make large contributions, therefore the government of the institution should be so organized as to appeal to the public for private benefactions. It was therefore decided to ask for the incorporation of a group of private citizens of British Columbia, gentlemen interested in such work, through whom the public at large might become interested in the enterprise.

To remove all doubt as to whether McGill had the right to do this work in British Columbia without its consent, it was decided to ask the local Government to give this permission. This bill has passed without opposition, as even the greatest enemies of McGill would hardly dare say she was not worthy of recognition.

The second Bill is a bill, the intent of which is, to call into legal existence a Board of Management. Its features are: To incorporate a number of representative men under the name of "The Royal Institution for the Advancement of Learning in British Columbia." The reason for the name is that the official title of the Board of Governors of McGill University is "The Royal Institution for the Advancement of Learning," an organization by whose instrumentality the University was called into existence. This Board will consist entirely of local men, with the single exception of Dr. Peterson, who will alone represent the parent institution. The Government will be represented by the Minister of Education and by the Superintendent of Education. The School Board will also be represented. To these men, residents in British Columbia, will be handed over the money McGill puts into the enterprise, and they take, under the Act, the responsibility. McGill has given her name, and under the Act her standard of work will be required.

The clauses of the Bill attacked were 3 and 8. The original clause 3 suggested that the name of the College to be founded be "The University College of British Columbia." It was objected that this was a name that should only be granted to a Provincial Institution controlled by the Government. It was agreed to amend the clause and call the College "The McGill University College of British Columbia."

There are just two things in clause 8. First, The Royal Institution is given power to negotiate with school boards with a view to taking over its higher educational work. Second, the school boards are given power to make an Agreement to have this work done.

For the purpose of founding a College the Royal Institution may act:

1st. Independently and anywhere it pleases.

2nd. It may, by agreement with a school board, take on its higher work and build upon that. In the latter case it is confined to three places in B.C., namely, New Westminster, Vancouver, Victoria, as these are the only High Schools trying to do higher educational work; Vancouver doing two years, Victoria one, and New Westminster, I believe, one. I call particular attention to this because of so much loose talk about control of schools. The Act confines its operations entirely to higher work, that is, work of a University character.

Doing such work does not touch the High School course except as provided in the Public School Act of this Province. The mistake has arisen from a misunderstanding of the meaning of ordinary educational terms. I would also call special attention to the fact that the Act gives only power to bargain, not to impose fees on high schools, or to affect courses of study in the slightest possible degree. All talk relating to such matters is absolute nonsense.

I would add that it was suggested to me that the clause might be made more rigid and the School Board, which is elected annually, be given the right to make an engagement for a term of years. My reply was that we were moving, we believed, in the public interest, and if any school board with whom we might associate and who might associate with us, desired to cut free at any time they should be at liberty to do so. I am satisfied that nothing more could be done to guard the public interest if endangering it were possible.

As to the plan of operation, it is the intention of those who will be incorporated under the Act to call their plans into operation. Of the details of these plans the public will be informed after the meeting and organization of The Royal Institution.

With regard to the attitude taken by a few of the Toronto graduates, I have nothing to say. I leave the public to judge in the matter between us. I am glad to believe that university men of British Columbia, as a body, are above sectionalism. Is the thing good for British Columbia or is it not, is the only question at issue. If it is, whether it is done by McGill University or Toronto is of no moment. I cannot see how any resident of British Columbia can take any other attitude.

Perhaps I ought to say a word to a few of those interested in the "Methodist Columbian College," as I believe that is the official title of that Institution. I have no quarrel with them. I am a Methodist myself. I pay to support its institutions. I cannot bring myself to believe that the Principal of that Institution was a party to the distribution of an unsigned circular, stating that Toronto University had spent $45,000 in education in British Columbia through Columbian College. The Methodist people of this country who are struggling to keep alive these institutions by paying their money earned by hard work, will not be gratified to know that their gifts are so spoken of. If the Principal is not responsible he owes it to the Methodist Church and to himself to repudiate it.

The following day, February 12, 1906, the *News Advertiser* published the following comment:

THE UNIVERSITY BILL

We publish elsewhere an interesting letter from Dr. Tory, the agent and representative of McGill University, on the action which that great and powerful institution is taking to forward the cause of higher education in this Province. Doubtless, not only Dr. Tory, but the authorities of McGill University are surprised at the attitude assumed by some persons in British Columbia towards a movement that it might have been supposed would have been met with unqualified approval and hearty support. The opposition in the Legislature to the Bill may be ascribed to more than one cause, which it is not necessary to mention. It may, however, be stated that Mr. MacDonald, the Leader of the Opposition, has not shown much sympathy with the violent and persistent efforts of some of his followers to defeat the Bill, and we have little doubt is in accord with a movement that promises much for higher education in British Columbia. There is no doubt that the Bill will be passed without any change from the form in which it left the Committee stage and the assurances of approval of its action in this matter which the Government is receiving from all parts of the Province are evidence that the measure is popular and that the people appreciate at its true value the generous offer that McGill University has made to British Columbia.

Dr. Tory, in his letter, has set out so clearly the history of the events that have culminated in the arrangement, embodied in Bill 23, that it is not necessary for us to repeat it. It may be well, however, to point out the care exercised by the Government in guarding against anything that might reasonably be claimed as discriminating against any other educational institution or putting any obstacle in the way of the establishment of a Provincial University. That the foundation of a Provincial University, on a scale that would be commensurate with the work that it should undertake, is beyond the present financial resources of the Province, cannot be denied. A small and weak institution with a scanty income and a small equipment, would be of little value. It could not give the facilities in those branches of education a knowledge of which is essential to success in some of the most important spheres of activity at the present time. Consequently while the youth without means would be denied the opportunity necessary to give him a start in his chosen vocation, the more affluent student would go to Montreal or Toronto.

This situation will now be changed by the exercise of that liberality and enterprise on the part of the authorities of McGill University, which has so frequently been displayed by them in various directions. McGill University among all the educational institutions of Canada, is alone able to undertake such a work and carry it to success. While there has been some criticism of the Bill and some opposition shown to it by men who were educated at Toronto University or other colleges, and who seem to think that the Bill gives the Montreal institution an unfair advantage, a perusal of the Bill shows that it contains nothing justifying such an assertion. The fact is that neither Toronto University nor other Eastern Colleges have the authority or resources to undertake such an enterprise. They are nearly all public institutions, either controlled by the Government or financially assisted by it. McGill, on the other hand, is entirely free from such obligations. Founded by a private citizen, its resources have been provided by a succession of men whose munificence and public spirit made them fit followers of the pious founder, and the millions thus bestowed have been administered with great skill and ability.

With a clear understanding of what is intended by the pending legislation and calmer reflection on the boon about to be conferred on the youth of British Columbia by the foundation of a University in the Province, we feel confident that the opposition manifested to the undertaking will disappear and be succeeded by the approval of it. In the report of an interview with him, Principal Peterson outlines the policy that McGill is pursuing and showed how foundationless were the suspicions about the motives actuating the University. When British Columbia can establish a Provincial university, Dr. Peterson says McGill will readily retire and bestow on its successor all the benefits which its action has conferred. That the action of the authorities of McGill is appreciated in British Columbia is beyond question. Their liberality will be an incentive to our people to give voluntary aid and we shall hope to see repeated in the West, and with like beneficent results, the wise liberality and munificence that have built up the great institution of learning in Montreal. The ultimate results of the present action can scarcely be estimated.

In the midst of the battle Dr. Tory received a telegram from Principal William Peterson of McGill dated February 8, 1906: "Hold the Fort"—Peterson. On the same day Dr. Tory replied: "Fort held, Bill passed third reading, Toronto making fierce onslaught."

On the passage of the Bill, February 22, 1906, the *News Advertiser* made its final comment as follows:

> Although its passage through the Legislature was bitterly contested, the Bill creating a Provincial corporation, under the name of "The McGill University College of British Columbia," passed its third reading. The opponents of the measure, as we pointed out on a previous occasion, consisted of those who desire the immediate foundation of a Provincial University and some of the graduates of various Eastern educational institutions who are resident in this Province. The former urge something that is practically impossible now or for years to come. The time may come, we believe it will, when the resources and progress of the Province will make it possible and feasible to found a Provincial University, one such as will provide satisfactory facilities for those who seek university training. But those who oppose the Bill on that ground must overlook the fact that for a number of years, perhaps for the best part of a generation, they would place an obstacle in the way of many who desire to avail themselves of a university course but have not the means to spend several years in Montreal or Toronto. The other class of opponents —the graduates of other universities—will doubtless come to the conclusion that, however much they desire to see the institutions at which they were educated taking a prominent place in the education of the youth of British Columbia, they have been injudicious and lacking in Provincial patriotism when they sought to put obstacles in the way of another institution—equal in every respect to its rivals —which was willing to lend its aid and give its resources for such a purpose.
>
> We are pleased to see that the Convention of School Trustees, in session on Tuesday last in Victoria, passed a resolution unanimously approving the action of the Government in carrying the University Bill through the Legislature. An endorsement by a body that directs the educational systems in our cities, of the offer made by the authorities of McGill, cannot fail to reassure people who may have been influenced by the bitter opposition manifested to the Bill. Time will show what great benefits to the Provincial educational system the movement initiated by the Bill will confer and we feel sure that many of those who have opposed the measure will come to be glad that their opposition to it was unavailing.

The Methodist Times sometime later published its views in the following terms:

WESTERN METHODIST TIMES

One of the best of signs in connection with our western progress is the attention which the claims of higher education are receiving from our public-spirited and progressive business men. Calgary has one of these institutions. Edmonton another, and from recent reports the citizens of Moose Jaw are stirring themselves for the establishment of one in their town. We think it would be an immense advantage if these colleges, at least in their beginning stages, could get into contact with such a magnificently equipped and endowed organization as McGill University of Montreal. One of the great weaknesses of these local institutions is that they have neither the staff nor the facilities for doing the best kind of work but in association with such an institution as McGill proper arrangements could be made to overcome this difficulty and we have no doubt such a wealthy institution as McGill would, if properly approached, help in the establishment of at least first and second year's work.

The short speeches made in the Legislature near the end of the debate seem worth recording.

Dr. Williams, a socialist member of which there were three in the House, said he took no great interest in the matter. The discussion seemed to have run along the lines as to whether McGill University was being given a preference to any other. It seemed to him that all universities were based on the same fundamental principles of teaching, and he thought opposition to it on the lines of loyalty to another institution could not be taken very seriously. He was not much interested in that, as his own university had been a logging camp. They also talked about hidden motives in the Bill, but he thought it was mere waste of time looking through the Bill with a microscope to hunt for these terrible hidden motives. They had been assured by the Government day after day that it would not interfere with the High Schools, and that it was not giving any special privileges to this particular university. If that were true, and there was no reason to doubt it, he could not see any reason in this bitter opposition to the Bill becoming law. If, on the other hand, it would reduce the cost of higher education and place it within the reach of the poorer people, that would be a sufficient justification for the whole measure. He saw no reason whatever for the amendments offered by the member for Yale. They were among those marvellous things that only found their home in the mind of a lawyer.

He was followed by Mr. J. A. MacDonald, leader of the Liberal Party, who said in part:

The only reason why the opposition had been so determined was because, in spite of anything that the government might urge, this bill did confer on McGill an advantage over other seats of learning, and the medium was the diversion of public funds to strengthen the monopoly of a private enterprise. He frankly admitted that for years to come the Province could not have a university of its own at all commensurate with McGill, but they had other educational institutions which would suffer in competition with McGill. He considered the provisions of the bill unfair to other seats of learning, unfair to the ratepayers and unfair to sister universities.

Hon. Richard McBride contended that this was the revival of a mainland versus island controversy, and an attempt to revive the old animosity, between McGill and Toronto universities. The opposition could not screen themselves behind principles because they consistently opposed the government even on measures which it was well known they really favoured.

Now, it was alleged that McGill was to get a preference. Well, if so, she proposed to pay for it, and why should she not therefore get something in return? Honourable members opposite lost sight of the immense benefits which would be derived by the young men of this Province, especially in respect of scientific learning for expert mining. What would be the position, if these advantages were repulsed? Toronto University could not offer them; a Provincial University could not give them for many years to come. This was a petty spirit and a narrow conception of the way to deal with a great public question. The proposal did not in the slightest degree clash with other universities. The government would hold out both hands to anyone who would offer similar advantages. But that was no reason for mistrusting McGill. Her reputation was second to none, and she had done more than all other Canadian institutions put together to give the Dominion a status in the eyes of the educational experts all the world over. What more did the opposition require? Something better? Where would they find it? Surely at this stage the opposition would cease and gracefully allow it to go through without party opposition.

Prompt action followed the passage of the two bills, and on March 19, 1906, the first meeting of The Royal Institution was held in the School Board offices, Vancouver. Members present at this first meeting:

The Hon. F. Carter-Cotton, Vancouver—*President*
J. W. Creighton, Esq., New Westminster
Hon. F. J. Fulton, Minister of Education
Dr. Alexander Robinson, Esq., Supt. of Education
William Peterson, LL.D., C.M.G., Principal of McGill University
A. C. Flumerfelt, Esq., Victoria—*Treasurer*
Col. Gregory, Victoria
S. J. Tunstall, M.D., Vancouver
D. Robertson, Esq., Vancouver
Ralph Smith, Esq., M.P., Nanaimo
W. P. Argue, Esq., B.A., Supt. of City Schools, Vancouver
Frank Eaton, Esq., D.C.L., Supt. of City Schools, Victoria
R. P. McLennan, Esq., Vancouver
J. Ramsey, Esq., Vancouver
J. P. Ferguson, Esq., Vancouver

The first step taken was the appointment of a finance committee. Immediately thereafter the Board discussed and finally adopted a statement which was released to all the newspapers on the following day. This was a comprehensive plan, with a great many provisions, beginning with the statement that:

The Royal Institution, although it has been called into existence through the instrumentality of McGill University is a British Columbia institution. The purpose was stated as being the promotion of higher learning, "especially in those branches of scientific study which lie at the basis of the industrial and economic development of British Columbia."

The College was to be non-denominational, without any religious tests for members of the Royal Institution, the staff, or the students. Although The Institution was to remain a private corporation, there was always to be government representation on the Board. The University College to be established would commence work in the fall of the year in the High School building, giving the first two years of Arts and Applied Science.

The complete Arts Course was to be supplied as soon as the number of students justified such an extension of services. The statement closed with an appeal for support from citizens throughout the Province.

With sufficient funds guaranteed for a start, and with promise of continued financial support, five additional staff members were taken on the College roll and work commenced in October, 1906.

In the following year there was an increased enrolment and Victoria College also came under The Royal Institution. Several new subjects were added and the workshop side of engineering was also provided. Early in 1908 an Act establishing and incorporating the University of British Columbia and repealing the old act of 1890-1891 was passed. This was consolidated in 1912, and a site for the University finally selected by a Commission which had been appointed in 1910. Preparations were not completed for several more years, however, and the McGill Colleges continued their work until May, 1915.

When the University opened its doors in the fall of 1915 these Colleges ceased to exist and were replaced by the University of British Columbia, a state-endowed institution which is famed throughout the English-speaking world for the beauty of its campus and the high standard of its academic work. When Dr. Tory's connection with the institution came to an end, in 1907, the Board of The Royal Institution passed the following resolution:

> The Board desires to place on record its appreciation of the eminent services rendered to the College by Dr. H. M. Tory. His energy and experience and organizing capacity have been of the greatest assistance to the Board, and to his efforts in no small degree must be attributed the satisfactory progress made already in the work which the College was established to do.

THE ARTS BUILDING AND MOLSON HALL, McGILL UNIVERSITY

THE UNIVERSITY OF BRITISH COLUMBIA

Top: The Library and Women's Gymnasium. *Bottom, left to right:* Agricultural Building, Arts Building, Administration Building.

CHAPTER X

BACK AT McGILL

AFTER HIS RETURN TO MONTREAL from British Columbia in the spring of 1906, Dr. Tory plunged with accustomed vigour into the affairs of McGill University. A mountain of unfinished business had piled up on his desk during his absence. There was a letter from Dean Moyse asking him to take over the Deanship of Arts during the absence of Moyse in England. The McGill Rifle Club, of which he was the founder and President, needed fifty rifles from the Department of National Defence, and plans had to be completed for McGill's participation in the annual intercollegiate rifle shoot.

In addition to all this, staff must be chosen for McGill College in British Columbia, and the Trustees of the Carnegie Foundation approached for a grant-in-aid for the new institution. There were preparations to be made for a quick trip to England in July, to purchase laboratory equipment for the College, and to fulfil a long-standing promise of a summer holiday for himself and Mrs. Tory.

Dr. Tory's correspondence at this time shows that his ranging, restless mind could no longer be confined to McGill, and its interests. In April, 1906, he wrote to every Minister and Deputy Minister of Education in Canada, and to all University Presidents and all Superintendents of Schools, stating that he proposed to make a study of the comparative costs of education in the various Provinces. This study would cover the whole field of educational expenditures from the elementary schools on up to and including higher education.

He had apparently felt cabined and confined by the fact that, as an ordained minister of the Methodist Church, he was obliged to report his activities to the Montreal Conference of the Church. He wrote on May 28, 1906, to Rev. W. R. Young, D.D., Chairman of the Montreal Methodist Conference, the following letter:

> I have been for some time contemplating withdrawing from the Montreal Conference and am now writing to tender my resignation. I have taken this action only after serious reflection, knowing that my action may be misunderstood, but I do not feel justified in remaining longer under the nominal control of a body whose dictates I would not feel justified in obeying if they were to order me to do work other than that I am now doing, work of which they take no cognizance and for which I receive no recognition. I write to ask you to place this matter before the Conference—my interest in the Conference will be continued but I shall prefer to class myself as a layman. I feel I must be free to act without reference to the Conference.

It is evident that the leaders of the Methodist Church in Montreal bore no resentment toward Dr. Tory as a result of his battles with the Methodist hierarchy over the McGill project in British Columbia. In full session the Conference passed the following resolution:

> That we, the members of the Ministerial Session of the Montreal Conference, desire to place on record our high appreciation of the work of the Rev. Dr. Tory, Professor of Mathematics at McGill University. We regard his influence in moulding the character, not only of our own students, but also of the students in general, as very great indeed. We also note with great satisfaction his growing influence in the educational affairs of both the Province of Quebec and the Dominion. We wish for him continued success and pray and hope that he may in future place Methodism under still greater obligations.

Before leaving for England Dr. Tory was happy to be able to write to his friends in Vancouver that $50,000 had been granted by the trustees of the Carnegie Corporation toward the support of McGill in British Columbia, on condition that they raise $50,000 of the total objective of $100,000.

When in Edmonton, on his way back from British Columbia, Dr. Tory had been greatly impressed with the work being done at Alberta College in Edmonton, and particularly with the energy and vision of its Principal, the Rev. Dr.

J. H. Riddell. He had agreed to approach Lord Strathcona, Governor of the Hudson's Bay Company, and request a grant of land to the College for a building site. But so deeply was Dr. Tory concerned about the growth of denominational colleges, and their threat to a unified system of education, that he wrote before leaving Montreal a long and confidential letter to Premier A. C. Rutherford on the subject. In the light of later events this letter is worth placing in the record at this time.

Dear Dr. Rutherford:

I hope you will excuse the liberty I take in addressing you with regard to the educational problem in your Province. I do so because of a feeling of fellowship which I have for you personally, as one called upon to solve for the Province of Alberta, its most difficult problem, namely the educational one—may I make as a further excuse, that I have been pretty well through all the phases of the problem in Canada of late years, and have seen the pitfalls into which the older Provinces have fallen. I would like to see these mistakes avoided in the new—.

Let me say first that I consider one of the greatest dangers to good educational work is the denominational spirit. In the Maritime Provinces that spirit in the early days was strong enough to prevent the establishment of a central institution of learning, and instead a group of small ones grew up, each with university powers, none of which is able to do first-class work. In these Provinces the separationist spirit has been so strong that all the denominations have decided in their educational work to keep apart. The result has been that men of first-class calibre will not stay in these institutions if an outside opening of any value offers itself.

In Nova Scotia and New Brunswick there are now seven institutions with university powers—these institutions have made it impossible for the government to support strong and worthy institutions in the interest of the state. The University of New Brunswick, the only real Government institution, is weak and struggling as a consequence.

Education along these lines was in some measure possible in the past; it will be practically impossible in the future. The older universities in years gone by, only offered courses in Literature, Mathematics and Philosophy. The modern university must be equipped scientifically to get any standing and to offer advantages which the student has a right to demand. When such institutions are situated near a great centre of learning they naturally dwindle.

A case in point is Bishop's College situated near McGill University. As the latter grew large and efficient the former grew small and today has only a handful of students. In a smaller way Dalhousie has had the same effect on King's College, Nova Scotia. The only hope of such institutions is that no large central place be permitted to grow.

Queen's university has held its own because of the great man who for years guided its destiny. The Methodist College, which was situated at Cobourg, was compelled, in self defence to get into Toronto under the shadow of Toronto University. Denominationalism in a new dress has presented itself in Manitoba, where they have a university as an examining body, but the denominations are doing most of the teaching. In its inception it was regarded as a splendid idea to have a university as an examining body as in London.

It was not recognized that London occupys a position which no Province in Canada can occupy for a hundred years to come, namely that a large body of highly educated specialists from Oxford and Cambridge; men engaged in higher educational work themselves, were available for examining purposes. Even London, however, has found it necessary to put its university on a teaching basis.

In Manitoba, however, the denominational spirit is at work again, and when the University is ready to take up teaching the Colleges are unwilling to allow such work being done. In justice to them it must be said that the University proper has waited a long time to organize its teaching and the pioneering work has been done by the Colleges—the natural tendency in Manitoba will be for the denominations to bring pressure to bear upon the Government to secure university powers for the individual colleges. Will the government be strong enough to withstand such pressure?

My judgment is that it would be a mistake that would take years to remedy if a university on an examining basis were started in your Province. It would be a quarter of a century before such an institution would have any significance outside your own Province.

If you take any steps in the direction of a working university and wish to avoid the mistakes of the past—you should start on a teaching basis.

I hope you will excuse the liberty I have taken in writing you in this way, but it seemed to me that one old McGill man might speak thus confidentially to another, more especially when the subject is of such importance. Let me add that nothing that I have said is to be in any way construed as reflecting upon denominations as religious institutions. I am thoroughly in accord with their work and aim. I am speaking of them only as educational institutions.

Believe me,

Sincerely yours,

H. M. Tory

One other task he completed soon after returning from British Columbia was the founding of "The Western Club of McGill University." The objects of the Club were three-fold:

1. to aid new students from Western Canada coming to McGill to find boarding places and in adapting themselves to university life;
2. to promote social intercourse among students from the West;
3. to give all possible help to the furtherance of McGill's interests in Western Canada.

Upon his return from England Dr. Tory spent three months in Vancouver helping with the organization of the first year's work of the College and the installation of the equipment he had purchased in England. Back at McGill in December, 1906, he proceeded to take up again his regular work of teaching. But his correspondence during the winter of 1907 shows that he kept in constant touch with what was going on at McGill in British Columbia. On January 17, 1907, he wrote to the Hon. F. Carter-Cotton as follows:

> Since coming home I have been actively interested in connection with a building project for our College. I have gone upon the plan that we would require for that enterprise the sum of $100,000. You will be pleased to know that Mr. Carnegie has agreed to give $50,000 if we can raise the full amount required. As we shall have two years to work that end of our scheme up, I think we can rest assured that the building project will be carried out as soon as we really need it. I should like to have a statement of Mr. Carnegie's gift made public as soon as you deem it advisable to do so.

Other correspondence during the winter reveals his continued preoccupation with the staff and curriculum problems of McGill in British Columbia. But meanwhile events were shaping up which would eventually change the direction of Dr. Tory's life.

In 1905 the Province of Alberta was organized under an Act of the Dominion Parliament, and at the first meeting of the Legislature, a University Act, to establish and incorporate a university for the Province of Alberta was introduced by the Hon. A. C. Rutherford, Premier and Minister of Education. The following year an amendment authorized the Lieutenant

Governor-in-Council to appoint a President, to whom would be given the responsibility in conjunction with the Senate of organizing and developing the university. It will be recalled that, on his way back to McGill in the spring of 1906, Dr. Tory had visited Alberta, and discussed the question of affiliation with Alberta College in Edmonton and Western Canada College in Calgary. On that occasion he had visited a number of high schools in the Province and met the leading educationists and professional people. He had also formed a warm friendship with Dr. Rutherford.

When, early in 1907, Premier Rutherford travelled East to find a President for the new university the name of Henry Marshall Tory was on his list as one of the people to be considered for the position.

Dr. Tory had now been at McGill as student and teacher for over twenty years, and had won a firm place for himself among the students, on the staff, and in the city. He was at this time, forty-three years of age, and he had settled down with every assurance that he could and would spend the rest of his life on the McGill campus. He had been the intimate friend of Sir William Dawson and now enjoyed the same relationship with his successor Sir William Peterson, and numbered among his friends were some of the most influential men in the city: W. M. Birks, President of Henry Birks and Sons, later a Governor of McGill; Arthur Wood, who became President of the Sun Life Assurance Company and a McGill Governor; John W. McConnell, noted financier, also later a McGill Governor; the late A. O. Dawson, and many others. All of these men had been close friends of Dr. Tory in the work of the Church, the Y.M.C.A. and the University. In the University itself he had won distinction as a scholar, teacher, and as the personal friend and adviser to hundreds of undergraduates.

When Premier Rutherford finally decided that Dr. Tory was the man he wanted, he invited him to lunch at the Windsor Hotel and promptly submitted his proposition. Dr. Tory asked for time to consider the offer; to discuss it with his wife and friends. At first everything possible was done to persuade him to remain at McGill. Dean Moyse even offered to resign the Deanship of Arts if he would agree to remain at McGill in that capacity.

The letter, already referred to, from Mrs. Walter Vaughan comments upon this difficult decision. She says:

> When the Principalship of Alberta was offered to Dr. Tory, he naturally had to give the matter careful thought before making his decision. McGill did not wish to lose him, and he was strongly attached to his work and friends here. I happened to come upon him and Dr. Charles Moyse discussing the question earnestly. Dr. Tory looking really perplexed turned to me and said more or less jokingly, "What do you say about it? Do I go or stay?" I, quite forgetting my unfitness to speak, but tremendously conscious that here for once I was seeing a great piece of work being offered to the right man, cried out excitedly, "But, of course, you must go! It is a tremendous opportunity." He laughed and said, "All right, I am off." Of course I do not flatter myself that I had anything to do with it. No doubt his mind was already made up, but it was one more joke between us. When I saw him in later years, he used to say, "You know you sent me out there."

It was a difficult decision. The Province of Alberta was just emerging from its pioneer beginnings, with a population of about 300,000 people strung out in tiny settlements from the Montana border to the Peace River, nearly 800 miles to the north. Edmonton was a raw, muddy city of some 15,000 inhabitants. The university was nothing more than a dream and a piece of legislation. But the pioneering instinct in Dr. Tory was stronger even than his love of teaching and research. It was in the nature of the man to accept any challenge that promised adventure in unexplored and undeveloped territory. He knew enough about the natural resources of Alberta to realize that it would become one of the great Provinces of Canada. As President of the University he would have scope for every talent he possessed—his scientific knowledge; his recognized ability for organization and administration; his love of teaching; his devotion to the cause of higher education. Beside all this he was a deeply religious man, and here was as clear a call from God as the call to become a minister of the Methodist Church had been in his youth.

When it was announced in the Press that Dr. Tory was

about to leave McGill a round of farewell parties and banquets followed. There was a banquet at the Engineers Club, of business and professional men, at which toasts were proposed and tributes paid by Mr. W. M. Birks, Mr. Abner Kingman, Dean Charles Moyse, Dr. Alexander Johnston, Dr. Frank D. Adams, Mr. H. B. Ames, M.P., and other noted men of the day. A faculty banquet was presided over by Dr. Peterson. A banquet of Y.M.C.A. and church people was given in the Y.M.C.A., where speeches were made by Mr. A. O. Dawson, Mr. E. E. Howard and Mr. John Torrance. On all these occasions presentations were made—a gold watch for Dr. Tory, two travelling cases for Mrs. Tory; a case of flatware, and various other gifts.

But the occasion which would perhaps warm the hearts of both more than anything else was the farewell party given by the students, when more than 200 undergraduates gathered to add their voices to the chorus of farewells and good wishes.

The final demonstration of affection and respect occurred on the Sunday before Dr. Tory left for the West. A mass meeting of students crowded the auditorium and the lounge of Strathcona Hall to listen to his farewell address. I was then in my third year in Arts, and, in company with a group of friends, attended the meeting. I had seen and heard Dr. Tory many times before but had never met him. On that occasion I was deeply impressed with the man and what he had to say. He spoke of the influence of Christianity in the history of the civilized world, and declared it to be the only solution of the social problems of modern society.

There had been a heresy trial in Montreal shortly before this and Dr. Tory referred to it in passing. I shall always remember his indignation at what he considered the wrong done to the defendant in the case. "It is this sort of thing," he said, "which compels many honest seekers after the truth, to be anti-ecclesiastic in order not to be anti-Christian." And he closed his remarks with this statement: "The ultimate teaching of all education is just this, that every man owes to the generation in which he lives the last full measure of devotion to whatsoever things are true."

Chapter XI

THE UNIVERSITY OF ALBERTA—BEGINNINGS

In January, 1908, Dr. Tory left McGill University to undertake his new duties as President of a university which existed only in name. Shortly after his arrival in Alberta he found himself in the midst of a bitter struggle over the proposed site for the institution. In his diary, Dr. Tory gives the historic background of this controversy:

> When the Province had been organized under an Act of the Dominion Parliament, in 1905, the selection of the site of the Capital was left to the Legislature of the Province, but it is only the truth to say, that the constituencies had been so arranged that the majority would favour Edmonton rather than Calgary as the site. Doubtless if a Conservative government had had the task of arranging the Province into constituencies, they would have been planned in such a way as to place the capital in the City of Calgary. On returning home from British Columbia in the spring of 1906 I had stopped in Calgary and had met a group of people interested in the subject, and I had suggested to them that, now that the question of the Capital had been settled, if they could only forget about the capital and ask for the university, they would stand a good chance of getting it, but they seemed so sure that they could still get the Capital that they refused to offer any compromise.
>
> The agitation was led by Mr. R. B. Bennett, himself, who was already one of the most prominent and powerful citizens of Calgary and a strong Conservative. Since I had been appointed to the Presidency of the new university by a Liberal Government, Mr. Bennett assumed that I had been responsible for the purchase of the site. Actually I had nothing to do with it. The university site had been purchased by the Department of Education, and consisted of 258 acres of land with a 2,000 foot river frontage across the Saskatchewan river from the city of Edmonton. Edmonton and Calgary at that time were real boom towns. Calgary had had a considerable start over Edmonton, largely because of the fact that it was one of

the main centres of the Canadian Pacific Railway; was on the direct line to the Pacific Coast, and had been for nearly thirty years the chief trading centre for the cattle and horse-ranching industry of southern Alberta. Edmonton on the other hand had been little more than a fur-trading post until 1898, when the Yukon gold discoveries brought a great influx of population and trade. This was due to the fact that there were thousands of gold-seekers attempting to make their way into the Yukon territory over an undeveloped trail running north-west from Edmonton and following approximately the present route of the Alaska Highway. There was a fund of stories in my early days in Edmonton about the Yukon boom. For example, some Englishmen from Yorkshire arrived at the railway station in Strathcona with a carload of baled hay, which they proposed to carry along with them to feed their animals as they made their way to the Yukon through what they apparently believed to be a burning desert. All sorts of ingenious methods of getting through had been devised. There was the case of a man who had packed all his reserve stock of supplies in a barrel, had strong hoops put around it, with shafts at the end so arranged that the barrel would revolve, and, with a horse between the shafts, undertook to roll to the Yukon, a distance of nearly 2000 miles. He got little further than the borders of the town when his barrel went to pieces.

Because of the intensity of the rivalry between Calgary and Edmonton, and the bitterness of the controversy over the site chosen for the university, I decided that the best thing for me to do was to get an institution started as soon as possible. I therefore began by visiting all the high schools of the Province, canvassing to see to what extent a new university would receive the patronage of the schools. Here I ran into an exceedingly interesting situation. The high schools were all manned by teachers from the East, men trained at Toronto, Queen's and McGill universities and a few from the Maritimes. These teachers had their own loyalties to the universities from which they came, and gave little encouragement at the beginning to any of their pupils to become associated with the University of Alberta. As a matter of fact, in the southern part of the Province, an outstanding citizen of Calgary went so far as to canvass the schools in order to prevent the pupils going to the university. After a full enquiry, however, I found that there were between thirty and forty students available for freshmen, and three or four would like to enter the second year.

Following this tour of the Province Dr. Tory decided, with the sanction of the government, to open the University for classes in the autumn of 1908 if suitable accommodation could be found. At that time the City of Strathcona had under construction a new high school building, which in due course would have classrooms to spare, as the building was being constructed with a view to the future growth of the city. In the meantime Dr. Tory was able to obtain the use of one floor in a public school building in Strathcona (The Queen Alexandra School), with the assurance that when the high school was finished later that fall ample space would be available until buildings were erected on the new university grounds. There was a bitter rivalry in those early days between the twin-cities, Edmonton and Strathcona, which faced each other at a distance of a mile or more across the deep valley of the Saskatchewan River.

Edmonton in 1908 had a population of about 15,000, Strathcona about 7,000, but the coming of the Canadian Pacific Railway into the latter city from Calgary, in 1891, had encouraged the belief that the larger development would take place on the south side of the Saskatchewan. This belief still persisted. The Saskatchewan River, flowing at a level of two hundred feet or more below the two cities, constituted a very definite physical barrier between them. The only connection between the two towns was what was called "the low-level bridge," and a scow capable of carrying three teams at once crossed the river at regular intervals near the university site.

Dr. Tory had left his wife behind him in Montreal, and one of the many first things that had to be attended to was the finding of a home. There was nothing available in Strathcona and the new President was compelled to live in Edmonton on the north side of the river. So great was the bitterness between the cities that it was years before he was forgiven this apparent disloyalty to Strathcona!

The University Act had stated, that the convocation of the University was to consist of all graduates of any British or Canadian university who had resided in the Province at least three months prior to the election of the Senate, and had registered at least one month prior to this election. Convocation was given the power to elect the Chancellor and five members of the Senate. Other Senate members were to be the Minister of Education, The Chancellor, The President and ten members appointed by the Lieutenant Governor-in-Council. The Senate was given control over both business and educational policies. Soon after his arrival it became clear to Dr. Tory that the Act would have to be rewritten.

Meanwhile as noted above, by authority of the Legislature (passed in 1907), River Lot, No. 5, containing 258 acres of bush-land, had been purchased on the south bank of the Saskatchewan River a mile west of the town of Strathcona.

In the original convocation of the University of Alberta, in 1908, approximately 350 names of graduates of various universities were enrolled. This was the number of those who had registered as members of convocation and had paid their fees.

From this group a ballot had to be taken for the election of representatives to the Senate. This was a tedious process, and before it was completed Dr. Tory began to realize something of the difficulties involved in starting a new institution in a new land. Among the persons elected to the Senate were graduates of McGill, Queen's, Toronto, Dalhousie, Dublin and Oxford. The result was an exceedingly mixed university tradition, and a deep suspicion among certain members that Dr. Tory would be bound to attempt to shape the new institution in the likeness of McGill. A further problem was the number of honour graduates of eastern universities, who were convinced that they themselves were exactly the right persons to head up one of the faculties, or at least be appointed to the teaching staff. Dr. Tory was determined that only highly qualified men would be appointed, and that he should have a free hand in making appointments. It so happened that one of the men elected to the Senate, a local high school principal, was himself a candidate for a professorship and at the first meeting of the Senate, he moved a resolution that the President be instructed to appoint men to the university professorships from among those already teaching in the Province. With this idea there was some sympathy, but not very much. Dr. Tory was sitting quietly taking little part in the discussion but always dominating the situation. The Senate as a whole agreed with Dr. Tory that, as far as possible, the professors should be Canadians, who had not only graduated with distinction from their own universities but had also taken post graduate work elsewhere. Before the resolution was put to the Senate some rather unpleasant discussion took place, and Dr. Tory stated that he would be satisfied with the passing of the resolution, provided that the mover would agree to one amendment, namely, that the President should appoint Albertans only if he was able to find men sufficiently qualified for their jobs.

Among the members of Senate was a very distinguished Calgary lawyer, Mr. P. T. Nolan, known all over Alberta as "Paddy." Mr. Nolan was a graduate of Dublin University, one of the outstanding barristers of the Province and noted for his wit. When Dr. Tory suggested the amendment, Mr. Nolan, who had been patiently listening to the discussion, spoke up: "Mr. Chancellor," he said, "the President has stated he would be satisfied with the amendment under discussion. Well, I am not, and I move that he be instructed to appoint *no one* from the teaching profession of the Province of Alberta." There was a roar of laughter in the Senate, the original resolution was withdrawn and the choice of teaching staff was left entirely in the hands of the President. That first meeting of the Senate was held in Edmonton on March 30, 1908, two months or more after Dr. Tory's arrival in Edmonton, and it was finally agreed that the President should proceed with the organization of the first faculty to be known as the Faculty of Arts and Sciences, with classes starting in September of that year.

Immediately after the meeting of the Senate Dr. Tory proceeded East with three objectives in mind: to gather together the nucleus of a staff, the nucleus of a library, and sufficient equipment for the teaching of the elementary courses in Science offered in the curriculum. The income available for the new institution at the time was an accumulation of approximately $25,000 through a percentage of Provincial succession duties made available by statute. Dr. Tory in choosing his staff had determined to appoint young men representing as wide a university tradition as possible from the outstanding institutions in the country. He was prepared to undertake the necessary instruction in physics and mathematics himself. After some weeks President Tory found the men he wanted.

William Hardy Alexander, who was then in a junior post at the University of Western Ontario, had a splendid record as a student in Honour Classics in the University of Toronto, and had taken his Ph.D. in California.

For English Literature he chose Edmund Kemper Broadus, a graduate of the University of Virginia, who had taken his Ph.D. at Harvard. For Modern Languages he found Luther Herbert Alexander, M.A., a graduate of Toronto, and at that time lecturer in Modern Languages at New York State College while pursuing his Ph.D. course in Columbia University.

His final choice was William Muir Edwards, a graduate in Engineering of McGill University, at that time a lecturer in Mathematics at McGill. These four men with the President constituted the original staff. At the second meeting of the Senate held in Calgary (July, 1908) Dr. Tory presented the names of these professors for appointment, and the University of Alberta was on its way to becoming a reality.

It is doubtful if the new President could have found better men anywhere than these to assist him in the difficult years that lay ahead. Each was an inspiring teacher, each entered into the spirit of the adventure and shared the President's infectious optimism. Each was in his late twenties or early thirties.

In an article in the University of Alberta student paper, *The Gateway*, published on December 15, 1927, when it was known that Dr. Tory was soon to leave Alberta to become head of the National Research Council, Prof. E. K. Broadus gave the following description of his first meeting with the President:

> It was across a luncheon table in a hotel in Boston in the early spring of 1908 that I first met the man (Tory). He was telling me of a University that didn't exist; in a province that I had never heard of; in a country that I had never been to, and then and there in an atmosphere of parker house rolls, and staid proprieties, I got an impression which has remained with me ever since as the peculiar essence of Dr. Tory. He dreamed a dream and there was a passion of fulfillment in him. He didn't quite seem to belong to Boston, and he didn't talk Bostonese. He seemed somehow to belong in a place

where things hadn't yet begun, and where his restless spirit could loose itself to the doing of them. And he had a way with him which made you want to go along and see him do it.

In the fall of 1908 the first session of the University met in the third-storey rooms of the Strathcona Public School. There were present a President, four professors and thirty-seven students, (8 more enrolled later in the season). Of this occasion Professor Broadus later wrote:

> In September of 1908, I found Tory ensconced in the attic of a small public school building. There assembled the four of us. We were to constitute the Faculty, veritable *philosophes sous les toits*, and he and we and it, were for the nonce the University of Alberta.

Before the opening a convocation was called and a suitable ceremonial took place. An address was given by the Honourable Dr. A. C. Rutherford, the Premier, and the Degree of Doctor of Laws was conferred upon certain distinguished gentlemen in the Province, including Chief Justice A. L. Sifton, who afterward became Premier of Alberta.

In his first convocation address Dr. Tory clearly stated his conception of the place of a University in a pioneer society:

> It is with a profound sense of responsibility that I come before you today for the first time in my capacity as President of your university. Positions of great responsibility and opportunity come to few men and when they do tradition has usually marked a way, a path, well trodden by other men which it is fairly safe to follow. But seldom is it given to a man or a group of men to lay the foundations of great institutions, and while doing so, to blaze a path into which an established order will compel other men to walk. Three years ago the Lieutenant-Governor, acting for His Majesty, the King, and the people of this Province, placed upon the shoulders of the Prime Minister and his ministers the task of making a tradition for the enactment of Law, in this part of Canada. With hands practically free, within the limits of the Constitution they were given an opportunity to show the world what responsible government could do for a country which begins its life with the effect of tradition reduced to a minimum. Similarly, to you, Gentlemen of the Senate and Convocation, and to me as your Executive Head has been given the responsibility to say what an educational institution starting unhampered by fixed traditions may become, as we build, unless we

build so badly that our work must be destroyed, others will build after us . . . .

The modern state university has sprung from a demand on the part of the people themselves for intellectual recognition, a recognition which only a century ago was denied them. The result is that such institutions must be conducted in such a way as to relate them as closely as possible to the life of the people. The people demand that knowledge shall not be the concern of scholars alone. The uplifting of the whole people shall be its final goal. This should be the concern of all educated men, it should never be forgotten.

It is the glory of our Canadian institutions that they have directed from the homes of those we are accustomed to call the common people, a steady stream of men into positions of responsibility among us. Without that which the university has to offer this would never have been possible.

It thus happens that the problems of our national life are being worked out, directly or indirectly, more largely by our universities than elsewhere. The university has become, in the words of the late President Harper, a prophet of the people. For from its walls must come forth the men who are to make their laws, who shall expound the principles of government, who shall soundly conceive the responsibility of the people. The men who shall see for the people, feel for them, hear for them, and lead them into those paths of life which make for stability and permanence.

It has been well said, "that there is a call for men trained by other agencies than the caucus for the discussion of public affairs; men who know what the experience of the world has been in the development of institutions and are prepared by intellectual and moral discipline to advance the public interest, irrespective of party, and indifferent to the attainment of official stations." Such men the universities should foster and nourish.

Mr. Chancellor, I consider that the extension of the activities of the university on such lines as will make its benefits reach directly or indirectly the mass of the people, carrying its ideals of refinement and culture into their homes and its latent spiritual and moral power into their minds and hearts, is a work second to none that can be undertaken by any government.

No truer application can ever be made of the words of the great Humbolt who said: "The State always acts wisely when in times of misfortune it uses its efforts to establish something looking to future good and connects its name with such work." The time will come when all men will recognize that the founding of the Provincial University in this Province was one of the great acts of the administration of the present government.

But Mr. Chancellor, I must hasten on to another question. You will expect me to say some word with regard to the direction in which we are now spending our energy.

Let me say in reply to such a query that here we have the past to guide us. The accumulated experience of past generations of educators and teachers has largely determined for us the materials of our courses of study and the direction in which our work must be started.

We have organized our first Faculty as a "Faculty of Arts and Sciences." In making our first appointments we have determined to begin with those subjects which everywhere by common consent are considered the subjects which should form the foundation upon which to build. These are: English languages and Literature, the Ancient and Modern Languages, History, Pure and Applied Mathematics, Physics.

To these at once will be added the natural sciences, chemistry, botany, and geology, and also philosophy. We shall rapidly push our scientific study into those practical fields which are necessary to meet the needs of the Province.

Permit me to say one word with regard to our staff. On them the success of the university depends. If we are to have a great university it will be because great men are upon our staff. Here we are confronted with the problem which confronted the First President of Johns Hopkins. He asked a friend what he was to do in this dilemma. "You cannot have a great university without great men and you cannot get great men without a great university. What am I to do?" This friend replied: "Your difficulty applies only to old men who are great; these you cannot move; but the young men of talent, learning and promise you can draw. They should be your strength."

Mr. Chancellor, it is from the young men of promise and learning of the continent that our staff has been selected. I will ask you to judge them by their work.

But before I leave them may I add one other remark. The members of the university staff must not be thought of in the ordinary way as state officers. They must rather be regarded in the light of independent thinkers and scholars who are to bring us into that appreciation of those higher things about which I was speaking a moment ago. For that purpose they have been selected and I am confident they will prove worthy of their high vocation.

One of the major concerns of the President, prior to the opening day, was to make sure that enough students would register to provide working material for the staff. There were a great many people in the Province who regarded the whole enterprise as premature. It is doubtful if there would have been a University of Alberta until many years later if it had not been for the vision and persistence of Dr. A. C. Rutherford, the first Premier.

It was important, therefore, in terms of public interest and good-will, that the University should start its work with convincing evidence that the action already taken was timely and that the institution would justify itself. Dr. W. H. Alexander writing of this period in the same issue of *The Gateway* mentioned above, says: "He (Tory) wisely satisfied himself first that there would be a student body; faculties can be had for the asking, but students, they are shy and diffident birds and may not come at all when you throw out the breakfast crumbs." Classes were opened on the 25th of September, 1908, and thirty-seven students appeared for registration, four of these had senior matriculation from Ontario or a year at a university and wished to take classes in the second year. As this was within the teaching competence of the staff as appointed, it was decided to offer the second year courses to the four students and three of these became the first graduates of the University of Alberta. Names of the graduates are: Decima Robinson, A. J. Law, and R. H. Dobson.

Among the students were some whose social background was extremely limited, as indeed is the case in the freshman year at any university, but there was perhaps less of an idea in this instance of what university life was like than in an Eastern university.

The Senate had decided that gowns should be worn by all students as was the custom in Eastern colleges at that time. It was believed that the disciplinary value in a gown would help to create a university tradition. Care had been taken to have gowns on hand to sell to the students at the opening. One of the students, not knowing how to accommodate himself to the situation, bolted into the President's office and wanted to know if it was necessary to take off his trousers before putting on the gown. On another occasion a student walked into a solemn faculty meeting presided over by the President and wanted to know where he could buy a fountain pen. Incidents of this sort undoubtedly helped the new staff members to realize that they had left Harvard and Toronto far behind them.

The quarters taken over were extremely small and crowded but there was a good elementary physics laboratory, even though the President had to set up his own office in one of the air shafts of the building which had barely room for a desk and one chair.

During the Christmas holidays the new high school building had been sufficiently completed to enable the university to move into more commodious quarters. The laboratories were extended and a place was found for the beginnings of a library. One of the tasks the busy President had undertaken during the summer of 1908 had been to get together not only a set of the ordinary texts required for undergraduate courses, but also a list of all the reference books then in use, in the other universities of Canada. Work was therefore beginning with a fairly substantial library on hand. Dr. Tory at once began to prepare a building plan upon which could be based such parts of a permanent structure as were within the reach of the prospective budget.

The President and other members of the staff were in constant demand for speaking engagements throughout the Province. Every club and social organization had to be visited. According to Dr. Tory the climax was reached when the undertakers' association asked him to address their annual meeting, the subject suggested being "What the undertakers can do to promote the prosperity of Alberta."

From the very beginning one of the questions facing Dr. Tory and the government was whether the University was to be a single institution with all its units in one place, or whether they were to be distributed among various parts of the Province. It was pointed out by those who favoured the latter plan, that many universities in the United States had the Faculty of Arts in one place, Engineering in another, and Agriculture in a third.

There were already bitter stirrings in the Legislature hostile to the government, and one of the items in the agitation was the university. Party loyalty was not as strong in this new country as it was in older and more settled communities, because people had come from all quarters of the globe and had brought with them many different traditions. Members of the Legislature were inclined to be suspicious of each other, partly because, in Alberta at that time, every community of any size was anxious to assist real estate promotion by bringing public institutions to the home town. Matters were complicated also by the fact that the Conservative Party was exceedingly weak, there being only two members in the Legislature. All other members were Liberals, and this tended to increase the demands upon the government since there was no effective criticism from the Opposition.

It was at this time that some of the members of the Legislature from the northern part of the Province began to promote the idea of more extensive railway development. Towns were springing up everywhere, as the beginnings of the notorious real estate boom of a few years later were getting under way. It was only a few years after this, for example, that the town of Athabasca nincty miles north of Edmonton on the big bend of the Athabasca River, where it turns north to flow into Lake Athabaska, had a population of 2,500 people, and was being referred to as the coming metropolis of the North. But when it was discovered that the direct line of railway from Winnipeg, as portrayed on the maps of real estate promoters, would by-pass the town, two thousand people folded their tents like the Arabs and silently disappeared, virtually overnight. This was the spirit of the times, and the men in the Legislature, backed by enthusiastic promotors—many of whom it must be said had a genuine belief in the permanence of the boom which was just beginning—were anxious that the great northland should be opened up.

This created sharp dissension in the Legislature, because the southern members within the Liberal party were against the idea on the grounds of local rivalry and the vast expenditures involved. The result was a gradual cleavage in the Party. The Prime Minister, Dr. A. C. Rutherford, was a gentleman of the old school, and not equipped by experience or temperament for the rough and tumble of western politics.

An additional factor making trouble for the Premier was the presence in the Legislature, after the election of 1909, of

Mr. R. B. Bennett whose intense ambitions for Calgary and the South and whose capacity for bitter criticism made the situation very difficult. There was no one in the House who compared with him in debate.

THE STRUGGLE FOR UNIFICATION

While this strife was going on the President of the University of Alberta had other things to think about. As previously stated, the University Act had to be rewritten as the original Act had been really nothing more than a provisional stop-gap. Under it the management both of the business and educational policy was left to the Senate, a considerable portion of which was elected by Convocation, and a small number by the Government of the day. This was clearly too cumbersome a plan. During the winter of 1908-1909 a great deal of Dr. Tory's time was given to the drafting of an Act with the necessary flexibility to make a workable scheme. This task was undertaken from the legal point of view by Mr. Sydney B. Woods, K.C., who was then Deputy Attorney-General of the Province. As a guide Dr. Tory and Mr. Woods used the report of a Commission which had just previously studied the whole problem of university management in the Province of Ontario, and the Act which resulted from the report of that Commission. In the new Alberta Act provision was made for a separate Board of Governors appointed by the Government to deal entirely with the business administration of the University, and a Senate which would have control of university policy, subject, so far as finances were concerned, to the final decision of the Board of Governors. The question of the personnel of the Senate was of some complexity in Alberta because of the variety of tradition among the university graduates of the Province. Provision was therefore made in the Senate for certain *ex-officio* members of the teaching staff, such as the President and Deans of Faculties, and for other persons elected by various faculties to represent their interests. On the other hand there were some special features of the Act as drafted by Mr. Woods and Dr. Tory that were intended to meet some of the special problems which Western Canada presented. For example, provision was made to bring the examinations for all the professions in the Province under the control of Boards appointed by the Senate of the University.

When Dr. Tory had been in British Columbia there was a great deal of unrest over the manner in which the medical examinations in that Province were conducted. The Medical Association of British Columbia appointed its own Board of Examiners from its members, to conduct the examinations of new candidates for the practice of medicine in the Province. At that time McGill graduates were in the majority, and it was openly stated that a McGill graduate found it much easier to get by the Board than those of other universities. The same situation existed in Alberta, only here the graduates were mostly from the University of Toronto. One story, which still persists among the old-timers of Alberta, is that a well-known official of the Attorney-General's department, in advertising for assistance in that department, stated that "only graduates of the University of Toronto who are members in good standing of the Zeta Psi Fraternity need apply."

Mr. Woods and Dr. Tory in rewriting the University Act were convinced that difficulties of this kind could be avoided if the medical profession, for example, would accept representation on the University Senate, and if the Senate were authorized to appoint an examining board made up of representatives of a university faculty of medicine and outstanding members of the profession in the Province.

It did not seem wise at that early date to make this feature compulsory, so a permissive clause was written into the Act which enabled the University Senate to negotiate, whenever it might see fit, for an agreement not only with the medical profession but with any and all of the professional associations of the Province. Under this plan all the professions which require teaching were eventually brought under standards established by the University. These included the medical profession, the dental profession, the chartered accountants, the land surveyors association, the Alberta architects association, the law society, the Alberta pharmaceutical association, and the nurses association. Concerning this aspect of the new Act, the *Edmonton Journal* later, in June, 1914, said in an editorial:

> It is probably true to say, that no such highly unified system of higher education exists elsewhere on the American continent as has been achieved in the Province of Alberta in the past six years.

In his convocation address at the University of Alberta in May, 1920, Dr. Tory referred to the success of this plan:

> When the University started to function all the professions of the Province were working independently of one another with regulations of their own prepared by their own bodies. This had led to considerable discussion from time to time in the public press, as to the justice of a state of affairs which allowed professional organizations to fix standards for themselves independently of public control. The question was finally solved by relating all these organizations definitely in affiliation with the University, and the responsibility for establishing standards of education was placed upon the University Senate by the second University Act passed in 1910. One by one the professions came into the scheme and today, through the University Senate, working in cooperation with the professions, educational standards have been established that have removed all possible grounds of complaint as to the fairness between an examining body and persons to be examined.

The acceptance by the professional bodies and the general public of this centralized plan was made easier by an event which took place at this time, and which illustrated the need for such a provision. An application had been made by a man from Southern Texas to practise medicine in the Province without examination. He had secured the backing in the Legislature of the Attorney-General and certain members of the Legislature. Dr. Tory went to the Minister of Education and called his attention to the case, as he was convinced that the man did not have the necessary qualifications. He had a certificate of graduation from some medical school in Southern Texas, and the argument used in supporting his application was the customary one, that there was a crying need for doctors in the rural districts, and that whatever his training may have been it would be better to have his services than no doctor at all. After a search was made it was discovered that the school was no longer existent; the principal having been imprisoned for selling graduation certificates to practise which had been obtained through correspondence courses. Some five hundred dollars was spent in tracing the history of the school, but the money was considered well spent, and the case was thrown out of the Legislature. The incident which was thoroughly reported in the Press served to emphasize the importance of Dr. Tory's demand for the university control of standards.

A further important provision of the new Act had to do with finances, as it was evident to Dr. Tory and his associates that a stronger financial basis would have to be established before any great expansion could take place. The new Act specified that fifty per cent of all succession duties should be turned over to the University Board, twenty per cent of the Corporation tax, and a portion of the Education tax. In addition the Board was empowered to borrow money or issue debentures, subject to the approval of the Lieutenant Governor-in-Council who could guarantee such loans.

The next question faced by the staff and the Senate was the question of standards. Was Alberta to be a small college, with standards little above those of a high school, or was it to become a great university?

If the latter position was to be achieved it would be necessary to assure three conditions:

(i) adequate matriculation standards;
(ii) a highly qualified staff of teachers;
(iii) freedom from political pressure in the matter of appointments.

Concerning the last two conditions there was complete agreement. The question of matriculation standards presented much greater difficulties.

The secondary school system of the Province was still in its infancy. Many of the students entering the first years at the University had been inadequately prepared, and the staff had found it necessary to work long hours in helping students to make up their deficiencies. It had been agreed at the beginning that matriculation requirements would be the same as those in effect at the major Canadian universities. But Dr. Tory's aim had gone far beyond this. He believed that all educational work from the elementary school to the last grade in high school should be integrated in such a way as to make the university the coping stone, and co-ordinating agency, of the whole educational system of the Province.

In a scheme of such far-reaching importance there was bound to be strong difference of opinion, and at first there were numbers of teachers and leaders in education who regarded such a plan as an invasion of their field by a group of university authorities who knew little about its problems.

A Curriculum Revision Committee was appointed by the Department of Education, and a large number of sub-committees were set to work upon different phases of the curriculum. The work of the committee, which consisted of representatives of public and high school teachers, inspectors and superintendents, and of the university, and which was presided over by Dr. Tory, extended over a period of two years, and resulted in the preparation of a report which was adopted by the Department of Education, providing for a revision of the course of studies. Later, with the support of Dr. Tory, a Joint Matriculation Board under the Chairmanship of the Deputy Minister of Education, and containing high school and university representatives, was established and this body continued the task of maintaining and improving curriculum standards.

Meanwhile, all during the first four years, there had been a rapid growth in the number of students enrolled at the University, a corresponding extension of faculties and departments, and the installation of new equipment of all kinds. There had been 37 students and four professors in 1908. In 1912 this number had grown to 320 students and a teaching staff of 26, and the University had moved into the first of its new buildings. The first faculty established had been Arts and Science, by 1914 there were in addition, Applied Science, Medicine and Law, a School of Pharmacy, a Department of Accountancy.

Dr. Tory's struggle to maintain the unity of the University centred largely on the question of a Faculty of Agriculture.

As most of the graduates in Agriculture in the Province were from O.A.C. at Guelph, there was a strong tradition in favour of a Faculty of Agriculture separate from the University. As the voluntary farm organizations such as the United Farmers of Alberta represented those most deeply interested in the question, Dr. Tory was asked to speak on the question at a number of farmers' conventions in various parts of the Province. For some time Dr. Tory had been carrying on a thorough enquiry with authorities in the United States and Great Britain, and found that all of them supported his own opinion that it was better, from every point of view, that a faculty of Agriculture should be on the same campus and an integral part of a state university. Mr. Bennett and his friends in Calgary were still planning for a university in the south of the Province, and were determined to have the faculty of Agriculture in that city. Since it was obvious that the new University Act had tied all other professional groups to the institution in Edmonton, there was a savage attack on Dr. Tory in the Calgary newspapers accusing him of playing politics by addressing farm organizations on the subject. The chief leader in the attack on Dr. Tory in this connection was a Mr. Tregillus who operated a large dairy farm outside the city of Calgary. There was such a commotion over the matter that the United Farmers of Alberta asked Dr. Tory to clarify the whole issue for them at their annual meeting which was being held that year (1910) in Calgary.

When the President arrived in Calgary for this important occasion he found himself in a hostile atmosphere, as those opposed to him and his plans had canvassed the delegates and pledged a majority to vote against his proposals. When the meeting was called to order Dr. Tory was hardly on his feet before the large and tense audience when the opposition took definite form. Mr. Tregillus immediately arose and moved that the President be given only five minutes to speak. Fortunately the Chairman was a fair-minded citizen who replied: "Dr. Tory knows we are very busy and will not take any more time than is necessary, but he certainly has the right to expect that much, since we ourselves have invited him here." As soon as Dr. Tory began to state his case, quoting from letters he had received from all over America, Mr. Tregillus rose in his place and asked why he had consulted American authorities instead of going to the farm people of the Province for advice. The Lord had delivered him into Tory's hands. Blazing with anger, the President arose and pointed out that he had addressed three conferences of Alberta farmers in the north and south, and had been accused in consequence by the speaker and his followers of playing politics. That was the turning point of the convention. A number of men sprang to their feet and stated that this was correct, and that Dr. Tory had dealt with the question at meetings they had attended on a strictly economic and scientific basis. Others said they had been compelled to cancel meetings he had agreed to address since he refused to speak on the subject after the hue and cry about political bias had broken out. That was the end of the interruptions. Dr. Tory spoke for an hour. He pointed out what educationists had long since realized, that the universities must forsake their ivory towers and concern themselves with the practical problems of every day life. He went on to say that where agricultural colleges had grown up apart from the university the tax-payers were compelled to support two institutions instead of one. This was not only very costly but created bitter rivalry in the legislature for public support and a resulting suspicion of the soundness of the work being done. By having a single institution, he pointed out, there is an opportunity to break down existing prejudices between rural and urban people through the mingling of students from the farm and the city in common classrooms, and students who were training to become school teachers would have an opportunity to take work in agriculture before proceeding to teach in a farm community. He quoted opinions from leading agriculturalists in Great Britain and America, all of whom agreed that the plan of consolidation being worked out in Alberta was by far the most practical and economical. In conclusion, Dr. Tory outlined plans by which the University intended to relate its research to practical production problems as well as the social and economic problems of farm people. The University existed, he said, to lighten the burden of their toil and to assist them in obtaining the maximum reward for their labour. The President's obvious sincerity and his convincing arguments carried the day, and at the conclusion of the conference the vote was 243 to 7 for consolidation.

About this time the Honourable Duncan Marshall, who had been appointed Minister of Agriculture, began to work out a plan for schools of Agriculture in the Province—a suggestion originally brought forward at one of the early meetings of the University Senate, and one which was of supreme importance in a predominantly rural region. After consultation with Dr. Tory and others it was decided that, instead of following the Ontario tradition of putting the study of Agriculture on the regular high school curriculum, three diploma schools of Agriculture would be established at strategic places throughout Alberta, and that a board of agricultural education would be set up under which these schools would function. Schools of Agriculture would serve as feeders for a University Faculty of Agriculture, and as soon as students began to go through the schools in significant numbers the university faculty would be started.

The Board of Agricultural Education was duly formed and Dr. Tory was appointed as Chairman, a position he held as long as Mr. Marshall continued as Minister of Agriculture. Three schools were established—one at Vermilion, one at Olds and one at Claresholm—in the north, middle and south of the Province. Farms were purchased, buildings were erected, and principals and staffs appointed. Later on two more schools were erected under the Marshall régime at Youngstown and Raymond.

In 1910 the mutterings already referred to over railways broke into fury against the Rutherford government. The trouble now centred around the decision of the government to guarantee the building of a railway from Edmonton to Fort McMurray, a distance of over two hundred miles. The first one hundred miles would pass through a fairly well established farming country, and one which was rapidly being homesteaded, but the last hundred miles was a wholly unsettled country of muskeg and forest. A Company had been formed headed by a group of men from Kansas City, and an Act was passed in the Legislature giving a subsidy of some seven million dollars toward the building of the railroad. Not only was the wisdom of the undertaking questioned by large numbers of people both north and south, but the soundness and integrity of the company was suspected. In addition the project intensified the bitter rivalry between the north and south; the southern members believing that an undue effort was being made to develop the north country. A complicating factor was that certain members of Legislature were in New York at the time when the bonds were sold, and that the price of the bonds advanced from seven to ten points the next day. All this looked very suspicious, and a tremendous agitation broke out in the Legislature with the leader of the opposition, Mr. R. B. Bennett, the chief antagonist to the whole scheme.

As Mr. Bennett was solicitor for the Canadian Pacific Railway, it was of course pointed out by the government that his was a dog-in-the-manger attitude. There were some spectacular scenes in the House as the debate proceeded. After several days of bitter discussion the government decided that the matter ought to be brought to a conclusion one way or the other.

On the last day of the debate, Mr. Bennett was not in his place at the afternoon session, and it was assumed that he had missed his train from Calgary, so an effort was made by the Government to get the Bill through its final reading as quickly as possible. Apparently Mr. Bennett had deliberately missed the regular train in order to make a dramatic entrance upon the scene. He came by special train from Calgary, and arrived in the House just in time to prevent closure of the debate. Mr. Bennett was always the best dressed man in the Legislature, and on this occasion he walked quietly down the aisle, bowed to Mr. Speaker and assumed his seat. He was dressed like a Bond Street business man, immaculate in morning coat, striped trousers, grey double-breasted vest, wing collar, grey silk tie and all.

When the Speaker called the question Mr. Bennett arose and made one of the most eloquent and remarkable speeches of his career. He spoke for four hours, and denounced with scorn, derision and fury, the American gentlemen who had formed the syndicate, the government which had backed the scheme, the uselessness of the territory through which the proposed railway would pass, and pointed out the impossibility of making it pay. Judging by newspaper reports there is little doubt that, if a vote had been taken after Mr. Bennett sat down, the Government would have been defeated on the spot, but the Hon. Duncan Marshall moved that the whole matter be sent for investigation to a commission under the Chairmanship of the Chief Justice of the Province, and this plan was adopted.

The opposition to the government was wider and deeper than the question of the railroad however. There was grave dissension in the Liberal Party and the government over the distribution of cabinet portfolios. The opposition within the government was led by the Hon. W. H. Cushing, the Minister of Public Works. He apparently had reason to believe that, if the Rutherford government went down to defeat, he would have the support of Mr. Bennett and dissident Liberal members in forming a new government with himself as Premier. There can be little doubt that Mr. Bennett took full advantage of the rift in the party and the government to further his particular interests—as indeed anyone involved in a hot political battle was bound to do.

Immediately after the Bennett speech, Mr. Cushing met his followers and was persuaded to continue his fight, with the understanding that he would be the next Premier. The result was that Dr. Rutherford tendered his resignation to the Lieutenant Governor, but the latter—The Honourable G. H. V. Bulyea, instead of calling Mr. Cushing to form a new government, to the surprise of everyone called upon the Chief Justice of the Province, The Honourable A. L. Sifton, to do so. This decision was reached after a hurried meeting in the home of John A. McDougall, M.P.P., which was attended by Dr. Tory, and it was the latter's advice which the Lieutenant Governor followed.

The real reason for this move—which proved to be a wise one—was that the Liberal party wanted someone in the House who was able to stand up to Mr. Bennett. That their confidence was justified was soon evident from the events which followed. Mr. Sifton at once secured the loyalty of the Liberal members; dealt with the railway matter in his own way; and proved himself well able to meet Mr. Bennett in debate. Mr. Sifton referred the whole matter of the railway agreement to the new Chief Justice, The Honourable Mr. Justice Horace Harvey, for investigation and report. When the House met again Mr. Sifton proposed a Bill transferring the whole seven million dollars to the general revenue of the Province, having decided that the railway would not be proceeded with. This action led to a court action, and ultimately went to the Judicial Committee of the Privy Council which gave a decision against the judgment of Mr. Sifton. The government was compelled to proceed with the project. A new contractor was called in and the railroad completed.

The relation of all this to the University of Alberta was very definite and very trying. Dr. Rutherford as Premier and Minister of Education had instructed the President to proceed with his building plans. Dr. Tory had spent considerable time looking over university building schemes both in the United States and in Great Britain. He had had long consultations with architects and had finally, in 1910, immediately after the passing of the new University Act, presented a carefully planned outline of a building programme, both for the present and the future.

Dr. Rutherford had assured the University bankers that they could advance the money to erect one building, which would be used later for a students' residence, and to proceed with the foundations of an Arts and Science Faculty building. Unfortunately, after the change of the government, the House closed without having passed a vote for either the buildings or the salaries of the staff. Sixty thousand dollars had already been spent on the authority of Dr. Rutherford, and Dr. Tory was now accused of having spent money which had not been approved by the Legislature. The President called upon the new Premier, Mr. Sifton, to explain the situation. Reporting on this interview later Dr. Tory declared it was one of the most disconcerting experiences he had ever had. Mr. Sifton was an exceedingly silent man, who could sit for hours with a cigar between his lips and never say a word. Dr. Tory talked for nearly an hour during which time the Premier stared at him without any comment. When he was through, Mr. Sifton told him the Board had taken a lot of responsibility on itself to spend money that had not been voted, and showed the President to the door without further remark. Dr. Tory went away feeling certain that Mr. Sifton had joined Mr. Bennett and his supporters in a plan to move the University to Calgary. It is altogether likely that if those who were advocating such a plan had gone about the matter sensibly, they might have succeeded. The only complications in the way were the money already spent on the University site, and the fact that Alberta College of the Methodist Church had been assigned a site on the University grounds and was planning to build. Even so, the amount of money spent was not very great, and a compromise might have been effected if the Calgary members had not changed their tactics and demanded a charter for a University of Calgary.

Meanwhile work on the first building (Athabaska Hall), started in 1910, had to be stopped. The money available from succession duties was soon gone, and the President found himself in the fall of 1910 without money enough to pay salaries and could get no promise from Mr. Sifton about the future. By pooling their personal resources Dr. Tory and a group of a dozen business men were able to get a loan from the bank sufficient to carry on until the Legislature met again.

The Sifton government now appointed a new Board of Governors, and at the first meeting it was apparent they had brought with them a good deal of the suspicion and hostility generated in the recent battle. Dr. Tory presented the first draft of his plans for a University building scheme and it was promptly attacked from all sides. It was clear that much of the opposition had its roots in the recent political agitation, while some was due to the fact that the first buildings proposed were not in a prominent place on the University site. One Toronto graduate on the Board wanted the Main building to look like University College, Toronto. Others were in favour of a plan similar to that of their own Alma Mater. One after another members of the Board condemned the plan. The only two members who had been on the old Board were the Chancellor,

H.R.H. The Prince of Wales and Dr. H. M. Tory leaving the University of Alberta.

THE ARTS BUILDING, UNIVERSITY OF ALBERTA

Mr. Justice Stewart of Calgary and Dr. Tory. The President was called upon to state his case. By this time he was fighting mad. He explained the plan in detail, why certain laboratories were here and others there, why the buildings were placed in certain positions, advantages of light, accessibility, etc., etc., and closed by saying:

> One of you gentlemen has referred to this as a "damn bad plan." I am going to tell you it is a damn good plan, and I am willing to submit it to any group of architects in Canada. This plan is not for tomorrow or the day after. It will require from thirty to fifty years to complete, and will grow with the growth of the Province.

The whole matter was submitted to an eastern firm of architects and finally adopted without change. It is a continuing tribute to Henry Marshall Tory's vision that every building that has gone up since that time has followed the original plan.

The original diagram of the campus and buildings as prepared by Dr. Tory and the architects was enlarged, photographed and framed, and still hangs in the President's office at the University of Alberta. Once, when Dr. Tory overheard a group of legislators examining the plans, one of them, to his amusement, said: "So this is Tory's scheme. Boy, he'll be a long time dead."

At one of the first meetings of the Senate the decision had been made that the University would be established on a residential basis. There were two main reasons for this. First, the traditional belief that a residential system helped to give unity to the University and added to the value of the tradition growing up with the institution. Secondly, it would be for a long time difficult to find suitable lodgings within easy reach of the University, as the site was across the river from the major part of the population and a mile or more away from the town of Strathcona as it had developed at that time.

The Senate had also decided at the same time that sites would be offered on the University campus to denominational colleges. This corresponded to the McGill scheme of residential theological colleges, with all Arts teaching being given in the University, as opposed to Manitoba and Toronto where denominational colleges undertook their own Arts courses, apart from those which required the use of laboratories. Mr. Sifton now suggested that it would be wise to proceed first with the residential buildings, postponing the erection of the main teaching buildings until later. The outcome of this was that the three residential buildings, which were completed in 1915, were erected according to plan. In 1912 the first building, Athabaska Hall, was completed, and that fall the University of Alberta moved to more commodious quarters. But even so Professor W. H. Alexander and Dean W. A. R. Kerr were forced to share an office designed to serve later as a lavatory.

> The floor says "Doc. Alex," was laid with an all round fall to the centre, and now those who have noticed all these years the slight limp with which those gentlemen walk will recognize it as the result of much hill-side ploughing.

By 1912, however, the student body had grown so rapidly it became necessary to proceed with a building devoted entirely to teaching. Plans were got under way and the Arts Building was completed for use in the fall of 1915. The university authorities seemed destined to live in a state of constant agitation over buildings. Soon after the Sifton government came into power, the question of a hospital for Strathcona to be situated beside the University became a subject of bitter controversy.

President Tory suggested to the Board of Governors that negotiations should be opened with the Councils of both cities, to see if they would agree to a union hospital built either on the university grounds or on the north side of the river on the grounds where the Parliament Buildings now stand, looking forward to the day when a medical faculty would be established at the University. But the idea of a medical faculty was regarded as so far in the future that Dr. Tory had difficulty in getting the matter considered at all. The major objection came naturally enough from the persons who were promoting a hospital project for the city of Edmonton.

When the matter was submitted to the Edmonton Hospital Board, the old cry about medical students practising on the poor was raised. Oddly enough the bitterest objection was led by a ladies hospital auxiliary led by Mrs. Arthur Murphy, widely known to the public by her pen name, "Janey Canuck." Dr. Tory visited Mrs. Murphy in her home and thought he had succeeded in converting her to his idea, but the next day she carried the campaign to the newspapers in an article blasting the President and all his works. This was in the year of 1912. After due consideration by the Board it was decided to go ahead with a hospital on the south side as close to the University as possible. The University had been offering courses in Science as a foundation for medical teaching, and had secured affiliation with eastern universities for recognition of the work done, thus making it possible to complete the medical course in an eastern institution in three instead of five years. The clinical work of the medical school was still some years away. However, a site was secured on the University grounds and the Town of Strathcona proceeded to build a wing, which when extended later became known as the University Hospital.

It became increasingly clear as time went on that the rivalry between Edmonton and Strathcona was harmful to both cities. A small group of citizens, of whom Dr. Tory was one of the leading spirits, began to discuss the possibility of Union with members of both Councils. The main arguments were: (1) the rapid growth of Calgary as the major city of the Province, and the fact that the two towns together actually almost equalled Calgary in population; (2) the union of the two cities would hasten the construction of railway facilities between them. There were of course many of the founding fathers left on both Councils, who still nourished the old antagonisms and would not listen to any proposals for union. A committee was appointed to draft the terms of an agreement, and Dr. Tory and O. M. Biggar, K.C., of the well-known law firm of Short, Cross and Biggar were chosen to represent the University's interests. It was largely due to the skill and tact of Mr. Biggar that Union was finally brought about. In the meantime the Canadian Pacific Railway had decided to build what is now known as the High-Level Bridge across the Saskatchewan River. This made it certain that the major part of the city would be on the north side of the river. This, together with the arrival of the Grand Trunk Railway, and the rumour that the Macdonald Hotel would be built shortly on the north side overlooking the river, changed the temper of both cities. The C.P.R. Bridge, when completed with streetcar service and a traffic section, made it possible for people doing business on the north side to have their residences on the south side. Gradually attractive homes built by professional people, who were interested in being close to the University, began to appear which served to bring a spirit of unity into the situation. Within a short time old antagonisms were forgotten, except in the case of a few of the old timers, and the two cities became one.

The above events had the effect of greatly strengthening the position of the University, and the clamour for a second institution in Calgary began to subside, although a start had been made and a University of Calgary in name at least had gotten under way. Pressure upon the government to endorse the establishment of a University in Calgary did not entirely cease after the proposal was voted on in the Legislature in 1910. As late as 1913, when the University in Edmonton had been in existence for five years and its building programme was well under way, the agitation for a similar degree-granting institution in Calgary continued.

The movement was now led by Dr. T. H. Blow, a medical doctor who was also a real estate owner and promoter. The plan was to build the University on some land several miles west of the city and thus create a fine residential district in that area.

The petition brought before the house, in 1910, for the incorporation of a degree-granting institution in Calgary was accompanied by a proposed Charter, which was in all essentials a copy of that drawn up by Mr. Sydney Woods and Dr. Tory for the Provincial university. The Legislature at that time gave incorporation to a College of Calgary, but withheld the power to confer degrees and to control the examinations required for admission to the professions. Two years later—in October, 1912—Calgary College opened in the Public Library, with a staff of four professors and an attendance of 24 regular students and 101 taking one or more classes. This was an encouraging beginning and the leaders of the movement again petitioned the government for incorporation as a University in 1913. When the application of Calgary College for University powers came before the Legislature on October 2, 1913, authority was given for the appointment of a Commission to enquire into and consider the proposals contained in the Bill.

The Commission was duly appointed on May 23, 1914, and consisted of: Dr. Walter C. Murray, President of the University of Saskatchewan; Sir Robert A. Falconer, President of the University of Toronto; and Dr. A. Stanley MacKenzie, President of Dalhousie University. The Commission turned in its report on December 29, 1914, and recommended:

(1) that degree conferring powers be not granted;
(2) that an Institute of Technology and Arts be established in the city of Calgary to be supported and controlled jointly by the City and the Province.

Calgary College lasted for three years 1912-1915, and closed its doors in the spring of 1915 with a deficit of some $6,000. Subscription pledges by private citizens had failed to materialize and no building was ever erected.

Chapter XII

THE UNIVERSITY OF ALBERTA— A TIME FOR EXPANSION

During the years 1908-1915 the University of Alberta witnessed a remarkable development. The Faculty of Arts and Sciences had been established first, and four years later, 1912-1913, Applied Science, Law, Medicine, Pharmacy and Accountancy were added. The Faculty of Agriculture was established in 1915. In this connection an article by Dr. Broadus in the special issue of *The Gateway* already referred to is of interest:

> In both these Provinces (Alberta and Saskatchewan) Universities were created at about the same time; and because both were prairie Provinces, depending upon essentially the same economic conditions, it might have been expected that their university development would have been on parallel lines. Instead, a curious paradox developed. The President of the University of Saskatchewan, who had been a Professor of Philosophy at Dalhousie, made it his first concern to establish Agriculture in the curriculum, on the principle that if the obvious thing was done first all things would be added unto it. The President of the University of Alberta, who had been a scientist at McGill, made it his first concern to establish and foster the Arts curriculum, on the principle that if he did first the thing that was hardest to do in a purely agricultural community the obvious things would come of themselves. Thus did *litterae humaniores* generate agriculture and Science become the father of the Arts.

In his first Presidential address to Convocation, in 1908, Dr. Tory had said:

> The modern state university is a people's institution. The people demand that knowledge shall not be the concern of scholars alone. The uplifting of the whole people shall be its final goal.

In order to establish a broader base of loyalty and support for the University among the people of the Province, a great deal of time and effort on the part of the staff had gone into extra-mural work. By 1912 Dr. Tory felt that the time had come for the appointment of a full-time Director of Extension Services to organize and direct all extra-mural activities. The demands upon members of the staff for extension lectures had grown steadily.

In addition to the original group of four there were now on the staff: Professors J. M. MacEachran, Philosophy; R. K. Gordon, English; W. A. R. Kerr, Dean of Arts and Professor of Modern Languages; J. A. Allan, Geology; E. W. Sheldon, Mathematics; Barker Fairley, German; Cecil Burgess, Architecture; Prof. A. F. Lehmann, Physics. These men were in constant demand, and some of them were away from the University for days at a time giving lectures to large and small groups of people in the towns and villages of the Province.

In an article written for *Queen's Quarterly* (Winter, 1951-1952) Prof. R. K. Gordon says:

> One might go and deliver a single discourse at, say Red Deer or Calgary, and go home, but there was also the grand tour; that was the great adventure. You gave seven or eight lectures and were away about ten days. Medicine Hat, Lethbridge, Macleod were the three largest places on the itinerary; and at them you were expected to face your audience in the full splendour of dress shirt and dinner jacket. The custom was to make one shirt do. At Macleod on its final appearance, it retained like Milton's Satan some of its original brightness but we relied on the hall being dimly lit.
>
> Our audiences were easy to please and extraordinarily large. Many of the small places had no theatre and these were pre-radio days. Even the young were willing to risk an hour. At one place I had supper at the parson's. Just before we were to go to the lecture hall, a young couple came in to be married. When they had been made man and wife, we went off to the hall—and the newly married pair came with us. Nothing was to interfere with the earnest pursuit of culture.
>
> But if there was a dance on the night of the lecture, the young at any rate did not hesitate. They knew where their pleasure lay. But there might be only one hall. At Nanton, South of Calgary, I arrived at the lecture-hall one night and found only the Chairman. He and I talked and looked at empty seats till well after the time

set for the lecture. Then he explained that there was to be a dance in the hall at half-past nine. It looked as though people were saving themselves for that and had decided to let culture go hang. I told him what an admirable idea this was. But his dancing days were long over and he was strong for culture. We were to have a lecture. The eager dancers trooped in only to find the barrier of a lecture between them and their fun. I have faced more enthusiastic audiences, and kept them from their waltzing as short a time as possible.

In this connection Prof. E. K. Broadus used to tell of visiting a small town not far from Edmonton to find the place plastered with notices which read: "Come and hear Dr. Broadus lecture on Shakespeare and enjoy yourselves afterwards at the dance."

Even the President, in the midst of all the pressures of his administrative duties, carried more than his share of extramural work. An item in the *Edmonton Bulletin* on February 13, 1912, states:

President Tory arrived in the city this morning after a ten day trip to the southern part of the Province. During his absence he addressed large audiences in Medicine Hat, Lethbridge, Cardston, Magrath, Calgary, Okotoks, Claresholm, Macleod and High River.

Dr. Tory had been at Cambridge at the time when British Universities were beginning to expand their services beyond the walls of the institutions. As early as 1883, in co-operation with organized labour, the old country universities had been giving lectures in the industrial centres of England. These were mostly on scientific subjects related to the rapidly developing industrial movement and its accompanying problems. In 1903, the Workers Educational Association was organized, which provided a direct approach for British Universities to the educational demands of the labour unions.

When Dr. Tory was in England, in the summer of 1908, he dropped in on an annual meeting of the W.E.A. which was being held that year at Oxford University. On that occasion, toward the close of the sessions, a Portsmouth millwright by the name of McTavish made a speech which, in spite of a certain quality of ranting, nevertheless made a great impression upon Dr. Tory and the large number of Oxford professors who were present. In part this is what he said:

> I am not here as a suppliant for my class. I decline to sit at the rich man's table praying for crumbs. I claim for my class all the best that Oxford has to give, claim it as a right, wrongfully withheld, wrong not only to us, but to Oxford. What is the true function of a university? Is it to train the nation's best men, or sell its gifts to the rich? Instead of recruiting her students from the widest possible area, Oxford has restricted the area of selection to the fortunate few. They come to her not for intellectual training but veneering. Not only are working people deprived of the right of access to that which belongs to no class or caste, but Oxford herself misses her true mission, while the nation and the race lose the services of its best men. I emphasize that point because working people could do far more for Oxford than Oxford can do for working people—Democracy will realise itself with or without Oxford, but if Oxford continues to stand apart from the working people then she will ultimately be remembered, not for what she is, but for what she has been. We want Oxford to open wide her doors to the best of our people. We want her to inspire them not with the idea of getting on, but with the idea of service to humanity—we need Oxford, and Oxford needs us.

In the main, that statement represented Dr. Tory's own concept of a University's responsibility to its constituency, particularly a state institution supported by the taxes of the people.

Ever since he had come to Alberta the President had continued to remind the people of the province that the university was their own institution. In one of his speeches at this time, he said:

> I believe the problem of rural life is the greatest problem we are facing today. If we create a keenness for intellectual effort through the use of our country schools we will do more to solve our rural problems than can be done by any other means.

Dr. Tory required a Director of Extension Services who wouldn't have to spend several years in experimentation. He wanted one with an intimate knowledge of life in a rural community and an understanding of its problems. He had no faith in the idea that popular education could follow traditional classroom methods, or that it could be doled out like a mail-order medical prescription without any knowledge of the patient's symptoms. The Extension Department would serve the known needs of people, not the fancies of a few.

In May, 1912, Dr. Tory called into his office a young giant by the name of A. E. Ottewell who had just graduated with honours in Classics. Ottewell had been brought up on a pioneer farm at Clover Bar, about fifteen miles south-east of Edmonton, and was on his way into the Methodist ministry. He had been in his early twenties when he enrolled with the first group of students in the fall of 1908, and was then nearly thirty years of age. There is no record of that first discussion between Dr. Tory and Ottewell, but the result was that Ottewell was offered the job of Director of Extension Services. Dr. Tory had an uncanny knack of choosing the right man for the job in hand, and the next few years proved that he had chosen wisely again.

With a battered old Ford car, some boxes of books, a slide projector—or magic lantern as they were then called—and the first portable moving picture machine in the Province, Ottewell began his work. He knew from his own experience that agricultural information of all sorts was available from the provincial Department of Agriculture. What the people in rural areas needed most was release from the loneliness and the hard grind of every-day work on the farm and in the home.

From the beginning Ottewell used a familiar but very effective technique. He used to get the people singing such old favourites as "Old Macdonald Had a Farm," "Alouette," "I'm a Little Prairie Flower." Or he might lead them in a square dance if there was a fiddler in the district. Then he would give them half an hour of comic films or a lantern-slide travelogue, after which the small children were stowed away at the back of the hall and Ottewell got down to serious business. He would tell the people about the University; what it had to offer them and their children. He would try to find out what they felt the University could do for their community. Together the group would talk far into the night on any one of a score of subjects—the Co-operative Movement, better schools, soil surveys, how to winter fall pigs. This method of approach made an immediate appeal, and within a year Ottewell was in demand all over the Province. Roads were bad and in many districts nothing more than prairie trails, but he drove his car day and night, summer and winter over the country, until almost every rural school-district in the Province was familiar with the boisterous, good natured giant of a man who gave the people such happy evenings. Ottewell was always on the look-out for promising young people, and soon there began to appear in the University classrooms students whose ambitions had been stirred and who had been started on their way to the University as a result of an evening spent with Ottewell.

When the writer joined the Department, in the fall of 1920, in spite of interruptions caused by the war, there were (1) some 200 travelling libraries in circulation, with over 12,000 books a year distributed by mail; (2) a package library of discussion and debating material serving nearly one hundred communities each month; (3) 900 boxes of slides (with type-written lectures included) on a great variety of subjects, available for schools, churches and young peoples societies; (4) a film library, which listed over one hundred 28 mm. films and was in weekly use in every part of the Province. Most of the film subjects were historical and literary, purchased in Great Britain and designed for use in secondary schools.

When Ottewell started on an extension trip he carried a formidable array of equipment, but of greatest interest to most of the people was the 28 mm. moving picture machine, powered by a 12-volt battery, and operated by a hand crank. It is interesting to look back from this distance and recall some of the films we carried: "The Lady of the Lake," "The Vicar of Wakefield," "The House of David," "Les Miserables." Some of them ran for two hours and were undoubtedly pretty crude stuff. We also always carried a half-hour of comics—Charlie Chaplin, Bobby Bumps, etc., for the children.

On one occasion I had been invited to come to a small town in the centre of the cattle-ranching country, south-west of Macleod. It was during the fall round-up of cattle, and the Women's Institute of the district was putting on an entertainment and dinner for the cowboys in their new community hall.

They had asked me especially to bring some Chaplin films, but they were all anxious to see "The House of David" film. I thought at the time this was a strange choice but I took it along. On the night of the show the hall was crowded with "cow hands." I ran off two Chaplin shorts and proceeded to put on the two-hour-long "House of David" film. As the scene opened on the quiet hills of Palestine, and shepherds with their flocks were seen against the sky-line, there were muttered imprecations in the audience and before long the cattle-men began to drift out of the hall. At the end of the show there were only the faithful members of the Women's Institute present and they were not very happy.

There was a famous baseball team called "The House of David" (after the religious sect to which they belonged) which toured the Province every summer giving amazing exhibitions of regular and trick baseball. The committee had made a mistake. They thought they had chosen a baseball film and instead they got a very dull historical sketch of the life and works of King David.

When Dr. Tory interviewed me prior to offering me the job of assistant to Ottewell, he emphasized, as he always did, that the people of the Province paid for the University; and that the Department of Extension existed for the purpose of relating the thinking and the research going on in the University to the needs and demands of the people of the Province. Then he went on to say a very significant thing: "The time may come," he said, "when the existence of a university will depend upon the public's assurance that its thinking and research are vital to the community." When the depression came, in 1929, the truth of that statement was realized to the full in more than one University in Canada.

From 1920 on, until Ottewell left the department to become registrar of the University in 1928, we continued to experiment with every new educational device we could find. In 1925 we persuaded Dr. Tory to allow us to proceed with the building of a radio station. The Farmers' Government was then in power, and was quick to realize the value of such a medium in serving the needs of remote parts of the Province beyond the reach of the University resources of entertainment and practical help.

A grant of $5,000 was provided and that amount, with the help of the Department of Electrical Engineering, was sufficient to erect a 100-watt transmitter which was later boosted to 500 watts.

The story of the Department of Extension is too long to include in all its detail here. It is enough to say that there has been a constant expansion in its programme of lectures, short courses, library services, moving pictures, classes in arts, drama, music and crafts. The Banff School of Fine Arts, founded in 1933 as a training centre for Drama, Music and Art, has won for itself an international reputation, not only as a school for training in the fine arts, but as a leadership training centre for almost every aspect of informal education.

In his last address to the University, in 1928, the retiring President was able to report:

> It is something to be able to say that the University influence through the Extension Department has been reaching fifty per cent of the homes of the Province of Alberta, and now that we have our own broadcasting station with our weekly lectures on practical subjects, it is possible that in the very near future a very large number of homes will be influenced for betterment through the activities of the University.

The outbreak of war, in 1914, had given a sharp set-back to the rapid growth of the University. The building plans had been completed, residential accommodation had been provided sufficient to accommodate new resident students *pro tem* with suitable classroom facilities, and the Arts Building was under construction. In the six years since the University opened, the student body had grown to 440 and the teaching staff to thirty-four. A plan for financing the necessary buildings had been adopted by the Provincial Government which authorized the issue of bonds against the University property, the Government guaranteeing both interest and principal. This had been done in agreement with the University's bankers, who had undertaken to advance money for capital expenditure until the first teaching building was completed.

The first effect of the war was to stop credit at the bank,

and all building operations had to be discontinued. With a half completed contract on his hands Dr. Tory approached the Government. He was instructed to see the bankers in Toronto, and arrange if possible for enough money to put a roof on the Arts Building. He proceeded at once to Toronto and to his astonishment found the head of the bank in a complete funk over the situation. Twenty-four hours passed before Dr. Tory was even permitted to see him. One whole day was spent in replying to notes of inquiry relayed to him by a bank official while Dr. Tory sat in an outer office. Finally he sent in a scorching note to the president of the bank, and left on the afternoon train for Montreal. There he took up the matter of financing with the head of another bank. The treatment he received was friendly and courteous, but the refusal to help was nonetheless definite and complete. While in Montreal Dr. Tory received a wire from the bank in Toronto offering a small advance but not nearly enough to save the situation. The University stood to lose heavily if the building could not be roofed before the winter storms began. The contract for the building had been given to the George Fuller Company of New York. Dr. Tory therefore decided to go to New York and place the whole matter before the Company. The General Manager of the Company received him at once, and when the situation was explained, said: "We will find a way to finance the contract. I have faith in Canada and will complete the building if the government will guarantee payment when the situation improves." Dr. Tory anxiously inquired about the rate of interest. "Six per cent," said the Manager. "We never charge more than that." At that time Canadian banks were lending money at eight and ten per cent rates. Under these conditions the Arts Building was completed and opened in September, 1915. In writing of this incident, Dr. Tory says:

> I mention this because I think it is worth recording the difference in outlook of an outside company and our own Canadian bankers. I have had to do with a good many contracting companies, but I never had such satisfaction as I had with the George Fuller Company. The extras on a building costing one half million dollars was only one thousand dollars, and not a single dispute took place between us that was not immediately adjusted.

By 1916 some 400 students and half of the professors had gone on active service. Others had been drafted for special work by the federal government. Dr. Tory himself was called away, in 1917, to organize the educational work already going on in sporadic fashion in the Canadian army. But it should not be assumed that these were sterile years in the University. The classes were kept going and in addition further construction progress was made. As already stated, in 1915 Agriculture had been set up as a full faculty. In 1917 the classes already established in Pharmacy became a School of Pharmacy. In 1918 Dentistry and Household Economics, and courses in Soils, Mining, and Economics were added.

From the beginning of its history the Science staff of the University had been in constant demand for advice on a number of practical problems. In 1911 an Industrial Laboratory had been established to provide practical help, but scientific developments resulting from the war had shown the need for greater emphasis in practical applied science, on the part of Canadian universities. A University Scientific Association was established, in 1919, and immediately set to work drafting a set of problems for research. Before a beginning could be made, however, additional funds were required and the Government was asked for assistance. The Government agreed to help and the first steps were taken.

The Scientific Association was then merged in a larger provincial organization called The Scientific and Industrial Research Council of Alberta. The University Farm became an experimental station related to the Department of Agriculture. Two research professorships were made available to the University at the same time. Space for the headquarters of the Council was provided in the University, and the staff of the Research Council constituted the Industrial Research Department of the University.

It was this development, fostered almost entirely by Dr. Tory, that paved the way for his work with The National Research Council in later years.

The steady growth of the University speeded up rapidly in the years immediately following the war. In 1921 Agricultural Engineering was added, and the training of public health nurses began the same year. A laboratory for plant pathology followed, and, about the same time (1927-1928), a long-cherished hope of Dr. Tory's was realized when the School of Education became a part of the University.

Meanwhile Dr. Tory had been struggling with problems involved in the establishment of a Faculty of Medicine. The University had been giving some work in Medicine for several years. Early in 1912 a working arrangement had been established with one of the city hospitals, and the provincial public health laboratories had been transferred from the Department of Health to the University. But there was no Faculty of Medicine until after the War, and then it came only after great pressure on the part of Dr. Tory and some of his supporters among the members of the medical profession.

In 1910, when the revised Education Act was passed, there had been some bitter controversy between Dr. Tory and certain leaders of the medical profession in the Province over the question of control, and such matters as the selection of medical students, the prescription of the work to be given and the way in which the courses were to be taught. There were a large number of doctors in the Province who felt that Dr. Tory was meddling with matters which were professional and not the concern of the University, even though the University Act had clearly empowered the University to exercise authority and control over standards. The President had very strong views regarding the place of a university in such matters. In one of his many public addresses on the subject he had made his position very clear:

> The function of the university in medical education became apparent the moment it was recognised that the chemist, the physicist, and the biologist must enter the field of medical instruction along with the anatomist and physiologist, as men of science and not merely as medical men. Then the university becomes a necessity, and not only a necessity but a first necessity for only there are these great sciences taught in their fundamental relations. The university must insist on the fundamental sciences being taught as university subjects with sufficient intensity to make the student realize that they are not incidental to, but fundamental to a proper

medical course; taught by full-time men who are masters of the subject they teach. My memory goes back to the days when physics and chemistry were regarded by medical students as a joke. The courses of study required in these fundamental subjects must be long and continuous courses to afford a firm basis for scientific knowledge. The standards of examinations must be university standards not special ones designed to help out members of a special faculty. If we are absolutely strict in this matter of intellectual standards I am sure half our task with respect to the equality of the men we train would disappear.

The University must also function in Medicine as the home of research; the university hospital becomes of necessity part of the Medical School. The first step must be the passing of the power of conducting examinations for the practice of medicine over to boards appointed by the University, thus freeing the medical profession from the charge of personal motive.

This was bitter medicine for the doctors of the Province, and some of them opposed every step taken by Dr. Tory in the direction of his fixed purpose. The terrible toll of the 1918 influenza epidemic indirectly helped to emphasize the need for a medical faculty at the University, and there was a considerable public demand on the part of the newspapers and the tax payers generally that the university should proceed at once to establish a medical faculty.

Dr. Tory had made a careful study of medical institutions in the United States and Europe, and was familiar with the enormous amount of money involved in the establishment and operation of an adequately equipped medical school. He was determined that no second rate institution should find a place on the campus. If he was to proceed with his plans there would have to be sufficient money forthcoming to make certain that the work done would be equal in quality to that of the other great medical faculties in Canada.

He went to New York and discussed his problem with the Rockefeller Foundation. He was assured that, if the equipment and teaching were up to the standards set by the Board of Directors, serious consideration would be given to his request for a grant. With this somewhat uncertain safeguard the Senate agreed that Dr. Tory might proceed with the selection of a teaching staff and the establishment of a Medical Faculty.

In 1921 the Liberal Government of the Hon. Charles Stewart was turned out of office and a farmers' government elected. One of the first demands of the new government was for an immediate investigation of the University's general expenditures, and the curtailment of the annual appropriation. On the very day the new Premier called on Dr. Tory to discuss the question of budget economies a cheque for $500,000 arrived from the Rockefeller Foundation. The government, impressed with this tangible evidence of confidence in the standing of the Medical Faculty and the work being done, withdrew its demands for further economies and the foundations were laid for a medical school which now ranks with the best in Canada.

For more than five years—from 1922 to 1927—Dr. Tory had been spending a great deal of his time with The National Research Council of Canada, of which he was a council member. His life-long interest in scientific research had been intensified by his observations of its practical values during the war, and more recently by the successes of the Alberta Research Council.

He had been elected President of the National Council in October, 1923, and had given vigorous direction to its activities ever since. In 1927 he was asked to give full time to the Council as its first President.

It was a difficult decision to make. In the twenty years of his Presidency, Dr. Tory had gathered around him a staff of highly qualified and exceptionally able men in every faculty. With his extraordinary gift for choosing the men best qualified to assist him in the realization of his dream of what a university should be, he had selected not only a company of able teachers but one which brought to the campus a remarkable *esprit de corps*. There was a warmth of friendship and inter-faculty co-operation on the campus which was unique. This sense of community was not confined to classrooms and administrative offices. It extended to the homes of faculty members and was a living thing among the students. The people responsible for this happy relationship between staff and students, between faculty members and the university community, were of course the professors themselves. They were for the most part a warm-hearted, gay and kindly group, committed whole-heartedly to the University and its future. Men like "Doc Alex" (Prof. W. H. Alexander), John MacEachran, Dean A. C. Rankin, John Allan, E. K. Broadus, Prof. E. Sonet, John Macdonald, Dean R. W. Boyle, Dean E. A. Howes, Dean W. A. R. Kerr, Dean R. S. L. Wilson, D. E. Cameron (librarian), R. K. Gordon, E. W. Sheldon, Douglas Killam, to mention only a few of the older men, brought to the University a wealth of experience, a knowledge of their subjects, and withal a gift for friendship which endeared them to students and staff alike. Back of all this were the Torys. Dr. Tory had chosen these men, and through the years had given them his friendship and confidence. His personal relationship with the staff was intimate, and with rare exceptions friendly and solicitous. But the person most responsible for the remarkable sense of family which prevailed on the campus was Mrs. Tory. The Torys had no children of their own, and Mrs. Tory lavished her motherly instincts upon students and faculty members alike. Her home was a happy meeting place for the wives and children of members of the staff. She was always first to call upon new arrivals to welcome them to the campus and make them feel at home in their new surroundings. She was respected and loved by everyone who knew her.

To leave all this, their home and their friends, to live in Ottawa and start again to make a new life for themselves when they were both in their sixties, was to tear up the very roots of a happy contented existence. But Mrs. Tory knew the man she had lived with for thirty-five years. This new challenge was as sharply defined in Dr. Tory's mind as any one of the Macedonian calls which had so often altered the direction of his life. The war had left upon him a lasting impression of the great value of scientific pursuits in the life of a nation, and ever since his return from overseas he had been tireless in his advocacy that governments, industrial firms, universities and voluntary societies of every kind should realize the enormous importance of scientific discovery; of the practical application of scientific devices and scientific techniques; and of the general guidance of society by scientific methods. It was not in Dr. Tory's nature to turn away from a position which would place him at the head of an institution dedicated to the purposes he had dreamed of and worked for all his life.

In his booklet Prof. W. H. Alexander writes:

> In April, 1928, President H. M. Tory reached a decision which had for some time seemed inevitable, that he must devote himself either to the problems of the growing University exclusively or relinquishing that obligation, give all his time and energy to the management and direction of the National Research Council. The call to the latter task, with its intimate relation to great industrial and commercial problems confronting the Canadian people, seemed of the two the more imperative and accordingly, as from June 1st, Dr. Tory laid down the reins of office which he had taken up a little over twenty years before. The event was felt to mark quite distinctly the end of an era for the University. It was the era of organization, construction and expansion over which Dr. Tory had so ably presided, an era for which his tireless energy and his indomitable optimism peculiarly fitted him. He came to Alberta to find a riverlot covered with scrub, on which he was expected to work out the plans of a permanent home for the University, and that is about all he found. He went boldly forth and literally discovered his first class of students. He wrestled with principalities and powers to get his scheme accepted, and was forced to call into play all his diplomatic talents more than once to avoid shipwreck. He replaced, before his term ended, the decaying log-barn on riverlot number 5 by teaching buildings, laboratories and residences valued at three million dollars, and began the great task of beating the campus into shape by ploughing, levelling and planting. He started his work with four professors and forty students, and ended it with a staff of one hundred and twenty-five and a student body of fifteen hundred. He began with the University of Alberta as a mere name and nothing more, and was able in his twenty years of administration to bring the institution to the point where a mere name had become a title of dignity and respect, which any alumnus may be proud to indicate as the origin of his degree.

For the men and women who graduated from the University of Alberta between 1912 and 1928 it would be difficult to think of the University without including in that thought the names of Dr. and Mrs. Tory. The latter will feel herself sufficiently praised in the praise accorded her husband, but it would be less than fair if this third episode were concluded without a mention of the kindly manner in which she sustained the arduous social duties that fell to her position. And so the third episode concludes in a shower of golden memories which the first President shares with the now extensive alumni body of the University of Alberta and the members of the staff, especially those associated with them in those early years, so trying oft times and yet so full of inspiration for the heart and laughter for the lips.

In 1928 at the age of sixty-five, Dr. Tory left the University of Alberta to undertake the most important, and in many respects, the most strenuous and difficult task he had yet attempted. But before that story is told it is necessary to return to 1917 and the Khaki University.

Chapter XIII

THE KHAKI UNIVERSITY

In an article which appeared in the *Montreal Standard,* in 1919, the following statement was made:

> The Khaki University was one of the most interesting developments of the war and one of which Canadians have special cause to be proud. Most things connected with the great conflict were destructive in character, but this was a great constructive effort, being at the same time a conception so striking in character that, when once seen in action in the Canadian forces, it was adopted in rapid succession by the Australians, New Zealanders, South Africans, then by the Imperial army and finally by the United States.
>
> In the standing army of Great Britain this educational work has now been made part of the regular training of every "British Regular."

Beginning in a small way, with a few study groups here and there at Canadian army camps in Witley, Seaford and Bramshott, the idea of providing educational services for the troops had caught on rapidly. Early in 1917 there were several thousands of men enrolled in voluntary night classes led mainly as discussion groups by chaplains and YMCA officers. The late Lt. Colonel Gerald W. Birks was then Supervisor of YMCA Canadian Overseas forces, with some two hundred commissioned and non-commissioned officers stationed at army bases throughout England and France. Under his direction a lecture programme had been set up, and some of the ablest lecturers from English and Canadian universities were already on tour throughout Canadian Army camps. Gradually the demand for regular courses of lectures and for text-books became so insistent that colleges were established on an experimental basis at Witley and Seaford Camps. By the summer of 1917 lecture courses and study groups were also being organized in France. At a YMCA staff conference at Col. Birks' headquarters in London, in the spring of 1917, it was felt that the time had come to give form and comeliness to this sporadic movement. It was decided that someone from Canada should be invited to come over, survey the situation and draw up a plan of action.

Col. Birks had known Dr. Tory for many years, not only when he was at McGill but later as an associate in the work of the National Council of the YMCA. In 1916 Dr. Tory had completed a report for the YMCA concerning the needs of men returning to Canada from the War, and what was being done to meet those needs.

Col. Birks was convinced that Dr. Tory was the man best equipped by experience and training to undertake the task he had in mind. He therefore returned to Canada in the early summer of 1917 and placed his problem before the National Council of the YMCA. It was agreed to proceed with plans for a properly organized and financed army educational system and Dr. Tory was invited to proceed to England to examine the work already being done and to prepare a plan for its further development. Dr. Tory accepted and arrived in England in July, 1917. He at once made a tour of all the camps in England and in France, inspecting the classes already in operation under the joint sponsorship of the YMCA and the Chaplain Services. He discovered to his amazement that these classes and lecture courses had an aggregate attendance of about 300,000, and were steadily growing in popularity. After a six-weeks survey he turned in a report to Col. Birks outlining: (i) a plan to meet immediate needs; (ii) a plan for the period of demobilization.

> There is a strong desire among the men (he said) to follow once again the old avenues of thought and particularly to think again in connection with the problems of civil life. The excitement associated with the beginnings of army life has passed away and the social and civil instincts are again asserting themselves . . . There is at present among a considerable proportion of the men, not only a willingness to take advantage of any opportunities for intellectual improvement that may be offered, but an anxiety to do so.

Dr. Tory had been particularly impressed with the results of a personal enquiry he had made in a class of two hundred men at Witley Camp. Fifty-seven men expressed a desire to take up the study of agriculture, thirty wanted a business education, fifteen wanted practical training in mechanics, forty wished to enter the university, eighteen wished to train as YMCA secretaries, one to teach, and the balance wanted to study without any particular objective.

He was convinced that an organized educational effort among both officers and men would, if wisely conducted, be greatly appreciated and would meet a genuine need.

The section of his report dealing with immediate needs called for the organization of a scheme of popular lectures, the promotion of small study groups within the units, and of reading groups in tents and billets. The topics he suggested for discussion were designed to give the men a better understanding of the war and the nations involved; the campaigns in the Balkans, Mesopotamia, Egypt, Italy, Russia, and at sea. Lectures were to be given on: (i) the British Empire and the Dominions; (ii) a thorough course of instruction on life in Canada after the war, for example, plans for land settlement and Canadian farming operations, with lantern slides illustrating types of farms from Nova Scotia to British Columbia such as; wheat farming and cattle raising; (iii) lectures on scientific subjects dealing with electricity and magnetism, the chemistry of explosives, the aeroplane, wireless telegraphy, the solar system and astronomy.

I. The immediate requirements of the programme called for the establishment of adequate libraries in all the Camps.

Up to the present, he reported, the library facilities offered in the huts have consisted of old books donated by friends and organizations. Too often these books have been of little value, being old and unattractive. I would strongly recommend that this practice be discontinued and that a library scheme be carried out along two definite lines.

(1) A definite reading library in the study rooms of the recreation huts with books covering all the topics prescribed for lectures; additional works on current history, books relating to the political problems created by the war; an encyclopedia of the type of

Nelsons or Everymans; a limited number of current magazines and of course a reasonable selection of novels, poetry, etc.

(2) Officers' libraries. The man most neglected today is the officer, due to the peculiar condition under which he carries out his work. I would strongly urge that small officers' libraries be provided wherever possible.

II. The second part of Dr. Tory's report dealt with the demobilization period. He pointed out in the beginning that this would be the most critical period of the whole war, and that consequently plans should be made at once. According to the best judgment available the time required for the complete demobilization of the armed forces would be a year or more. During that time discipline would be relaxed and the men would be anxious to get home. He therefore recommended that plans be put on foot to establish an educational institution in one Central Camp, to be called "The Khaki University of Canada," where all branches of study that could possibly be arranged would be offered, and with an extension department providing services for every other camp in Great Britain. The University would consist of the following faculties:

(1) An agricultural College, offering a full year's work in; animal husbandry; field husbandry; dairying; farm mechanics; operation of tractors and motors; elementary chemistry and physics.

(2) Matriculation courses for the younger men who wished to enter Canadian universities.

(3) A business college teaching arithmetic, business correspondence, stenography, telegraphy.

(4) Work of college grade for undergraduates of universities, in History, Literature, Languages, Economics, Political Science. In this respect an attempt would be made to have the universities of Canada agree to the acceptance of such work.

(5) Engineering: courses in mechanics, drawing, higher mathematics, descriptive geometry.

(6) Normal School Training: In this connection Dr. Tory pointed out that in one Province in Canada there were vacancies for 800 teachers, and there would be a great many men in the army who would like to enter the teaching profession. Here again recognition would have to be obtained from Departments of Education.

(7) Medical Instruction: There had been during the war a vast accumulation of medical experience by a limited number of medical men, but a great many doctors in military units had probably lost ground as general practitioners. For these men provision should be

made for medical instruction to bring them up to date. Some of the ablest practitioners in Great Britain and from the Army he was sure would co-operate in such a plan.

(8) Legal Studies: classes for lawyers and law students on recent advances in Law, International Law.

It was characteristic of Dr. Tory that the plans he outlined were far ahead of the thinking of the men actually engaged in the work, or the people at home in Canada who would have to provide the money for the project. His reach always did exceed his grasp, and Dr. Tory presented his report with some trepidation before the National Council of the YMCA.

The first question was how much would all this cost? There was the matter of equipment, operating expenses, the provision of an adequate library. How many students would be likely to enrol? How much of the teaching staff could be recruited from the Army, and how much would have to be taken from Canadian universities. There was also the cost of scientific apparatus and laboratories, agricultural machinery and general administration. This was an enormous undertaking. These were some of the questions asked by the business men on the council who would be responsible for raising the money.

Dr. Tory replied that the whole plan was based on the idea that military authorities would provide one big central camp for the university, and prospective students would be sent from their units to that centre and returned to their regiments when the time came for demobilization. So far as equipment was concerned, much, if not all of it, could be obtained from the army. Dr. Tory also believed that the big agricultural implement companies would contribute modern machinery for demonstration purposes.

Army huts and YMCA huts now in use could be moved and set up as classrooms, living quarters and laboratories. The cost of the whole enterprise was difficult to estimate until it was discovered how much of the teaching power could be obtained from the Army itself, but it would probably not be safe to estimate the cost at less than one million dollars. If the plan was acceptable it was suggested that an Educational Advisory Board composed of representatives of the YMCA, Chaplain services, the Army, and a group of distinguished Canadian laymen should be established and if necessary incorporated.

One man should be appointed as Executive Head, to whom would be given the responsibility of perfecting the plan both with respect to the courses of study and the choice of staff. To Dr. Tory's surprise his report was received by the YMCA with enthusiasm. Plans were set in motion to raise the necessary funds, and Dr. Tory was asked to become Executive Head of the undertaking. He at once returned to Canada to secure leave of absence from the University of Alberta, and to get support for the project from Canadian universities and Provincial departments of education.

While Dr. Tory was in Canada making these arrangements, the educational work in Great Britain was moving forward under the direction of the late Capt. Clarence Mackinnon of the Chaplain Services (Principal of Pine Hill Theological College, Halifax) and Col. G. W. Birks. The work in France was directed by Major Ernie Best of the YMCA and Lt.-Colonel E. H. Oliver of the University of Saskatchewan, also a Chaplain.

Meanwhile General Sir R. E. W. Turner had appointed a military Education Committee as a first step in the direction of formalizing and co-ordinating the undertaking. The relationship of the YMCA to the proposed Khaki College was revised, with the result that the former agreed to relinquish control of the project, but would continue to co-operate: (a) by loaning its secretaries and officers; (b) by placing its purchasing and supply department at the disposal of the Military Education Committee for securing and handling of equipment and supplies; (c) by keeping the books and handling the funds; (d) and most important of all, by agreeing to raise the necessary money to carry on the work.

While this was being done, Dr. Tory had obtained his leave of absence; had met with the Canadian University authorities, and the provincial Departments of Education, obtained the approval of his plans from the Prime Minister, Sir Robert Borden, and was on his way back to England in January, 1918.

An advisory Board, under the chairmanship of Sir Robert

Falconer representing Canadian Universities had been appointed to provide additional teaching staff where necessary and to accept the certificates of men returning from overseas.

When Dr. Tory arrived in England to commence his new duties he found that, as a result of his earlier visit and the report he had turned in, the work of organization had been pursued with great energy and enthusiasm by the YMCA officers, members of the Chaplain Services and a large number of officers and men of the Army with educational experience, who were teaching and helping with administrative and organizational work both in England and France. Military authorities at Argyle House, headquarters of the Canadian Army, were supporting the programme in every way possible.

One of the first tasks undertaken was a census of the camps to find out what kind of courses of instruction were most desired by the men themselves. One of the results of the census was the discovery, that there were a surprisingly large number of soldiers in the Canadian forces who were illiterate. This condition was later found to exist in all the other allied armies. Arrangements were immediately made to meet this situation, and during the next year over 3000 men were taught to read and write.

Dr. Tory was particularly anxious to get university students back into their work, and to this end began to plan for a single centre for all students of university grade where courses in the first and second years in Arts, the preliminary sciences in Medicine, the first years in Engineering, Theology, and Law could be given.

The census revealed the fact, that there was almost enough teaching power in the Army to undertake the work outlined except in Theology and Law. Dr. Tory had planned to bring to England a number of men from Canada to assist in the work. He now wrote to Dr. Walter Murray, President of the University of Saskatchewan, and Dr. Frank Adams of McGill, asking them to come to England. Dr. Frank Adams came but Dr. Murray because of conditions at home found it impossible to do so. One or two men from Oxford, including Sir William Osler, joined Dr. Tory at this time, and together they planned the more advanced courses and obtained the necessary library books.

Provision was made for the use of army huts for classrooms, and at base depots officers and men of high educational qualification were seconded on formal request to assist in the work. Progress had been made in France under Lt.-Colonel the Reverend E. H. Oliver and Major Ernie Best of the YMCA through the co-ordination of all educational work under the spectacular title The University of Vimy Ridge, and this famous institution continued its work in the battle area until the German break-through in April, 1918. At that time the Director reported that "the University of Vimy Ridge still exists, but our books are packed and stored. As soon as this little business of fighting is over we will carry on again."

In the summer of 1918 reorganization of all the work in both England and France took place. The educational work of Khaki University became the "Educational Services of the Canadian Overseas Forces," under the General staff of the Canadian Army.

This was accomplished by a Government order-in-council of September 19, 1918. The government made no direct grant to the "Educational Services," but authorized the transference to the services from other Army units of two hundred and forty officers and other ranks for the purpose of organization and teaching. The establishment for France was to be ninety officers and one hundred other ranks. The administrative staff at this time consisted of Col. H. M. Tory, Director of Educational Services; Lieut. Col. Frank D. Adams, Vice-Principal of McGill University, Deputy Director; with Major Clarence Mackinnon and Major L. W. Gill as Assistant Directors for England, and Lieut. Col. E. H. Oliver as Assistant Director for France.

Six weeks after the above reorganization was completed the Armistice was signed.

The financing of the scheme from the beginning was undertaken by the YMCA. When the financial campaign was organized, in the spring of 1918, the National Council of the YMCA added $500,000 to its budget to be spent on the educational effort and the people of Canada gladly subscribed the full amount. In raising the money the Chaplain Services, under the leadership of Dr. Clarence Mackinnon who was home in Canada, gave great assistance.

Meanwhile Dr. Tory had not been successful in obtaining formal official approval of his plans. In a letter written to Colonel Gerald W. Birks, who was in Canada in connection with the money raising campaign, he complained bitterly of official inertia. Colonel Birks showed the letter to Sir William Peterson who was about to leave for England. It so happened that Sir William travelled on the same boat as Sir Robert Borden, who was on his way to attend a war cabinet meeting in London. The letter was shown to Sir Robert who immediately took action on arriving in London. The morning after his arrival Dr. Tory was called to a meeting of Sir Robert, Sir Richard Turner and other officials of Argyle House. The outcome of this meeting was that with the consent of the YMCA, through whose agency the scheme had originated, the Khaki University was established as a part of the regular army.

During these discussions Dr. Tory had expressed the wish not to put on a uniform, as he was over the fighting age and did not wish to be classified officially as part of the fighting forces. He was informed, however, that if he was to work in the Army with officers and other ranks, he would have to take Army rank. A few days later he was gazetted as "Colonel, Director of Educational Services."

At this point in his Diary Dr. Tory pays a special tribute to Sir Robert Borden who, in the midst of the uncertainties of the summer of 1918, and the possibility that the war might continue through another year, was able and willing to give time and thought to the educational services.

The establishment which was given to the educational services consisted of a Director and governing body with the right to secure such teaching assistance from the Army as was considered necessary. The scheme when set up was similar to that of a modern university. A teaching organization was to be established with a headquarters and an officer appointed to direct that centre. A Director of Educational Services for England was appointed in the person of Major L. W. Gill, who was convalescing in England and unable to return to his unit. Major Gill was Professor of Engineering at Queen's and later head of the Hamilton Technical School. Lt.-Colonel E. H. Oliver of the Chaplain Services was appointed Director for the Army Areas in France. Major Clarence Mackinnon was appointed Director of the Forestry Corps in France. In addition Major James Weir (later Minister of Agriculture in the Bennett Government) who had been wounded and was unfit for further active service, was appointed head of the correspondence department. These men were seconded to the education establishment from the Army.

The correspondence department devoted itself to meeting the growing demand for books from persons who desired to keep up reading but could not get away from official duties. The division undertook to supply any text-book or reference work asked for by any competent officer. In addition libraries were provided in a great many camps in France and placed under the direction of YMCA officers or of an interested Chaplain. By September, 1918, nineteen centres of education had been organized in the camps and hospitals of England.

During all this time there were in London between three and four thousand men belonging to the pay corps who were permanent residents of the city.

At the head of the University of London was Sir Gregory Foster who became greatly interested in the Canadian Army educational effort. Through his good offices, accommodation for evening classes was obtained in University College, Gower Street. The result was that the full facilities of University College for evening class work were placed at the disposal of the Canadian establishment until the end of the war. Here matriculation classes as well as classes in business training were carried on.

It was during this time, also, that the publication known as *The Beaver* was launched. This was a weekly publication distributed to the whole Army free of charge, giving them the story of what was going on in Canada and especially the activities of the educational establishment. To round out the scheme it was necessary to obtain a headquarters for the administrative staff and teachers. A small office was obtained in Bedford Square, but by Armistice Day expansion had taken place so rapidly that three houses were fully occupied. The Prime Minister of Alberta, the Hon. Charles Stewart, who had been in England during the summer of 1918, closed the Alberta offices on Trafalgar Square and turned them over to Dr. Tory for use in the educational effort, and incidentally left him the responsibility of handling any unfinished business belonging to the Alberta government. After the Armistice was signed, Dr. Tory joined Colonel E. H. Oliver at Bonn where the Canadian Corps was settled. It was then believed that the Canadian Corps would remain for some time in Bonn, and that it would take a much longer time to get the troops home for demobilization than turned out to be the case.

Colonel Tory and Colonel Oliver had an interview with the President of the University at Bonn, and, with the permission of Sir Arthur Currie, the University was taken over for teaching purposes. Since the University authorities were fearful that the buildings might be used for barracks they gladly consented to have them used only for teaching purposes. Evening classes were immediately organized for the teaching of the German language and the professors of the University were employed for the purpose.

After the Armistice there was growing unrest among the soldiers, not only on the continent but throughout the whole Army. When Colonel Tory returned to London he discussed the problem with Sir George Foster who was then in London as a member of the War Cabinet. It was decided to prepare a document to place in the hands of the soldiers, outlining demobilization plans and the land settlement projects prepared by the demobilization board. This was done and the booklet was in the hands of the Army in France within two weeks. Also a carload of books was immediately shipped to Bonn for teaching purposes.

To follow up the work that was organized in Bonn, classes were established in practically all the regiments. This work continued with more or less regularity throughout the winter of 1918-1919, but the restlessness and discontent among the men

COLONEL H. M. TORY
[1918 - 1919]

Photo by National Film Board.

in the Army was steadily increasing. The Demobilization Board was convinced that the condition of shipping would make it impossible to get the soldiers home inside of eighteen months. This idea was strengthened by the fact that there was an enormous number of American troops in England and on the continent who were equally anxious to get home. When the American Army had first come over their officers had studied the Canadian educational plan, and following the Armistice a great organization was set up in the South of France. A farm was purchased and special instruction in agriculture was planned. Their experience, however, was the same as the Canadian, the war being over the men wanted to get home.

All this made Dr. Tory more determined than ever to find a central camp site where students who wished to devote time to study could be brought together. It was clear that if these men were allowed to scatter, a whole year would be lost and many would give up their intention of finishing their courses.

The plan was to get good ambitious students together, and keep them at Camp in England until a year's work had been accomplished, allowing others to go home. Dr. Tory wished to have another survey made. This time he wanted to discover how many men, who had been university students before the war, were willing and anxious to continue their studies—and to discover also the number of university teachers who were available in the Army. But the restlessness was so great that regimental commanders, particularly in France, were loath to allow those of the quality required to leave their units, as they were men of the highest morale and necessary in the trying days ahead. Dr. Tory's request for a survey was refused, and he began to despair of being able to proceed with his plan, but an incident occurred which changed the outlook—an incident, by the way which indicated that particular quality of mind which made General Sir Arthur Currie head of the Canadian Corps and later a great Principal of McGill University.

In the midst of Dr. Tory's perplexity, General Currie came to England and sent for Dr. Tory to come and see him. During their discussion Sir Arthur learned of the difficulty of the survey and immediately said: "I can see that this is a necessary step in the direction of your plan for a University establishment, and the order will go out tomorrow." Meanwhile a section of the military camp at Ripon in Yorkshire had been assigned as an educational centre. The men of university grade in England were removed to this centre, and teachers were brought together so that by the first of December, 1918, the Khaki University was ready to begin instruction.

The camp consisted of living quarters for over a thousand men and a number of hutments that could be turned into lecture rooms. It wasn't long before laboratories in Physics, Chemistry and Biology were set up sufficiently equipped to give elementary courses. A large central hut, under the control of the YMCA, was handed over as teaching headquarters and as a library centre. During the summer a curriculum had been drawn up and a library had been collected. Courses were included for those who wished to complete matriculation and for first and second year in Arts. There were a considerable number of men who had already completed one year in Arts, but a much larger number who had only their junior or senior matriculation.

After the survey was made, men began to pour into the Camp from France. Of course there were some who had simply used the opportunity to get out of France; and a great deal of sifting had to be done, but when the classes were finally organized there were between eight and nine hundred registered for the courses.

Dr. Tory was fortunate in that there were a number of professors from the University of Alberta in the Army, and he was permitted to call upon them as a nucleus of a teaching staff. Other men were brought from Canada and a number of representatives from other Canadian universities were found in the Army. Among those who made application for admission were many students who had already completed their second and third years of university work. In order to meet their demands the matter was taken up with the British universities, all of which gladly agreed to take a limited number of men for one year's work.

Edinburgh, for example, started on the first of January,

1919, a full year's course for Canadian students and accepted 110 for a year's work. The time requirements would be met by continuing courses through May and June. Oxford, Cambridge and University College, London, all took some Canadian students. Altogether between 400 and 500 men were placed in this way and thus saved a college year. These men were given certificates which they brought back to Canada and were accepted by Canadian universities. Some of them who had taken the equivalent of the fourth year were granted their degrees.

The interest taken in this work by English educators like Sir Robert Lodge in Edinburgh, Dr. Haleworth in Oxford, Sir Gregory Foster in London, Dr. Shipley of Cambridge, to mention only a few, was a source of great help to Dr. Tory and his staff.

A curious circumstance arose in that there were quite a large number of men who wished to study Theology. In order to meet this situation Dr. Tory communicated with the United Theological College, Montreal, and asked Dr. Irving P. Rexford, head of the Anglican College, if he would come to England and bring with him a representative of each of the other colleges in the Union. Dr. Rexford came bringing with him representatives of the Presbyterian, Methodist and Congregational Colleges.

It so happened that there had once been a Theological College in Ripon, associated with the Cathedral. The whole establishment was available at a very reasonable rent, and a course of studies was established based upon the work of the Union College in Montreal. A substantial library was assembled and about seventy students registered. In connection with this latter move some unpleasantness arose for which Dr. Tory publicly took most of the blame. He had, to use his own words, thoughtlessly failed to recognize the fact, that in the Chaplain Services there were already a number of Theological professors whose services could have been called upon to take over that section of the work entirely. For this oversight Dr. Tory was not soon forgiven by certain members of the Theological hierarchy in Canada and in the Army.

That the teaching in the Khaki University was up to Canadian University standards is evident from the following list of the heads of the various departments:

Department	Head	University
History	Prof. George Wrong	Toronto
Mathematics	Prof. Douglas Killam	Alberta
Classics	Prof. Herbert Rose	McGill and Oxford
Modern Languages	Prof. Edouard Sonet	Alberta
English	Prof. MacDonald	New Brunswick
Drawing	Prof. Cecil Burgess	Alberta
Physics	Prof. Rennier	Birmingham
Chemistry	Prof. Cowper	London

Most of these men had been in the Army in some capacity or other. There were also Dr. James Robertson, former head of Macdonald College, McGill, in charge of Agriculture, and A. E. Ottewell of Alberta in charge of Extension Services. In addition there were a large number of teachers who had been either full professors or juniors in Canadian universities before the war began. Altogether, including the work in the various departments of Khaki University and the camps, over 700 competent teachers were being used.

It became necessary to prepare a considerable number of text-books for junior work. These were printed in London. Altogether, during the 1918-1919 period approximately 250,000 of such text-books on agriculture, elementary physics and chemistry, etc., were used throughout the Army. During the winter of 1919 His Majesty, the King, visited the College, and as a result of his visit he made it possible for the agricultural students to visit the Royal farms and to be given instruction in the judging of livestock. Large classes were taken to agricultural centres in England and given an opportunity to study and compare English methods with Canadian.

During all this time Dr. Frank D. Adams of McGill, second in command to Dr. Tory, acted as liaison officer between the university and the general commanding the camp. Among those who visited the camp frequently and gave it enthusiastic support, was General Sir Richard Turner, V.C., Chief of Staff of the Canadian Army. His interest in Khaki University had been continuous since its inception, and when rioting broke out, in 1919, he placed the men taking courses at Ripon under arms for the purpose of bringing the riots under control—sufficient evidence that he considered them worthy of trust.

The financing of the whole undertaking, as we have noted, was a part of the budget of the Canadian YMCA in the amount of $500,000, but this would not have been nearly adequate were it not for the fact that the teaching staff cost the YMCA almost nothing. The teachers taken from the Army were allowed to continue their army pay. This did not involve any loss to the people of Canada since these men stayed in England for the purpose of teaching, but their places were taken on the ships by other soldiers going home. There was no delay in the total of men demobilized. Under the Khaki University arrangement certain men agreed to accept demobilization at a later date, and thus allowed others to take their place.

The commissioned officers received only their Army pay. The non-commissioned officers who were teachers were paid a small amount extra as compensation for the extra work which they had to undertake. None of the headquarters officers was paid other than the regular pay. Those who came from Canada received only their travelling expenses. Their salaries were continued by their universities. Neither Lieutenant-Colonel Frank Adams nor Colonel Tory received any compensation, not even the pay of their rank. The $500,000 given by the YMCA was spent on rentals, books, equipment, travelling expenses, printing, and so on. When the whole enterprise was finished $100,000 was left over. Part of this was returned to the YMCA for winding up their work, and part was devoted to the establishment of a system of scholarships in the universities of Canada for the purpose of making loans to soldier students.

For a long time Dr. Tory had been anxious to see the way opened for graduate study by Canadian students in British universities. The only definite connection existing at the time was through Rhodes scholarships. But a graduate of a Canadian university going to Oxford or Cambridge was compelled to take work leading to the same degree he already had. This was part of the old tradition that to carry a degree from a university meant attendance at that university for a full course of study. The question of granting graduate degrees to students from overseas had been previously raised at the Imperial Universities Conference of 1912, a conference Dr. Tory had attended.

Up to that time most graduate students from Canada went either to the United States or to Germany . If they went to the United States and did at all well, as most of them did, they received appointments in the U.S. and did not return to Canada. The small number who were able to study in Germany was not sufficient to meet the needs of Canada's teaching profession.

All the time he was in London, Dr. Tory kept this situation in mind and talked to a number of British professors about it. He was convinced that if the British universities could be persuaded to plan for graduate studies somewhat after the fashion of German and American universities, the flow of students from the North American continent previously going to Germany would change to the British Isles. The late Dr. Damie, at that time principal of Liverpool University, and Dr. Shipley, Master of Christ's College, Cambridge, felt as strongly in the matter as Dr. Tory did. A conference was called early in the fall of 1918 to discuss the question. There were several American professors at Cambridge at the time who stoutly supported Dr. Tory's ideas, and for this reason it was decided to hold the Conference at Cambridge. It became apparent that all of those who had travelled and studied in Canada and the United States were in favour of the plan, but, on the other hand, the representatives of British universities who cherished the old ways were opposed. During one of the sessions, when Dr. Tory had presented his case with his usual enthusiasm, a Cambridge Don spoke up and said: "Tory, you are asking us to gain the whole world and lose our own souls." The Conference was an intimate and friendly affair, and no one took offence when Dr. Tory replied with a broad smile: "Then I would suggest that you inquire whether the particular soul you are trying to save is worth saving."

Shortly after this a Conference was held in South Kensington which was attended by representatives of all the English and Scottish universities. At this meeting Dr. Tory was asked to present his scheme and outline its advantages. He pointed out; (a) that Canadians were anxious to continue the British educational standards and traditions; (b) that it was a waste of time for Canadian graduates to repeat courses in Britain they had already taken in Canada; (c) and that the same thing applied to the United States. He emphasized the value of building up good-will and understanding in this way throughout the Empire.

A warm discussion followed in which, to Dr. Tory's surprise, Sir Ernest Rutherford, afterward Lord Rutherford, his old friend and associate, took exactly the opposite point of view, and made a speech the essence of which was that one could not expect the English universities to change their whole *modus operandi* to suit the convenience of the universities of the Dominions. Others took the point of view that the British universities could not afford to ignore such a progressive suggestion. Nothing much came of this campaign at the time, and it is mentioned here merely to show the extent of Dr. Tory's interests, and the fact that, even while burdened with the responsibility of the army educational programme, he could never quite lose sight of the larger problems of the whole wide community of higher education.

In an undertaking as extensive and involved as the army educational scheme there was bound to be a good deal of criticism of the curriculum, the teaching staff, and the sponsoring organizations. There was friction between the Chaplain Services and the YMCA because the former felt that they had not received full credit for the part they had played in the initiation of the work at the beginning when it was a purely voluntary and largely unco-ordinated effort. Much of the work done in the camps was of a casual and haphazard nature. The draft system made it almost impossible to keep students and teachers together for more than a few weeks at a time. During the battle of Passchandaele the College at Seaford was literally wiped out over night when both students and teachers were drafted for reinforcements. Another source of unrest and criticism was the arbitrary way in which young professors and teachers were seconded for duty with the educational units. They had enlisted and been trained to fight a war, and many of them bitterly resented being transferred from active service to teaching jobs.

It was therefore inevitable that much of the work done prior to the Armistice, and the establishment of the Khaki University at Ripon was spotty and in many instances superficial. The quality of the courses differed a great deal in the different camps, depending upon the staff available and the support given to the undertaking by the commanding officers. The whole system was tightened up and became vastly more efficient after Dr. Tory's arrival in January, 1918, and the arrangements had been completed for the transfer of responsibility from the YMCA to that of a recognized army establishment.

The great value of the project, in its early development in 1917, was that it prepared the way for the more solid and lasting values which followed with the establishment of Khaki University. It stimulated large numbers of men to make a start, at least, in preparing themselves for a return to civil life. Reports show that from 1917 to 1919 upwards of 650,000 men attended lectures and 50,000 were enrolled in classes.

After the Armistice, when the Khaki University settled down to its regular work at Ripon, over 2,000 men registered in classes of university level in the various faculties. As men returned home Canadian universities were informed of the progress each had made and arrangements were made for them to continue their studies, some of them on scholarships provided from unexpended funds. There was scarcely two years between Dr. Tory's original survey in the summer of 1917 and the closing of the Khaki University in the early summer of 1919. And yet, this "University" can claim an important place among Canadian educational institutions. It had a large share in three important results: (i) the development of educational programmes among the armed services of many other countries; (ii) the maintenance of a healthy morale in the Canadian Army during the difficult period of demobilization; (iii) and the encouragement of a great many Canadians to continue their education which otherwise they might have abandoned. There can be no doubt that the enduring benefits of the scheme owe more to the vision, enthusiasm and administrative ability of Dr. Tory than to any other individual.

CHAPTER XIV

THE NATIONAL RESEARCH COUNCIL

OF ALL THE ENTERPRISES to which Dr. Tory devoted his time and his rare organizational ability, none has had such a far-reaching effect upon the economic and industrial development of Canada as that of the National Research Council.

The history of the Council dates back to 1916, when, on the request of the Government of Great Britain, the Canadian Government established both a committee of the Privy Council for Scientific and Industrial Research and an Honorary Advisory Council for S.I.R. Before World War I, facilities for scientific research in Canada were limited almost entirely to the universities. As early as 1882 Sir William Dawson of McGill had been urging upon government and university authorities in Canada the need for some unified plan of research and the interchange of findings among Canadian scientists.

In the *Proceedings and Transactions of the Royal Society of Canada* for that year he has this to say: "With the exception of the somewhat meagre grants to the Geological Survey and to the Meteorological services, the Government of Canada gives nothing to the aid of scientific research. What is done for local societies must, under our system, be done by the separate Provinces, and is necessarily unequal and imperfect. Few large endowments have been given anywhere for scientific purposes. We have no national society or association comparable with those in other countries, and yet we are looking forward to a great future."

The Canadian people were at that time a pioneer society and the rewards of painstaking research lay beyond their immediate interests or concern. Even at the beginning of the 20th century, when the work of Rutherford (later Lord Rutherford) at McGill was attracting the attention of scientists all over the world, neither laboratories nor trained men were available in any numbers in Canada.

The growth of scientific research under Dr. Tory in Alberta had begun as early as 1910, but had not gone very far before the war put a stop to plans for its development. Scientific teaching in Canadian universities was sound enough, but their budgets were almost entirely absorbed in undergraduate teaching. With few exceptions, staffs were appointed on a basis of teaching ability; graduate schools were slow in developing and, even where graduate schools existed, the time available from class-room duties for graduate instruction and research was limited. In addition, there was no adequate system of scholarships to assist bright students proceeding to post-graduate degrees.

Outside the universities very little research was done, although many of the larger Canadian companies had analytical laboratories for testing and process control. Difficulties in the way of a sound plan for the promotion of scientific investigation, provincially and nationally, included public indifference and in many instances strong opposition on the part of those who were suspicious of anything in the nature of change or who feared that some particular interest might be endangered.

Following a speech by Dr. Tory in Alberta in the early days of his efforts to establish the provincial council for research, the chairman of the meeting said, "We have listened with pleasure to the Doctor but I want to tell you people that God made the world and I suggest He knew what He was doing and the good Doctor can't change it and even if he could, what would we do with all the stuff we would grow if we followed his advice." Later, when speaking on the possible development of the Alberta tar sands and the problem of separating the bitumen from the sand, one of his listeners protested: "God has been mixing those tars and sand for thousands of years and probably knows more about it than the fellows at the University."

Nor was the attitude towards research radically different in England. On a visit to Europe in 1912, Dr. Tory had been greatly impressed with the status of research students and workers in Germany as compared with those in Great Britain. In his report to the Canadian National Research Council covering the years 1916 to 1926, he makes the statement that in 1914 "under the stress of the war the call went out throughout the British Empire for highly qualified research men and it was then discovered that there were more trained scientists in a few of the great German industries than could be found in the whole British Empire." It was this situation which led to the creation of the Department of Scientific and Industrial Research in Britain and to a request from the British Government to each of the Dominions to set up similar organizations. As a result the Canadian Government late in 1916, established the Honorary Advisory Council for Scientific and Industrial Research. Some years before the War, Sir Clifford Sifton, who was out of office at the time, had persuaded the Federal Government to appoint a "Conservation Commission" to make a study of Canada's natural resources and to make recommendations regarding their protection from undue exploitation. Sir Clifford was made Chairman of the Commission and over a period of several years was responsible for much of the effective work done in estimating the quantity and quality of Canada's natural wealth and in promoting public interest in conservation.

The new Council, which had the strong backing of the universities of Canada and the Canadian Manufacturers' Association, was brought into operation in 1917 under the chairmanship of Dr. A. B. Macallum, professor of biochemistry at the University of Toronto. He was assisted by a council of eleven scientists, most of them men from the universities, plus a few from industry, all serving on an honorary basis. The Council was charged with the promotion of researches which would develop industrial production and the utilization of the natural resources of Canada. Postwar trade was also a primary consideration, but few thought that the war would last long enough for the Council to be of much assistance.

One of the first jobs undertaken by the Council in 1917 was a survey of the work already being done in Canada. As was expected, the report of the survey revealed two things: First, that industrial research in Canada was practically non-existent, and secondly, that the number of research men available with the kind of post graduate training necessary to qualify them for independent investigation was entirely inadequate. To meet this deplorable situation two proposals were drawn up by the Council. One called for the immediate establishment of a national scholarship and assisted research plan which would bring Canadian universities into the enterprise on a co-operative basis; the other proposal called for the provision of national research laboratories which would complement the research activities of the universities. These proposals were forwarded to the Government in the fall of 1918 and were referred to a special committee of the House in the spring of 1919. There is every evidence that serious consideration was given to the recommendations of the Council. Witnesses were called from Canada and abroad and the matter was apparently studied with some thoroughness during the sessions of Parliament. The special committee had given unanimous approval to the Council's proposals and added a strong recommendation, "that a National Research Institute for Canada endowed with the functions and of the character indicated be established in the vicinity of Ottawa on a site fifty acres in area and conveniently located for water, gas and electric power. That there be appropriated to Parliament $500,000 for the purchase of the site and construction of the building, $100,000 for the scientific equipment of the Institute, and $50,000 for salaries and maintenance during the first year of its operations; that legislation be enacted at this session to provide for same."[1]

Unfortunately, just when it seemed that the Council's four years of planning were to be rewarded, the project was killed in the Senate. It is true that a grudging approval was given to the Council's proposal for scholarships, but the debate on the second part of the measure dealing with the establishment of the Institute showed that many of the Senators had no understanding of the economic possibilities of the plan. One Senator said: "Now, honorable gentlemen, there was just one value in the former research institution in Canada and that was the salary paid to the chief. That is all there was in it for anybody. It is absolute nonsense."[2]

The section of the bill dealing with the building and equipment of laboratories was therefore vetoed, mainly on the grounds of expense, and with the mistaken idea that the former

[1]Report of the Special Committee of the House of Commons to consider the matter of the development in Canada of Scientific Research. April 27, 1920.

[2]Debates of the Senate, 1921. P. 506.

Conservation Commission had not been of much value. The action of the Senate had a most unfortunate result. It deprived Canada of national scientific laboratories for more than ten years. Meanwhile, in March, 1921, the Chairman, Dr. A. B. Macallum resigned in order to return to academic work, and he had left for China for the Rockefeller Foundation before the Bill was considered and passed by the Commons and later killed in the Senate in May, 1921. When Dr. Macallum resigned he thought the Research Institute was assured.

In 1923 Dr. Tory was appointed to the Council. Ever since his return from overseas he had campaigned throughout Western Canada, preaching the need for, and the practical values in, scientific research. His life-long enthusiasm for scientific investigation and for the scientific method in meeting the problems of the modern world had been vastly stimulated by his observations of its value during the war and by the successes of his own Alberta Research Council. When Dr. Tory was elected a member of the Council so deep-seated was the frustration and discouragement of the members following the action of the Senate that only a small portion of the $120,000 which had been voted from year to year by the government was being used. In October, 1923, by unanimous vote of the Council, Dr. Tory was nominated President and appointed by the Government, taking office on October 5th of that year.

In the light of the developments which immediately followed his appointment there can be little doubt that Dr. Tory had come into his kingdom for such a time as this. He fully realized and made the Council realize that no government was likely to authorize the building of national research laboratories and entrust them to a group that had not demonstrated its ability to organize and carry out research on a national scale, and he immediately set to work to rectify this situation. His first action was characteristic, he set in motion a survey of the major problems facing industry at that time. Within a year a long list of projects was drawn up and organized researches in certain fields were undertaken. The second thing to be done was to secure the passage of an Act which would give the Council definite standing as a government institution with the right to receive and spend not only the money voted by Parliament, but the income from industrial researches.

The members of the National Research Council originated the idea that the Council should become for Canada not only a research institution but a department for standardization, following the pattern of the Bureau of Standards in Washington. This, they submitted to the Government in 1918 and it was approved by the Special Committee of the Commons in April, 1920. Dr. Tory carried on the original idea. Although many members of the House of Commons and of the Senate were unconvinced regarding the value or the necessity of the Council's work, the new Act was passed in 1924 and the way was open for immediate progress.

Dr. Tory made a clear distinction between: (1) researches carried out under scholarships, whose primary purpose was the training of research workers, (2) assisted researches, mostly in the universities, in which the primary consideration was the nature of the problem and the fitness of the applicant to tackle it, and (3) researches of associate committees, in which many groups or companies were frequently interested, and to which the Council voted money which could be allocated by the committees themselves.

The Council's first laboratory investigation was carried out by an Associate Committee under the direction of Frank Lathe, who was at that time the only technical employee of the Council. It was an experiment repeatedly referred to by Dr. Tory in his public addresses and serves to illustrate several phases of the Council's activities during its period of rapid growth under his direction. Dr. Lathe gives the following account of the work:

> In the spring of 1925, three years before Dr. Tory went to Ottawa on a permanent basis, the Canadian Government was approached by representatives of the companies mining an impure magnesite rock in the Grenville district of the Province of Quebec. They brought out the fact that during the war, when Canadian steel companies' supply of Austrian magnesite—then the standard material used for steel furnace linings—was cut off, the less pure Canadian deposits were opened up, and this material, burned at a high temperature, had helped to meet the essential requirements of Canadian steel companies and those in the eastern United States. After the

war, however, the Austrian magnesite again became available, and most of the companies reverted to its use, hence what had been a key industry during the war lost substantially its whole market and was threatened with a permanent shut-down. The companies' representatives asked the Government for a duty on imported magnesite; this was refused, but the Minister of Finance offered instead to provide a grant of $25,000 to the National Research Council (then without laboratories of any kind!) in order to finance an investigation of the companies' technical problems, and the offer was accepted.

Dr. Tory immediately set up a small committee to organize the investigation, appointing to it Dr. Charles Camsell, then Deputy Minister of Mines, representatives of the companies concerned and several other technically qualified persons, himself assuming the chairmanship. Dr. Camsell generously offered the Council the use of the laboratories of his department until other provision could be made, and within months several men paid by the Council were working there. Their progress was such that work on a larger scale was called for, and late in 1926 Dr. Tory took over several floors of a small office building in the business section of Ottawa, set aside the top floor as a laboratory, and moved his own office from the west block of the parliament buildings to the new quarters. Dr. Tory considered this a very important step in his plan to acquire large laboratories for the Council.

While the magnesite investigation was the only major one carried out in this building, Dr. Tory proceeded to organize many investigations under committees, and by 1928 had convinced the Government of the urgent need for laboratories suitable for investigations of a national character. Indirectly, the Ontario Government at this time lent weight to Dr. Tory's campaign by their own activities in the creation of the Ontario Research Foundation. The Canadian Government acquired property on Sussex Street, and in 1929 the Council's offices and laboratories were moved to it and set up in old buildings of the Edwards Lumber Mills. Another very important step had been taken, and Dr. Tory now improved the opportunity to appoint the future heads of several of the laboratory divisions of the Council, in order that they might themselves proceed with the organization of staff and get researches under way.

The magnesite investigation was now prosecuted with even greater zeal. Patents on new magnesite products and processes were taken out, and strong financial support was forthcoming from the companies co-operating in the investigation. When the new main building was erected, the magnesite work was moved to it, and continued for more than a decade on an expanding scale, until the industry built its own research laboratory at the mine and the work was transferred there; at the same time the industry undertook to pay back the Council's total expenditures on the investigation, including even the original grant of $25,000.

This work pleased Dr. Tory in many ways. Not only had it played an important part in the campaign to get National Research Laboratories, but an important industry had been established on a sound basis, the merits of government research in co-operation with industry had been fully demonstrated, research had proved a more powerful weapon than tariffs, and a constant stream of men trained in the magnesite investigation had gone out into the industry to apply their skill and knowledge. This last function was, in Dr. Tory's opinion, one of the most important services the Council could render to the nation. Were he alive today, he would be delighted to find that his efforts had helped to establish the largest basic refractories industry in the British Empire, exporting some fifty different products to about thirty countries, and would rejoice to see the company's senior technical staff—from the president down—made up of men trained in his own magnesite investigation.

From the beginning, the job of training students in research methods and techniques had been one of the major concerns of the Council, and for this purpose bursaries, studentships and fellowships had been established. This method of procedure was recognized everywhere as fundamental in the establishment of competent research organizations and was especially valuable in Canada because the universities had never had an adequate system of scholarships, with the result that most brilliant students had been going abroad to study. This was particularly true of the United States where there were a great many scholarships open to American and Canadian scholars alike. An investigation showed that to one Canadian university alone scholarships amounting to $16,000 had been provided by two of the larger American universities.

It was quite clear that until laboratory facilities could be provided at Ottawa it would be impossible to build up a proper technical staff. It was also clear that neither the Parliament nor the Government would be willing to vote large capital sums for laboratories until public demand for them became more or less irresistible. The defeat of the original scheme had to some extent fixed in the minds of the Council members and the Government the idea that the time was not ripe for such a move. Many of the universities were lukewarm in their attitude, because they feared competition from government laboratories.

Several government departments were also bitterly opposed to the establishment of the National Research Laboratories. For these reasons the Council under Dr. Tory's direction began to enlarge the scheme of assisted researches in Canadian universities.

In the University of Alberta a list of problems had been drawn up on which work was proceeding. Outstanding among these was a set of biological problems having a very definite relation to the agricultural prosperity of the country. A conference had been held with distinguished American investigators who were dealing with similar agricultural research projects in the Western States. The programme adopted as a result was carried out mainly in the University of Alberta but was applicable to all the Western Provinces and some of it applicable to the Eastern Provinces as well.

At this time also the Federal Department of Agriculture was carrying out investigations in connection with cereal rust in the West. It had been estimated that the loss in the Northern States and in Canada due to rust amounted to some $25,000,000 a year and that Canada's loss in certain years was not less than one hundred million bushels of wheat. Here was a practical problem of such dimensions that a successful attack upon it would not only save Western farmers a vast amount of money but would be a striking demonstration to the Canadian public of the economic rewards of scientific research. Dr. Tory discussed the matter with the officials of the Department of Agriculture and urged that the investigations already going on be enlarged and placed under a general committee including representatives not only of the National Research Council and the Department of Agriculture, but of the biological departments of the universities as well. He persuaded the Department of Agriculture to join with the Council and the western universities in a joint attack on cereal rust. Dr. Robert Newton, later President of the University of Alberta, and at that time on the staff of the National Research Council gives the following account of this investigation:

In order to familiarize themselves with the work being done in the United States on this problem, Dr. Tory and Dr. J. H. Grisdale, then Deputy Minister of Agriculture, visited the Universities of Wisconsin and Minnesota to see how far they had succeeded in their work. As an outcome of this visit the Minister of Agriculture called a conference in Winnipeg in 1924 at which representatives from the Department of Agriculture, the Council and the universities of the Western States and Western Canada were called into consultation on the subject. At this conference a general plan of attack was drawn up, resolutions were passed urging the construction of a rust laboratory in Winnipeg, a general committee to guide the research was agreed upon, and the organization of research staff initiated. The Associate Committee on Cereal Rusts, a joint committee of the Research Council and the Department of Agriculture, was set up promptly, and in a short time the Winnipeg laboratories were completed on the campus of the University of Manitoba. All three universities of the prairie provinces co-operated actively in the investigations, though the University of Alberta confined itself mainly to certain theoretical aspects of rust resistance, since this disease was not a serious practical problem in that province.

It soon became apparent that the researches should be extended to other plant diseases causing important losses to Western farmers, and the Associate Committee on Field Crop Diseases (with which the Rust Committee soon merged) was established in 1928. Meanwhile, three wet harvest seasons in a row had led to the establishment in 1926 of the Associate Committee on Grain Research, with the immediate object of investigating the drying of damp wheat without injury to the baking quality. This was done successfully, and the committee went on to the broader task of investigating the industrial qualities of all western grains, especially the milling and baking quality of the many new varieties of wheat introduced or produced by plant breeders in the effort to get rust resistance.

The Board of Grain Commissioners had for a good many years been maintaining a grain research laboratory in Winnipeg. The Board now joined forces with the National Research Council in carrying on and supporting financially the programme of the Associate Committee on Grain Research. Further support soon came from another source. For some years grain "overages" had been accumulating in the public terminal elevators, the allowance under the regulations for losses in handling being slightly greater than required. This surplus grain really belonged to the farmers of Western Canada, and the then Minister of Trade and Commerce, the Honourable James Malcolm, promptly accepted Dr. Tory's suggestion that the proceeds of its sale should be turned over to the National Research Council for the use of the Grain Research Committee. The amount realized was about $220,000. The committee decided to budget this sum over a period of ten years, in the hope that by that time some of the major problems would be solved and the value of the work recognized by additional financial support.

Happily this proved to be the case. Though the Great Depression began in 1929, the Committee, with the help of the grain overage fund, was able to continue its programme without restriction till better times came.

Throughout this entire period the production of rust-resistant wheat occupied the centre of the stage, the first limited distribution to farmers of thoroughly tested varieties taking place in 1936 and 1937. The first variety was actually a production of the University of Minnesota which, with the University of North Dakota, had co-operated actively with Canadian workers, and indeed anticipated or inspired not a little of the Canadian work. The Associate Committee on Cereal Rusts met annually at Winnipeg, under the joint chairmanship (in the early years) of Dr. Tory and Dr. Grisdale, who often welcomed representatives of the United States workers to the meetings. On each of these occasions the whole work of the previous year was reviewed and plans laid for further progress. It was known when the investigations began that the common wild barberry was the essential host of one stage in the life cycle of the rust organism. An effort had been made to eradicate this plant from the Western wheat-growing region of the United States, and a campaign had been initiated about the same time to do this also in Western Canada. But it was discovered that the rust spores causing our epidemics blew up from the United States, in successive waves beginning in the South, where the spores survived the winters, and progressing northward as the wheat crop developed. An aeroplane device for picking up spores found them 5,000 feet up in the air as far north as Fort Churchill on Hudson's Bay. Dusting by aeroplane with sulphur was partially successful in controlling rust on wheat, but was much too expensive a treatment to cover the vast grain areas of Manitoba and Saskatchewan. Plant breeding to develop resistant varieties seemed the only answer. This was complicated by the existence of more than forty different physiological races of rust, so called because, although they looked the same, they differed in their capacity to infect different varieties of wheat. It was decided to concentrate on producing a type of wheat resistant to the most destructive races. This was bound to be a long and tedious process, and the problem was shown to be more complex than it first appeared when Dr. J. H. Craigie, the head of the Dominion Rust Laboratory at Winnipeg, discovered that new races of rust were arising by old ones crossing at the stage on the barberry bush. Ultimately the problem was solved for existing races by crossing some of the lower forms of wheat, which were already immune or highly resistant to most races of rust, with the bread wheats, and out of many thousands of plants in the progeny selecting those which had the rust-resistant character of the lower wheats and the milling and baking quality of Marquis wheat, the standard bread wheat grown in Western Canada. A constant watch is still maintained for new races of rust and when these appear the plant breeders take whatever additional steps are required to meet the new threat.

The total cost of this investigation over a period of years, taking the Canadian and American expenditures together, was probably several million dollars, but it has been estimated that the total loss to Canada from 1916 to 1930 due to rust averaged approximately twenty-five million dollars a year—a total of over two hundred and fifty millions. Actually, as Dr. Tory pointed out in 1945 in one of his many speeches on the value of research: "The saving in one year as a result of the rust control research project was sufficient to repay to Canada the total cost of the Research Council from its foundation to the present time.

The full story of this particular investigation is recorded in the annual reports of the Research Council for 1924-1935. As the report recognizes, the actual research work done on this problem was carried out mainly by the Federal Department of Agriculture.

Another example of the enormous value of scientific research in the industrial development of a country was the Trail Smelter Smoke Investigation. In 1928 the Canadian Government called on the Council to undertake an investigation which eventually proved to be one of a major character, lasting for about ten years. Action against Canada was taken by the United States Government to secure compensation for damages alleged to have been suffered over a wide area in the valley of the Columbia River in the State of Washington, owing to smoke blown down the valley from the smelter of the Consolidated Mining and Smelting Company of Canada at Trail, British Columbia. Damages were claimed for the destruction of forests, field crops, orchards and pasture lands, the loss of livestock, abortion in cattle, and illness and possible death to human beings, the total compensation demanded running to many millions of dollars. The International Joint Commission was authorized by the governments of the two countries to adjudicate the question and recommend a settlement, and the Council was asked to investigate conditions and report to the Commission. In a comprehensive investigation, in which eventually about 10,000 trees were bored and the width of their annual growth rings measured over the period of alleged damage and previously, and crops and forests were surveyed by experts, the Council found that sulphur dioxide in the smoke had caused severe damage to vegetation in a limited area and slight damage elsewhere, but none to animal life. The Commission recommended that Canada be required to pay the United States the sum of $350,000 to cover all damage to the end of 1931.

The smelting company undertook to eliminate the nuisance. This it did as a result of extensive research by solving the problem of recovering elemental sulphur from the smoke, and by using all but a fraction of the remaining sulphur dioxide in the manufacture of ammonium sulphate and other fertilizers. Undertaken to eliminate a nuisance, this research eventually proved highly profitable. In the meantime, additional claims were made for damage in 1932 and subsequently, leading to some years of research by the Council on the effect of sulphur dioxide on vegetation, and eventually to the payment of another $78,000. When the Council published a book covering its investigations, it was acclaimed as a classic on the subject. Dr. Tory was chairman of the committee in charge of this work until his retirement, and always insisted that all the facts be brought out, regardless of their bearing on the case. Fortunately this was also the position of the smelting company.

Meanwhile Dr. Tory had initiated a campaign through the press, the universities and on the lecture platform to inform the public of what was being accomplished and the nature of the problems being attacked, in an attempt to convince thinking Canadian people of the need to spend more money on research. In Parliament itself the difficult task was to convince some members of the House and the Senate that the programme of the Research Council was not just another political game. One member of Parliament had protested against government grants to universities for research work, claiming that men thus engaged would consider themselves pensioners of the state and would idle away their time.

It should be noted, however, that a number of newspapers

and industrial organizations were now urging upon Parliament a more generous provision for research. On June 15, 1926, the *Toronto Globe* stated:

> We are lamenting the departure of university trained men from Canada. Many of them have been drafted by countries spending millions of dollars annually on research work while we spend not more than a quarter of a million. The field awaits them at home to their own profit and that of their country, but we do not provide it.

The *Globe* went on to point out that although rust had cost the Western farmers millions of dollars, Parliament would only authorize a salary of $2,700 for a trained pathologist to study the problem. After noting that the Canadian Manufacturers Association had been urging more government attention to industrial research, the same editorial goes on to say:

> It might surprise even the C.M.A. to hear Dr. H. M. Tory state that a government department of science, industry and commerce "could in a few years be made to mean more to industry than all the petty tariff changes about which there is so much agitation." There are scores of questions, demanding solution, having to do with industry, agriculture and natural resources requiring the employment of specialists, and each of them offering a return to the country of many millions of dollars a year. It is a typical case as Dr. Tory points out that more time and attention are given to the expenditure of three million dollars on the Hudson's Bay Railway than on the elimination of wheat rust in Western Canada—During the past four years the country has paid out three million dollars for cattle slaughtered because of tubercular trouble. Yet it is not willing to pay for research to wipe out the malady—The separation of bitumen from the tar sands of Northern Alberta is another case in point—Research in this area will eventually run into wealth which cannot be calculated at present. Britain is now spending five million pounds a year in learning the secrets which scientific research will disclose, but Canada is hopelessly immovable.

These petitions and editorials had their effect, but it was not until 1928 that the government agreed to a substantial expansion of equipment, staff and services. On April 24th of that year, the Honourable James Malcolm, Minister of Trade and Commerce, outlined a new plan for the Council in an interview with the Canadian Press. A full report of this interview appeared in the Montreal *Gazette* of the same date, as follows:

The council (Mr. Malcolm said) was to have these functions:

First, the coordination and standardization of research work in Canada.

Second, the granting of financial assistance to qualified research workers to carry on investigations of approved problems of national importance. This work has been carried out mainly in the laboratories of the universities, and of federal and provincial governments and has been made possible through the cooperation, without remuneration, of the highly trained staffs of these laboratories.

Third, the building up in Canada of a corps of highly trained scientific workers by the awarding each year of approximately fifty scholarships for training in science and research.

Fourth, it has been decided to establish under the Council, national research laboratories.

Up until this time Dr. Tory had been commuting at regular intervals between Edmonton and Ottawa. He had plenty of problems guiding the destiny of the rapidly growing University of Alberta, but for five years he had served the Council as President in an honorary capacity. Under pressure from the government and his associates on the Research Council he now decided to give all his time to the latter and he resigned as President of the University of Alberta to become President of the Council on June 1st, 1928. Immediately after taking office Dr. Tory started off on a world tour to study scientific laboratories in the United States, Great Britain, France and Germany. A large part of his time was spent in the National Physical Laboratory and with the Advisory Council of Science and Industrial Research of Great Britain, the Kaiser Wilhelm Institute at Dahlem, Germany, and the Bureau of Standards and the Mellon Institute of the United States. He spent more than a year on this survey and he declared later that he studied and worked harder than he had done at any other period of his life.

The results of this investigation were not only soon apparent in the general plan and laboratory equipment of the new building but were made available to the public during the next few years in dozens of speeches and official papers given before service clubs, scientific societies, and university faculties all over Canada. In these reports to the public it was Dr. Tory's custom to tell of the enormous progress being made in industrial research in Germany, Great Britain and the United States, and of the results of a study he had made of the situation in Japan in connection with his visit to the Pacific Science Congress in 1926. No nation in modern times, he said, had risen so rapidly from a position of comparative obscurity to become one of the most highly productive industrial nations of the world. In addition to the work being done in vocational schools and the six Imperial State Universities, he found sixty-nine specific research institutions in the country working on the problems of industry and agriculture, most of them under government auspices. In these institutions nearly 4,000 scientific experts were employed. Every year 300 of the most brilliant graduates of the universities were selected and sent abroad at government expense to study in Great Britain, Germany, France and the United States. Travelling scholarships alone were costing the nation close to one million dollars a year. In Russia, similar progress was taking place.

It must be clear to everyone, he said, who considers the matter seriously, that if Canada is to maintain her place in world trade in competition with countries provided with the scientific machinery he had described, her greatest need was the provision of adequate laboratory facilities where the work of standardization could be done, and where researches of an industrial character could be carried on. Constant appeals, he said, were being made to the Research Council for assistance, which it was impossible to consider because of the lack of laboratory facilities. The result of this was that Canadian manufacturers were forced to have much of their research work done in the United States because facilities were not available at home.

This kind of enlightened propaganda had its effect in awakening the Canadian people to the need for increased expenditure of government funds on scientific research.

At sixty-five years of age Dr. Tory was starting life all over again and bringing to the challenge of his new position all the vigour and euthusiasm of youth. Plans for the new building to be erected on the site already purchased, overlooking the Ottawa River, were in his mind wherever he went. He was convinced that the laboratories should serve two primary functions —a bureau of standards, and a centre of research for industrial purposes. Dr. Tory also insisted on the provision of adequate library facilities which he recognized as fundamental to the work of a research organization. As a result stacks were built for about 500,000 volumes in the central part of the building where they are most readily accessible to the staff.

Meanwhile, the depression which had started in 1929 settled heavily over the land. It is a tribute to Dr. Tory's generalship and to the government of the day that in spite of protest from certain quarters a vote of three million dollars was passed and plans accepted for the splendid structure with 270,000 square feet of floor space, which is still the headquarters of the National Research Council.

Many newspapers and some members of Parliament maintained that the whole project was a luxury Canada could well do without. They mocked at the size of the building and prophesied that it would never be fully used. Stories were published in the opposition press describing extravagances in the purchase of equipment, of furnishings such as desks, wastepaper baskets and rugs. But the Council had kept itself free of political entanglement of all sorts and the result was that when the Liberal Government was defeated and a Conservative Government took its place, the work of completing the laboratories continued without interference.

On August 10th, 1932, His Excellency the Earl of Bessborough opened the new building. He was introduced by the Prime Minister, the Right Honourable R. B. Bennett, who stated during his remarks that "the purpose of this building is to determine how industry and mankind can best be served." On the same occasion Dr. Tory in his opening address referred, as he always did, to Canada's need of trained men and pointed out that it had been the aim of the Research Council "to assist the universities in maintaining a standard of graduate training which would make possible a succession of trained men capable of dealing with the problems of the nation."

A broad base for the work of the Council had been progressively established through committees composed of experts in the respective fields, drawn from the various Canadian universities, government departments and industry. Every one of these committees was dealing with practical problems in the solution of which fundamental research was essential. This plan of decentralized responsibility did much to refute the criticism which Dr. Tory was constantly facing, that the work of the Council was too theoretical. The problem in public relations was to make ordinary laymen understand that the foundation of all progress lay in the discoveries of fundamental sciences applied to particular problems.

Dr. Tory now had two major tasks: the development of the work of the Council by gathering about him a staff worthy of the magnitude of the undertaking, and the creation and maintenance of favourable opinion among parliamentarians, business men, industrialists and the general public. He continued to make speeches throughout the country wherever the opportunity occurred and published regular reports interpreting the work of the Council.

In one of these reports specially prepared for the Senate in 1932 to meet the criticism of members of both Houses, Dr. Tory disclosed that a thorough study of scientific development in every major country was being made; the council had brought together a corps of highly trained specialists to the service of the state, and a national library of science had been developed both for the use of the Council staff and for all scientists in Canada; the publication of the *Canadian Journal of Research* was bringing recognition to Canadian research workers and providing them with information about scientific progress within Canada; almost two million dollars had been expended during the life-time of the Council in direct grants to individual investigators, and a scheme of co-operation between governments, universities and industrial concerns had been worked out. "The results of these efforts," he said, "are seen in the fact that even in these depression years, the Council has continued to grow in effectiveness in spite of the fact that many of its activities have had to be curtailed."

Meanwhile Dr. Tory's hand was strengthened greatly by the recognition the Council was receiving from the scientists of other countries. In a radio address broadcast from the Cavendish Laboratories to the Fifth Pacific Science Congress at Vancouver in 1933, Sir Ernest Rutherford congratulated Canada on its Research Council and prophesied that under the direction of his old friend, Dr. Tory, it would prove invaluable to the welfare and development of Canada. No such institution had been established by the national government of the United States and at conferences of scientific men references were constantly being made to Canada's fortunate position in having a government institution capable of establishing throughout the country a co-ordinated plan of scientific research. All this helped to establish the Council and its work in the esteem of thinking people and Dr. Tory was able to report in 1933 that grants in aid of research projects in eleven universities carried out in twenty-five departments of science, amounted to $167,000 and that the same year scholarships to the value of over $38,000 had been awarded. These major research projects, which were being worked out by professors in Canadian universities, were for the most part investigations into such practical problems as the production of magnesite, aeronautical design, weed control, the training of research workers.

Perhaps the most noteworthy contribution of the Council was its success in raising the standards of graduate work through the granting of scholarships and fellowships. Four classes of scholarships had been established. There were bursaries of $500 a year available for students just entering upon graduate work, studentships of $1,000 for students having one year of graduate work, fellowships of $1,200 for those whose work gave evidence of high intellectual capacity and a few travelling fellowships of $1,500 for students whose studies involved foreign travel. Dr. Tory had always stressed the importance of graduate work in Canadian universities. As President of the Research Council he was able to persuade his associates to agree to a system of grants to universities for the development of their graduate schools. Grants and scholarships enabled a number of Canadian institutions to expand their graduate work, particularly in the departments of chemistry, physics and biology, where most of the scholarships were awarded. Before Dr. Tory retired from the presidency of the Council in 1935, close to $600,000 had been spent on scholarships to some 400 students, and grants in aid of research to universities were over one and three-quarter millions of dollars.

In a paper read before the Royal Canadian Institute on January 31st, 1953, the President of the National Research

Council, Dr. E. W. R. Steacie, reported that since its inception the Council has made some 2,500 awards at an overall cost of about $1,800,000 to 1,500 individuals. "It is generally conceded," he said, "that the programme of scholarships and grants supported by the Council over the past thirty years has been the most vital factor in building up organized science in Canada. This support is being maintained and the Council is now spending over two million dollars per year on scholarships and grants."

When the Second World War broke out, the total staff of N.R.C. was only about three hundred, servicing four main divisions, biology, chemistry, physics and mechanical engineering. The total budget was about $800,000 (including scholarships and grants.) Today (1953) there is a staff of 2,500 with a total budget of fifteen million dollars per year. There are eight laboratory divisions: physics, applied biology, pure chemistry, applied chemistry, radio and electrical engineering, mechanical engineering, building research and medical research. There are, in addition, two regional laboratories, one at Saskatoon and the other in Halifax.

Dr. Tory in his life-time had seen this institution, which his vision and energy had helped to create, become one of the greatest organizations of its kind in the world. His contract had been for a period of seven years and his time was up in June, 1935. He was now seventy-one years of age, but his strength was not seriously impaired and his spirit as active and progressive as it had ever been. His correspondence at this time shows that he would have liked to carry on as President for another two years. This was the time he felt he required to round out the various projects he then had on hand. On April 18, 1935, the Prime Minister, Mr. R. B. Bennett, called Dr. Tory on the telephone. Unfortunately there is no record of the conversation which ensued, but the same day Dr. Tory replied in writing as follows:

Dear Mr. Bennett: Re offer of C.M.G.

When you spoke to me over the phone today I was presiding over a meeting and hence found myself somewhat embarrassed how to answer without informing others of the nature of the conversation.

For a moment I did not recognize your voice nor realize it was you who was speaking.

Please believe me when I say that I am grateful for the thought you entertained concerning me, and that I regret that I felt I had to give a negative answer to your suggestion. I would not, however, want my refusal to be interpreted in any way a criticism of any action on your part, nor that I think lightly of Imperial relationships. I believe that I am one of the old school who believe intensely in the British Empire and that our future, both because of tradition and of economic circumstances, must lie with her; nor would I regard any effort on my part too great, as I think I showed during the Great War, in promoting that ideal. I am very glad indeed to know that you are sufficiently recovered in health to join in the Jubilee Celebration and hope that the additional respite which your visit will give you will result in complete restoration to health.

Very sincerely yours,

H. M. TORY

Writing of this episode, Dr. John E. Robbins, who was a close friend of Dr. Tory for many years says:

My recollection of the story of the telephoned offer of a decoration from the Right Honourable R. B. Bennett was approximately as follows:—

BENNETT: Hello, Tory. Do you want me to get you a C.M.G.?

TORY: No, thanks. Good-bye.

This offer came about the time that R. B. Bennett was elbowing Dr. Tory out of the National Research Council. Part of the resentment over the offer was due to the manner in which it was made, but beneath it all was the fact, according to Dr. Tory (which R.B. must have known) that he was slated for knighthood fifteen years earlier just at the time when the Nickle resolution put a stop to all titles, until the Bennett government came. Bennett had been handing out a few titles and Dr. Tory interpreted his offer of a C.M.G. as tantamount to saying, "I think you were over-rated fifteen years ago."

Dr. Robert Newton, at that time a close associate of Dr. Tory in the National Research Council, and later President of the University of Alberta, gives approximately the same account of the incident:

When Prime Minister Bennett called Dr. Tory on the telephone on April 18th, 1935, he offered to put his name on the Honours List for the C.M.G. Dr. Tory was understandably reluctant to accept favours from Mr. Bennett though in recounting the conversation to me soon afterwards he admitted he might have been tempted by a higher honour. If I remember rightly, that was the final batch of Canadian Knighthoods, including F. G. Banting and Ernest MacMillan.

On March 7th, 1935, Dr. Tory had written to the Honourable R. B. Hanson, then Minister of Trade and Commerce in the Bennett Government, pointing out that the time of his appointment, i.e. seven years, would expire as of June 1st, but since there was still much to be done he would appreciate an extension of two years in order to clear up a number of projects then proceeding under his direction. This letter was not answered until May 29th, when Mr. Hanson wrote as follows:

Dear Dr. Tory:

With regard to the question of your reappointment as President of the National Research Council. . . . I personally regret indeed to have to inform you that the Council has decided that on the expiration of your term of office on June 1st next, you will not be reappointed, but that a successor will be named in due course . . .

As you know the term of your office as President of the National Research Council expires under authority of Order-in-Council P.C. 597, dated April 28, 1928, which covered a period of seven years and until a successor has been appointed and by reason of your being over 70 years of age, Council did not feel justified in extending your services beyond the date mentioned.

I want to thank you for your services . . . The Government appreciates, etc. . . . I hope you will continue to enjoy good health . . .

Dr. Tory replied to Mr. Hanson on May 30th as follows:

I have your letter of May 29th. From its contents I am not sure whether you desire me to continue after June 1st until my successor is appointed. Under my agreement I would so continue. There is a great deal to be done in rounding out the work of the past year. I would be grateful for immediate instruction as to whether I am to leave the office on June 1st.

On May 31st, Mr. Hanson wrote to Dr. Tory:

Further to my letter of May 29th in regard to the question of your retirement, please be advised that the decision of Council is that the term of your service expires as from May 31st, 1935.

The above correspondence speaks for itself. It is unlikely that there have been very many occasions in the history of Canada when a distinguished public servant had been so shabbily treated. The action of the Privy Council in deciding that, since Dr. Tory's contract had expired and he was over seventy years of age, his position should be held by a younger man was to be expected. But to give him only two days' official notice and refuse his request that he be allowed to continue (as was his right by contract) until his successor was appointed, surely constitutes an unforgivable departure from ordinary amenities and official procedure. It had taken R. B. Bennett twenty-five years to catch up with "that man Tory" as he was wont to refer to him. He waited a long time to avenge himself upon the man who had defeated him too often and too thoroughly in Alberta.

When the Canadian Press carried the story of Dr. Tory's retirement and the appointment of his successor, Major General A. G. L. MacNaughton, the daily press from coast to coast carried tributes to the work of Dr. Tory and the worthiness of the man who was to succeed him, but there was strong resentment among members of the House over the manner of his dismissal. On request of Major Fred G. Sanderson, Liberal member from South Perth, the correspondence noted above was tabled in the House but the early letter of March 7th from Dr. Tory to Mr. Hanson and marked "personal" was not tabled for the reason, said the minister, that he was not able to reach Dr. Tory to ask for permission to release it.

On June 4, 1935, the *Border Cities Star* (Ottawa correspondent) reported:

> A great deal of resentment, even among Conservative members of Parliament, was expressed today over the summary dismissal of Dr. H. M. Tory as Chairman of the National Research Council and his succession in that office by Major-General MacNaughton, Chief of the general staff of the Department of National Defence. Dr. Tory, who left the Presidency of the University of Alberta to organize and establish the Research Council and under whom it has grown to its present proportions, received curt and formal notice under date of last Friday that his services would be dispensed with on Saturday.

In all this controversy Dr. Tory himself took no part, but it was an injury he felt deeply as did his many friends throughout the Dominion. Shortly after this he and Mrs. Tory left for a long and much needed holiday in Nova Scotia.

Almost a year later, on May 20th, 1936, a reception to Dr. and Mrs. Tory was held in the National Research Council Building when a portrait by Lilias Torrance Newton of Dr. Tory was unveiled. On that occasion the presentation address was given by Dr. Frank D. Adams, his old McGill friend and associate for many years on the National Research Council. His speech, in part, follows:

> When asked to deliver the presentation address on this happy occasion, I accepted the invitation with pleasure for Dr. Tory is one of my most intimate friends and I have known him from the time when he was a very young man, when we were lecturers together at McGill University, and I have from that time until quite recently been closely associated with him in connection with the work of the Commission of Conservation, the Research Council of Canada, and on other committees and commissions.
>
> A friend of mine told me that he was at a funeral recently and when the minister in his funeral address commenced to enlarge upon the good points in the character of the departed, a young lawyer who sat next to my friend, leaned over to him and whispered—"The case for the defence is now being opened." Here, however, there is no funeral. Dr. Tory is in sound health and has many years of productive work ahead of him; nor does the defence here need to attempt to put forward any case, for Dr. Tory's career needs merely to be set forth in order to win from everyone a high meed of approbation and praise.

There followed then a survey of Dr. Tory's youth, his years at McGill University, his work in establishing McGill in British Columbia, his Presidency of the University of Alberta, his experiences as President of Khaki University, the Royal Commissions on which he had served, and special emphasis upon his accomplishments as head of the National Research Council. In conclusion Dr. Adams said:

> A greater change has taken place in human society the world over, within the past fifty years than in any other period of equal duration in the history of the world since man appeared upon the globe. This has been brought about chiefly through the discoveries

Photo by Malak, Ottawa.

CARLETON COLLEGE, OTTAWA

FAMILY GROUP

Front row, left to right: Mrs. John A. Tory, Mrs. Robert Kirk Tory, Mrs. H. M. Tory, Mrs. James C. Tory. *Back row, left to right:* Dr. John A. Tory, Hon.

and applications of modern science. Furthermore this period of scientific discovery and advance is not drawing to a close. It is evidently in full flood and some of the most remarkable discoveries have been made within the past few years; while others, not less remarkable, are in the act of birth at the present time. All the leading nations of the world are vying with one another in programmes of scientific research. The development of their resources and the efficiency of their manufacturing process depends upon it and these are of vital importance to their very existence.

Canada must keep pace with other nations in these critical times, or fall behind and lose her place in the sun. And so, we should all realize the importance of this great centre of research in our Dominion, and would, I am sure urge upon the government and all the thinking people of Canada the vital necessity of giving it adequate and indeed abundant support.

Dr. Tory's friends, desiring that a suitable memorial of him should be placed in this building, which owes its existence largely to his efforts and in which some of his fondest hopes are enshrined, have had a portrait painted of him by Mrs. Lilias Newton of Montreal. This is to be hung in the library of the Research Council, and it now gives me much pleasure to unveil this portrait.

In Dr. Tory's reply, he began by stating that all his life he had been a pioneer in the field of education and then proceeded to review as briefly as possible the successive steps of his career, from the time he entered McGill University as a freshman, until his retirement as President of the National Research Council. Speaking of the early years of his association with the Council he said:

One of our first acts on completion of a staff was the drafting of a programme of problems on which we considered research should be undertaken. This grew out of the fact that constant appeals were being made to us to answer questions related to possible material development to which no ready-made answer could be given. On the staff of the Research Council are two men who worked with me on the drafting of a set of problems for research, Dr. R. W. Boyle and Dr. Robert Newton.

We took the ground from the beginning that *the basis of all real development must be knowledge.* We stated a set of problems on which we considered research should be undertaken, and presented them to the government of the day. If the University of Alberta flourished and early became recognized as a worthwhile institution, it was because we relentlessly pursued the policy of working at those urgent problems. We did not consider that it was our duty to wait until we were asked to do something. We considered ourselves to be in the best position to decide what should be done.

Naturally such an aggressive policy brought us both friends and foes. Those who were wedded to ancient ways were, of course, opposed, but fortunately the type of people who settled in Alberta was virile enough to realize that such work as we were undertaking would ultimately be to the advantage of the Province. I am happy to think that the organization under the direction of my successor, Dr. R. C. Wallace, still carries on. . . .

I have always been a "Canada First" man, if by "Canada First" is meant creating the conditions which will enable Canadians to do their own intellectual work, thus assuring their intellectual equality with the whole world. There are a lot of little Canadians who think otherwise. They see in expenditure for the extension of research and education only money wasted unless it brings grist to their own particular mill. With such I have no fellowship.

Before these laboratories were built an intensive study was made of the laboratory systems of Europe and America. Perhaps the eighteen months that were associated with the preparation and building of these laboratories were the most intensive period of study in my life. I had only the beginnings of a staff under my control and the right to secure appointments was exceedingly slow in coming.

There are three men, however, whose vision of the future especially, made possible these laboratories. I refer to the Right Honourable William Mackenzie King, the Honourable James Malcolm and the Honourable Charles Stewart, all of whom sensed the importance of the research move and backed the activity of the Council in trying to realize upon it. . . .

I know there are some who have spoken as if it were unnecessary. A civil servant, high in the service, meeting me on the street when the building was nearing completion said, "You are building a white elephant." A certain cabinet minister, speaking to me concerning it, in a not unfriendly way, said, "You know very well this effort is too great for Canada." Such statements are the result of utter ignorance of the whole forward movement of research that is going on in the world, and the complete absence of understanding of the place which research has in the material and intellectual development of a country.

I rejoice tonight in the fact that Canada does possess the facilities which the Research Council and this institution offer, and that no matter what short-sightedness may be associated with policy connected with it, its future is secure.

May I add a final word. For forty years I have given my life, the best that is in me, to the development of those aspects of our national life which I have been emphasizing tonight. . . . In a letter sent me by one who was an old student of mine in McGill days and who has later worked with me at the head of one of the divisions of this laboratory, are the following words:

"We who worked for you and for the cause which you yourself had at heart, have greatly profited by that association. No one could long be in contact with you without sensing the driving power in your life, or without being stirred by it to greater effort. You never urged us verbally, the urge of your example was always with us."

I could wish for no greater reward than that my own activities should have so affected those with whom it was my good fortune to be associated.

I had hoped that when the time for retirement came I might have remained associated with some of those aspects of the Research Council's activities which lie outside the immediate work of research. That opportunity, however, has been denied me and I am content. *I just want to say to you that I do not regard my work as yet done.*

Any man who has studied as intensely and has worked as diligently as I have tried to do, cannot but sense the immensity of the problems that lie before the people of Canada before she realizes her national destiny. In the solution of some of these I hope I may still be permitted to participate.

Again permit me to say, I am profoundly grateful to the friends who have made this gift to the Research Council possible. A great English statesman who visited us some years ago referred to this building as a "Temple of Science." If the men who work here toil with a sense of devotion to truth, aiming at the well-being of Canada, then the name suggested, with its implied religious ideal, may well be regarded as intensely appropriate. I shall continue to watch the progress of this institution with the keenest interest.

Nearly three hundred people contributed to this farewell tribute to Dr. Tory. Almost all of them had been associated with him at various times in his career. Among the hundreds of letters he received at this time expressing appreciation of his work and regrets at his retirement were warm personal messages from the Right Honourable Mackenzie King, Sir Robert Borden, the Honourable J. L. Ralston, the Honourable Charles Stewart, the Honourable James Malcolm, the Honourable H. H. Stevens, and many other men distinguished in public life.

That night when Dr. and Mrs. Tory returned to their home in Rockcliffe Park and before retiring for the night discussed the events of the day and looked through the letters and telegrams piled high upon the table, Dr. Tory got up and walked around the living room until he was able to say in a voice choked with emotion: "Well, Annie, my dear, it's been a long hard pull, but at last 'The Word has been made Flesh'."

Chapter XV

CARLETON COLLEGE

There is a legend to the effect that President Garfield once said his idea of a college was Mark Hopkins on one end of a log and a student on the other. Another legend has it that Carleton College started on a street corner one day in 1941, when Dr. H. M. Tory and Mr. W. M. Connor stopped to exchange greetings in downtown Ottawa.

The need for a non-sectarian institution of higher learning had long been recognized in Canada's capital. The University of Ottawa, established in 1849, had an enviable reputation for scholarship in certain academic and scientific fields and there was also St. Patrick's College, providing courses leading to the Arts degree. But these were Roman Catholic schools and Ottawa even in normal times had a population of over 80,000 Protestants. In 1941, with the war on, that number had greatly increased. A great many civil servants were university graduates and were anxious to have their children enjoy the same opportunity they themselves had had. But this meant, for the non-Catholics, sending them away from home to Queen's, Toronto, McGill, or elsewhere, which was beyond the financial capacity of many people.

For some years there had been a strong committee at work in the Ottawa YMCA headed by Dr. H. L. Keenleyside (now Administrator of the United Nations' Technical Assistance programme) working on plans for the development of a college which would at least provide for the first two years of university work and at the same time supply courses in professional training for civil servants. Very substantial progress had been made in securing public interest in the project when the Second World War put a stop to the plans because of the drain on YMCA funds following its immediate assumption of auxiliary services for the Canadian Army, Navy and Air Forces.

In the meantime it had been necessary to appoint a programme secretary to look after the educational work already going on in the YMCA. Under the direction of Mr. L. R. Shaw, the new secretary, the idea of such an institution was kept alive. Shaw visited a number of colleges and universities in the United States and spent some time examining the work of Sir George Williams College in Montreal, particularly its evening class programme.

It was at this time that the conversation between Dr. Tory and Mr. W. M. Connor, who was chairman of the Council of Social Agencies in Ottawa and a member of the YMCA Board, took place. Dr. Tory had retired some years before as President of the National Research Council, but was fully occupied in a number of voluntary and official activities. Both men were convinced that the war had provided an urgent reason for continuing the work of the original committee. Thousands of young people from all over Canada were crowding into Ottawa to take up work created by the war. Many of them would be eager to continue their interrupted education. It was agreed that the committee should meet at an early date to explore the situation and the possibilities of taking immediate action.

On December 2nd, 1941, a meeting was called and it was decided to revive the committee on College Grade Education, with Dr. Tory as chairman. He was then seventy-seven years of age, but he assumed this new responsibility with the kind of enthusiasm and energy which had characterized his youth.

The first regular meeting of the committee under Dr. Tory's chairmanship met on January 28th, 1942, and the question of making a start with a new educational institution in war-time was thoroughly discussed. It was estimated that there were some fifteen thousand temporary civil servants in the city, most of whom had considerable leisure time on their hands. Even if the attendance was not large during the war, at least a start would have been made and there would undoubtedly be a wide-spread demand for training facilities after the war, as a result of the rehabilitation programme already under consideration by the government.

It was unanimously agreed to proceed with the plans for

the establishment of a college and an objective of one hundred evening students was adopted for the first year. Only Junior College work would be provided; but if the students were to be accepted by Canadian universities, a special study of the law in Ontario regarding the chartering of colleges and the granting of degrees would have to be made. A special committee was appointed to make such a study and a sub-committee on curriculum, consisting of Dr. Tory as chairman, Dr. John E. Robbins, of the Dominion Bureau of Statistics, Mr. Frank Patton, business administrator for the Ottawa Collegiate Institute Board, and L. R. Shaw of the YMCA, was set up.

There were large numbers of professors in Ottawa on special war duties of various kinds, so the matter of a staff of instructors appeared to present no difficult problem. Temporary quarters in one of the city collegiates were obtained and a campaign to secure funds was initiated. Dr. Tory agreed to undertake the responsibility of obtaining recognition from Eastern Canadian universities for the work of the first two years of the College.

Once it became known that a decision to proceed with the original plan had been reached, there was a heartening response to the appeal for financial support and general assistance.

At a meeting on May 28th, 1942, the original YMCA Committee on College Grade Education became the Carleton College Committee. In order to facilitate an appeal for support to all classes and creeds in the community, the Ottawa YMCA relinquished control of the project and a new board was established called "The Ottawa Association for the Advancement of Learning."[1] Pending an Act of Incorporation, Articles of Association were drawn up as follows:

(1) the name of the Association shall be the Ottawa Association for the Advancement of Learning.

(2) the Association shall be deemed to have commenced on the eighteenth day of June, 1942.

(3) the Association shall have for its purpose and objects:—

(a) The promotion of learning in all its branches;

[1]The name was of Dr. Tory's proposal, and derived from his early association with McGill University, the Royal Institution for the Advancement of Learning.

(b) the organization and establishment of a non-sectarian college of higher learning in the City of Ottawa;

(c) the organization and establishment of an Institute of Public Administration;

(d) the promotion of the intellectual, social, moral and physical welfare of its students, graduates, teaching staff and others interested in the Association and of the community in which it operates.

(4) the Association shall have its seat at the City of Ottawa.

(5) the Association shall be governed by a Board of twenty-one, to be known as the "Board of Governors." In acknowledgement of its interest and assistance in the organization and establishment of the Association, the Ottawa YMCA shall have the right to name and be represented by four members on the Board of Governors at all times.

(6) any person of good moral character may become a member of the Association or otherwise admitted to interest or participation in the activities of the Association, subject to approval by the Board of Governors. Members may retire from membership upon three months written notice to the Chairman. The executors or administrators of deceased members shall be relieved and indemnified against all liabilities of the Association by continuing members.

(7) the interests and activities of the Association shall be open to men and women on equal terms.

(8) the Association shall otherwise be governed by a constitution and by-laws which may be amended or repealed or added to, in the manner and under the provisions therein stated.

It will be noticed that the foregoing articles gave the Association the right to undertake work in the general public interest as well as to establish a college.

Immediately following the adoption of the Articles of Association, a Board of Governors was appointed, with Dr. Tory as Chairman, and it was decided at its first meeting that the new college would open its doors to students on September 14, 1942.

Once again Dr. Tory was back where he was at his best; at the head of an educational institution. He took on at this time, the look of a man who has been born again. He begged, borrowed, and—to use his own term—scrounged desks, tables, benches, typewriters, blackboards—anything needed for the College. But it was not an easy undertaking. Writing of this time, Mr. Walter Herbert, Director of the Canada Foundation, who was in close touch with the project from its inception, says:

> Dr. Tory had to meet and overcome objections from a number of sources. Some people were not in favour of a "third college" in Ottawa, for reasons which were neither academic nor economic; while others expressed the view that it was a "lot of damn nonsense" starting a thing like this when Queen's, Toronto and McGill were so close at hand. I think, too, that Dr. Tory must have found it necessary to overcome indifference among highly-placed people in Ottawa. I say this because I remember several occasions when he expressed annoyance, even anger, over the petty attitudes of some of the people he had turned to for help and encouragement. I feel very strongly that no one else could have done the job. If Dr. Tory had not been in Ottawa, and available, in spite of all the other factors, Carleton College would not have come into existence in 1942 —his great talent for personal leadership was a tremendously important factor in the creation of Carleton College.

In September, 1942, when the College opened, no one could keep up with Dr. Tory night or day. The whole administrative staff was made up of himself, L. R. Shaw, the Acting Registrar, and one assistant. They had anticipated an enrolment of one hundred and fifty at the most, but within a few weeks of the opening, more than seven hundred students had registered. There were freshmen and graduate students, young and old, some under twenty and some over fifty. They came for various reasons—to begin college; to follow some study, hobby or special interest or to train themselves for advancement in the government service. For the first several weeks every day and every night new emergencies presented themselves, new classes had to be organized, additional instructors had to be found, new classrooms opened. In a letter written on March 4, 1953, Senator Cairine Wilson says:

> The founding of Carleton College was a godsend, for Dr. Tory entered into it with all the zest of a young man and several amusing stories are told of the early days. One of the students, Ian Campbell, said that he registered before a kindly old gentleman whom he later met at the Bursar's wicket when he paid his fee, and then he took his first lecture from the same man, who turned out to be Dr. Tory,

President of the College. Dr. Tory told of a young husband and wife who arrived with a three weeks old baby to register for the course in Child Psychology and he held the infant while they registered.

There was an enormous appetite in the Capital for classes in languages. To meet the demand, courses were offered in Spanish, Russian, German, French, Italian and oriental languages. Most of the instructors were professional teachers and professors.

At the end of the first year of work the Board of Governors felt that the time had come to fulfil one of the original purposes of the founding fathers. From the beginning it had been recognized that there was a unique opportunity in Ottawa for the specific training of civil servants in public administration. It happened that a former Canadian at the University of Pennsylvanian, J. C. Miller, had, in 1939, made a scholarly study of the Canadian system of education. This study had been published under the title *National Government and Education in Federated Democracies.* In his report Miller urged that "Public Administration" should receive high priority in future developments in Canadian education and pointed out that Ottawa was the logical centre for such a course of training. On April 23, 1943, the Board of Governors approved a plan for the establishment of such courses at Carleton College under the name of "The Institute of Public Administration" classes to start during the session of 1943-1944. Separate educational directorates were set up for the two schools, both under the supervision of the Board of Governors.

In the fall of 1943 a number of courses of instruction demanding no special academic requirements were offered and others were promised as time went on and trends became apparent. The first series of lectures covered such subjects as: Principles and Practices of Personnel Management, Introduction to Statistical Method, Population Trends and Social Policy, Advanced Calculus and Differential Equations, World Organization, Advanced Accounting, Social Science and Town Planning. It was anticipated that some fifty or sixty students would register for the work. But the response was the same as the year before when the general college courses were started. Instead of the expected fifty or so, more than two hundred students enrolled for these special courses.

In the meantime application had been made to the Ontario Government for a Charter and Incorporation. In June, 1943, the application was approved and the Letters Patent granted. Thus, "The Ottawa Association for the Advancement of Learning" became an incorporated body under the laws of the Province of Ontario for the purposes already set forth in the "Articles of Association" with all necessary powers for the making of by-laws and the administration of the Corporation.

The officers appointed as Directors of the new undertaking were: Dr. Tory as Chairman, Dr. Hugh L. Keenleyside, Vice-Chairman, Dr. John E. Robbins as Secretary, and W. M. Connor as Treasurer.

By the end of October, 1943, classes were well under way and the first convocation exercises were held. Of this occasion *The Ottawa Citizen* remarked:

> Impressive in its individuality was the occasion last evening as Carleton College and the "Institute of Public Administration" held its initial commencement exercises in the Assembly Hall of the Glebe Collegiate. Unlike convocations at older, more seasoned colleges, there were no presentations, no decorations to distinguish last night's gathering. Instead there were many people all interested in the furtherance of education in Canada's capital, doing honour to the institution on its first anniversary.

On this same occasion, the Earl of Athlone, then Governor-General of Canada, referring to the importance of education for adults—a cause always close to Dr. Tory's heart—said:

> What matters is not the amount of information that is offered, but the amount that is absorbed and the great value of adult education lies in the fact that the mind, being more mature, is more likely to retain what it learns than it is in earlier years. I should like to congratulate Dr. Tory, through whose vision, and if I may say so, youthful energy, the remarkable success of Carleton College is so largely due.

Throughout the second year of operation, 1943-1944, the Board of Governors decided upon the provision of additional services. Dr. Tory had been urging further expansion in the firm belief that the educational facilities offered to service men and women under the government's rehabilitation programme would have the effect of crowding the Canadian universities as they had never been crowded before. In this attitude, as usual, he was looking into the future and mentally planning how to meet new demands. Dr. Tory was satisfied that there would always be a place in Ottawa for an evening college; and the experiment thus far had convinced him that Carleton College had come to stay, and that it would continue to grow in importance as a night school as time went on. With adequate public support he believed that nothing could stop the work already under way. But for Dr. Tory's driving spirit this was not enough. He was convinced of the need for a degree-granting Arts College with a much wider scope than the present establishment provided. This would involve a permanent building and staff and large capital expenditure—Dr. Tory was dreaming again—but if this was a far-off event, a start could be made. In June, 1944, he persuaded the Board to appoint a committee to consider the question of day classes to meet the requirements of service men and women returning to Ottawa. The hope was that the college might be in a position to offer day classes in the fall of 1945.

The Board of Governors report for June, 1944, showed that the College and Institute had been carried for the second year without a deficit. A major advance planned for the season 1944-1945 was the establishment of a Department of Extension. Dr. Tory's experience in Alberta had convinced him of the value of extension services, not only in terms of good public relations but as a medium through which the college could broaden its base of operations and its usefulness beyond the walls of the institution itself. A properly constituted Department of Extension could provide a two-way channel of communication between the college and the community. From the beginning, it was decided to relate extension services at Carleton College to the regular teaching programme of the college. The department would not be, as is usually the case, a separate division operating more or less independently of the staff and with an administration of its own. The Extension Services of Carleton College began and have continued as an integral part of the basic college activity. To this end extension courses are limited, as a rule, to those which merit and receive the sponsorship of regular departments of the institution. This means that the instruction department sponsoring an extension course assumes responsibility for the content of the course, the leadership, and a major part in the planning and promotion. This policy adopted at the beginning has meant that the Extension Services of Carleton College are the concern of every member of the faculty and not just of one staff member or one department.

The calendar for 1944-1945 offered five courses as an extension service, these were: Modern trends in Education, Town and Regional Planning and Housing, Journalism, The Far East, and the Evolution of Knowledge. These courses carried no admission requirements, no examinations and no credits. The lectures were given by the professors of the college and by specialists recruited from various government departments and other professional sources.

In addition to all his administrative duties as President of the College, (for which, incidentally, he received no salary) Dr. Tory took this opportunity to return to his first love—teaching. This incredible man now gave the extension course on "The Evolution of Knowledge." I have the notebook in which this whole series of twenty weekly lectures are outlined. The first three are written out word for word in the clear, firm handwriting so well-known and easily recognized by Dr. Tory's friends. (It is further proof of his enormous vitality that up to the last days of his life there was no change whatever in the bold firm sweep of Dr. Tory's handwriting.) After having written in longhand the first three lectures the President apparently decided he could rely upon his memory for the rest of the series, and from there on he used only scribbled notes. Some idea of the work involved in the preparation of the series of lectures may be gathered when it is noted that they covered, in popular language and style and with the use of illustrated charts, the whole history of knowledge from man's first appearance on this planet to the present time. The taking on of such an assignment in his eightieth year gives some idea of the inexhaustible energy of Dr. Tory and it illustrates the conviction he had always held that the public was entitled to instruction on the same basis of sound scholarship required in the classroom,—an educational philosophy which explains the fact that the extension services of Carleton College have continued as much a part of the life of the institution as any of its work in Arts and Science.

In the 1944-1945 period changes and additions were made in the curriculum of "The Institute of Public Administration." It had been recognized from the beginning by the Board of Governors that *ad hoc* courses would not be satisfactory. They must be integrated with a programme of practical work. Preferably they should be on a post-graduate level. A fully integrated plan of study leading to the certificate of Bachelor of Public Administration (B.P.A.) was now instituted. The requirements for the certificate included: (1) Holding a Junior College graduation certificate from Carleton College or having obtained equivalent standing elsewhere, including two courses in Economics, Political Science, Psychology and Philosophy. (2) Obtaining satisfactory standing in ten of the courses outlined. (3) University graduates desiring to obtain the B.P.A. Certificate might do so by selecting courses supplementary to the courses already taken in Arts. Credits for courses in Arts will be arranged on application in each individual case. Sixteen courses were offered under the following sections:

A. Personal Problems
B. Public Finance
C. Accounting
D. Political Science
E. Economics and Sociology
F. Statistics
G. Advanced Calculus and Differential Equations

Here was an astounding record to present to the world. In the midst of war and financed only by fees and a limited number of private donations, with a total administration staff of four or five, with no permanent teaching body, make-shift physical accommodation and equipment, the Ottawa Association for the Advancement of Learning was in its third year of existence operating two institutions of higher learning with an enrolment of over one thousand students.

The vision, determination, and sound judgment of a small group of men led by an eighty-year-old Chairman had established a college for the people of Ottawa which provided educational opportunities for hundreds of young people during the war years when they would otherwise have missed the chance, had developed what has been called the most unusual modern language department in Canada, and had started an institution by which professional training of the highest standards could be provided for civil servants.

In the early months of 1945 it became obvious that special arrangements would have to be made to accommodate the large number of young war veterans returning from overseas. On March 19, 1945, the College opened the first of a series of nine intensive courses each of from four to five months duration. These special courses in matriculation subjects were given in day classes, the first day-time classes in the history of the institution. It was for these courses for veterans, also, that Carleton College employed its first full-time instructors. By the end of August, 1946, when the special courses were discontinued, more than twelve hundred ex-servicemen and women had taken advantage of the facilities offered in making their first approach to rehabilitation.

Meanwhile, the needs of the civilian students were not being overlooked. It was impossible to accommodate them in the day classes, but new teachers were engaged and new courses offered in the evening classes and the civilian registration in September, 1945, was over one thousand.

It was not until September, 1946, that Carleton College came into possession of a building of its own. Early in the war, the Department of National Defence had purchased the Ottawa Ladies College as a barracks for the Canadian Women's Army Corps.[1] This building now became the home of the College, and full-scale day and evening classes were opened here in the fall of 1946.

Two major advances in the teaching curriculum were made

[1]Dr. Tory had been a member of the Board of the Ladies College, and had retained the idea of "reincarnating" it as an educational institution.

at the beginning of the academic year 1945-1946. In response to many requests, mostly from discharged service personnel, a Department of Journalism was established as a two-year course with two years in Arts as the entrance requirements. Requests from other ex-servicemen resulted in a decision to offer subjects in Engineering.

During 1945-1946 the various courses offered by the College were consolidated in a Faculty of Arts and Science and the following year the Institute of Public Administration was absorbed by the Faculty of Arts and Science. The first degrees, three Bachelors of Journalism and three Bachelors of Public Administration were conferred at the Convocation exercises of October 23, 1946.

A few months later the President was dead, but he had lived to see the youngest of the five educational institutions he had helped to establish on its way to become one of Canada's great universities.

At the time of his death, February 6th, 1947, the newspapers of Canada from coast to coast carried tributes to the great Canadian who had just passed away. Of them all perhaps the most moving was that published in *The Carleton*, the twice-monthly publication of the students of Carleton College and reproduced on February 13th in the *Ottawa Evening Citizen.*

THE CHIEF DEPARTS

Faith is the substance of things hoped for,
the evidence of things not seen
—Hebrews XI, 1.

We shall remember Dr. Tory as he appeared at his last Convocation, a striking figure in his academic robes, every inch a fighter for "whatsoever things are true, whatsoever things are just, whatsoever things are pure, whatsoever things are of good report."

He challenged us "to think on these things." With fists clenched and robes whirling he challenged us to participate actively in his great adventure of seeking knowledge and of seeking to use knowledge for the common good. He challenged us to carry on the great work he had started. He expressed the hope that he would live till the day that Carleton was more than a single building, but he fervently exhorted us to ensure that Carleton would become, with or without "Old Tory," the great university that he envisioned. A very great Canadian challenged the people of Ottawa and the students of Carleton College to carry on a great work of tremendous importance in a world that cries for enlightenment.

It has been rightly said in tribute to Dr. Tory that he never lost his "boyish enthusiasm and fervour," he never grew old.

This tribute recalls the story of the professor who was walking across a campus when he suddenly saw a flag at half mast and wondered if it might be for him. The professor realised that he had gradually withdrawn from the daily activities of the world about him. "You don't die all at once," the professor mused, "you die gradually. You're never completely alive or completely dead. And then some day something gives you a little shove over the borderline, and you're more dead than alive, and people say you're dead. You don't really die, you commit death on yourself. You run away from life." Dr. Tory did not die gradually—he died all at once.

To old men in their teens, to very old men in their middle age, to men who think that their life of usefulness is ended in their later years, Dr. Tory presented a moving challenge. He would have left many a young man panting for breath as he flung himself into the task of building great institutions where no immediate material seemed to exist.

A great heart has stopped beating but a great spirit is left for us to benefit from.

To complete the story it is only necessary to add that under Dr. Tory's successors, Dr. M. M. MacOdrum as President, and Mr. H. S. Southam, C.M.G., as Chairman of the Board of Governors, together with an able and devoted staff, the work so well begun has continued with the same energy and vision with which Dr. Tory had inspired the undertaking during his régime. It was decided to proceed without delay to the execution of plans made in the autumn of 1946 for raising by public subscription the $500,000 needed to pay off the debt on the recently acquired building, to enlarge it and to provide necessary equipment. The campaign was launched in mid-February, 1947, immediately after Dr. Tory's death. During the campaign one hundred and eighty-nine subscribers contributed $337,463 to the building fund. A second three-year campaign, the Carleton College Development Fund, was begun in February, 1951, with an objective of $511,000. Subscriptions in the first four months totalled $304,952.

Beginning with the year 1949-1950, support was given by the Province of Ontario—the allocation for the year 1951-1952 being $100,000.

In preparation for the academic year 1947-1948, complete four-year Pass courses and five-year Honour courses were organized, leading to the Bachelor of Arts, Bachelor of Science and Bachelor of Commerce degrees. Enrolment in the winter sessions 1951-1952 in day and evening divisions included 414 full-time students and 683 part-time students in courses for academic credits, and 344 registered in non-credit extension courses, a total of 1441.

On April 10, 1952, Royal Assent was given in the legislature of Ontario to the Carleton College Act, 1952. By it the College is endowed with university powers, with authority to grant degrees, honorary degrees and diplomas. Thus in the short space of ten years another Canadian institution of higher learning has taken its place among the great universities of Canada.

A member of the staff of Carleton College said to the writer recently: "For nearly fifty years Dr. Tory strode like a giant through this country and wherever he stopped he left a monument to remind us of his greatness. Carleton College was the last of them, but it has the same quality of timelessness that characterized the life and works of its founder."

CHAPTER XVI

THE EDUCATOR IN PUBLIC LIFE

THERE IS A LONG-STANDING TRADITION in Canada to the effect that ministers of the Gospel and educators should keep out of politics. Whenever, in our history, the parson or the professor has entered the political field, with rare exceptions the result has not been impressive. Dr. Tory undoubtedly could have been a highly successful politician. He had all the necessary gifts of organization and persuasion. In fact on more than one occasion he was urged to accept political office. The late Jim Cornwall, famous northern leader and promoter, once said to the writer: "Tory could be Prime Minister of Canada if he would concentrate on skinning his own skunks." Through his work on Royal Commissions, and by constant speaking and teaching outside the classroom, Dr. Tory kept closely in touch with public opinion, and there were many occasions when the success or failure of a major undertaking depended upon his genius for winning public support for his plans.

Dr. Tory's enemies, and he had many of them, were for the most part people who resented his influence and activities outside the classroom. His work in promoting the establishment of McGill in British Columbia; his vigorous direction of the struggle for unification of higher education in Alberta; his participation in the move to amalgamate the cities of Edmonton and Strathcona; his administration of the Khaki University, are cases in point.

There were undoubtedly many occasions also, both in Alberta and in Ottawa, when his advice was sought by political leaders. Among his most intimate friends in Alberta were men like the Honourable Charles Mitchell, the Honourable Charles Stewart, Senator W. A. Buchanan of the *Lethbridge Herald,*

Colonel J. E. Woods of the *Calgary Herald*, the Honourable J. E. Brownlee and many others prominent in the political life of the country. In Ottawa, among his friends were the Right Honourable Mackenzie King, J. S. Woodsworth, M. J. Coldwell, the Honourable Thomas Crerar, the Honourable Paul Martin, the Honourable L. B. Pearson, and the Honourable Brooke Claxton, to mention only a few. When his advice or assistance was requested, he gave it willingly, but avoided involvement in party politics.

It was Dr Tory's belief that the educator as a trained citizen has a duty to the state, and few have been more active in their country's service than he was. The voluntary agencies to which he gave generously of his time and energy were, in themselves, an indication of the general direction of his public interest—The Associated Canadian Clubs, The League of Nations Society, the YMCA, the Canadian Citizenship Council, and others.

He was one of the founders and a lifelong member of The Associated Canadian Clubs, and in the early days he vigorously defended the movement against those who suspected it of being a separatist activity. In one of his addresses entitled, "The Canadian Club Movement," he said:

> I would suggest that in no country in the world is an intellectual understanding of the meaning of loyalty more necessary than in Canada. With regard to this I am bound to say that, having lived at various times in five Provinces of the Dominion, and knowing something of the reaction of the parts, one to the other, I am confident that the necessary unity of feeling and sentiment is slowly being brought about. But we must turn from our narrow provincialism. Some of our political discussions do not help in this regard.
>
> I remember distinctly my feeling when one of our foremost public men, speaking in a town in the West referred to a certain place in Nova Scotia as a "God-forsaken place in Eastern Nova Scotia." It happened that the place mentioned was the town and district in which I was born and spent my boyhood, one of the most beautiful on the North American continent. About the same time, a distinguished Canadian, speaking in Montreal, was joyously cheered when he referred to the men living on the prairies as " the prairie parasites."

Canadian unity and Canadian citizenship were subjects to which he returned again and again in his public addresses. One of the problems which gave Dr. Tory constant concern was the Canadian "inferiority complex," which he believed was largely due to our dependence upon the United States. He made a speech on this subject before the New York Canadian Club, in 1926, and was roundly rated by the Toronto *Mail and Empire* for his pessimism about Canada and Canadians. In the same year the Toronto *Globe*, reporting a speech of his in Toronto, underlined this passage:

> I say to you that if we would throw off the mantle of pessimism which has possessed us in the past, and risk the use of the trained and trainable intelligence of our own people, in one generation we would add to the national assets of our common country the equivalent of our national debt.

This confidence in Canada's potential man-power, and her capacity to develop her own natural wealth, was the motivation of his life-long effort to provide training facilities for young Canadians. There was no let-up in the addresses he continued to give on this subject. Month in and month out he told audiences of farmers, business men, school trustees, service clubs, lodges, women's clubs and anyone who would listen to him, that their struggle to develop this great new land would be fruitless unless they made provision for the training of their young people. A reporter in *The Financial Post*, May 4, 1928, wrote of him:

> Tory has the gift of luminous speech. No man can portray the achievements of science to a popular audience better than he, for he has, in an extraordinary degree, the power to articulate technical facts in common terms.

During his life-time Dr. Tory served on a great many public commissions. As early as 1913 he had spent some time in Europe as a member of the American Commission for the study of Agricultural Credits, and had made a thorough study of the European land-bank system. As a consequence he was a natural choice when someone was needed for a study of agricultural credit in Canada. On August 23, 1923, he received the following letter from the Honourable W. S. Fielding, Minister of Finance in the Federal Government:

Dear Dr. Tory:

In connection with the recent revision of the Bank Act representations were made that there was need of some system of rural credits, something perhaps between the chartered banks and the loan companies. The Banking and Commerce Committees, while making no formal representation on the subject, were impressed with the view that there ought to be some inquiry into it.

Another committee of the House of Commons dealing chiefly with agricultural matters, considered the same subject and made recommendations concerning it in a report, copy of which I enclose.

I have already discussed the matter with the President of the Canadian Bankers Association and with representatives of the principal loan companies. They are giving the matter consideration and I am not without hope that they can devise some scheme which will meet the needs of the people. In the meantime I will be glad if you will undertake to conduct such an inquiry as is indicated in the committee's report.

I do not think the inquiry should take the form of a Royal Commission of a number of people. My preference is to select one man to do the work and leave him free as to his methods of inquiry. I shall be glad to receive an intimation from you that you are willing to undertake the work along the lines herein suggested.

Yours faithfully,
W. S. Fielding

Although the administrative demands of a growing university were sufficiently arduous, and he had recently been appointed Chairman of the National Research Council, Dr. Tory cheerfully accepted this additional responsibility. The inquiry involved a thorough investigation of the agricultural credit situation in all of the Provinces, as well as a complete understanding of the systems operating in Europe and the United States. He had been serving as Chairman of the Alberta Tax Committee, which was particularly concerned with the way in which education could be more adequately supported, and was thoroughly familiar with the credit needs of that Province. His work with the American Commission, in 1913, had given him a good working knowledge of the operations of the European land-banks, and of the work of the state organizations in the United States which had been established to assist farmers. But the study which continued for two years, 1923 and 1924, involved painstaking research into the whole Canadian situation.

In order to refresh his understanding of the progress being made in the United States as a result of the 1913 Commission Report, Dr. Tory spent several weeks in Washington in the fall of 1923. On December 31, 1923, he wrote to the Honourable Herbert Greenfield, Premier of Alberta, as follows:

Dear Mr. Greenfield:

I have been in Washington for some time, and I think I have pretty well completed my studies with regard to the American systems—One thing has become quite clear to me, and that is that a general plan involving the coordination of provincial effort into a general national scheme is the only feasible system.

State organizations in the United States for assisting farmers have not so far been a real success and the effort made has been a costly one. The Federal scheme, on the other hand, has been a great success to date, both from the point of view of meeting a pressing need and of securing lower interest charges.

I am writing this letter to let you know that I am hard at work and to express the hope that if you are contemplating any legislative changes affecting agricultural credits, it will not be necessary for you to bring down such legislation until after there is a chance for a conference with you on the subject. With all good wishes for the New Year,

Sincerely yours,
H. M. Tory

At the same time Dr. Tory wrote to the Honourable Charles Stewart, Minister of the Interior, at Ottawa. Apparently Mr. Fielding was ill at the time and he reported briefly to Mr. Stewart instead.

I have been here in Washington making a survey of the operations of the American system of agricultural credit, and have been tremendously impressed with the whole scheme.

In the few years the farm loan banks have been in operation they have loaned one billion and a quarter dollars; have returned to the Federal Government almost the whole of the original investment and have a surplus of $50,000. The losses are practically nil. It is a bold and venturesome scheme, but it appears to have amply justified itself in its effect on agriculture and in public confidence.

I expect to be back in Ottawa about January 12, and I think we should have a conference with some of the Government members who would be responsible for any action that might result from a report. If you think I should go ahead on my own without reference to other members of the Government, I will do so. I think there is no doubt I can have a report ready for March 1st, at least a good preliminary one.

Sincerely yours,
H. M. TORY

His report which was turned over to the government in April, 1924, shows an intimate understanding of the problem of farm debts, the resulting loss of farm productivity in Canada, and the serious effect upon rural people. He urged more generous federal assistance and a closer co-ordination of federal and provincial planning.

In 1930 Dr. Tory prepared important submissions for the Price Spreads enquiry.[1] In 1936 his report as Royal Commissioner on anthracite coal dealt sharply with monopolistic practices in that industry.[2]

In 1930 he accepted the invitation of the Nova Scotia government to serve as Chairman of a Royal Commission to investigate the apple industry of Nova Scotia. The Commission held its first meeting in Halifax in February, 1930, and the final report was completed in August of the same year. Public hearings were held in Windsor, Hantsport, Wolfville, Kentville, Berwick, Middletown, Lawrencetown, Bridgetown and Annapolis. In all, 164 witnesses were heard, representing the production and shipping phases of the enquiry. All this was an exhaustive undertaking for a man actively involved in the planning and construction of the National Research Council building in Ottawa. It is a tribute to the thoroughness of the work done by Dr. Tory and his fellow commissioners, Rev. H. P. MacPherson of St. Francis Xavier University, Horton W. Phinney, Esq., of Halifax, J. W. Boulter, Deputy Minister of Agriculture, Prince Edward Island, and F. W. Swindells, Esq., farmer of Princeport, Nova Scotia, that the report is still

[1]*Report on Price Spreads.* Ottawa: King's Printer, pp. 5091-5144.

[2]*Report of the Royal Commission on Anthracite Coal,* Ottawa: King's Printer, February 3, 1937. P. 120.

referred to in connection with the recurring problems of the apple industry.

A letter to the writer from F. W. Walsh, Deputy Minister of Agriculture for Nova Scotia, dated January 30, 1953, states:

> I have read this report many times and still refer to it—the statements contained in the preamble to the recommendations were in my opinion sound when they were made and still are applicable today, although there have been many changes and readjustments since that time, implementing many of these recommendations.
>
> Some of the changes which have taken place as a result of the investigation and subsequent report have been: compulsory inspection and improvement of grades; a shift over from the barrel to the box for apple packing. At the time the report was made there were over 150 varieties of apples being marketed; as a result of the Commission's work plus the "Tree Pulling Assistance Policy" instituted by the Dominion and Provincial Governments from 1946 to 1950, the commercial varieties have been reduced to some twenty-five. Other recommendations dealt with such matters as spraying, freight rates, refrigerator charges, ventilation, pruning and thinning, financing and marketing.

Under the latter heading, Mr. Walsh says:

> This is most interesting in that it called for the establishing of an overall consolidated company with compulsory powers. It suggests that which many of us believe is proper, namely a large, strong cooperative, handling some sixty to seventy per cent of the apples and the establishment of some type of Marketing Board (which was unknown then) to force the minority to cooperate in a way that would not harm the whole industry.

On the question of ventilation, Mr. Walsh states:

> This recommendation was probably the first of its kind to indicate that ordinary common storage and care was not satisfactory for the holding of apples. I believe that the suggestion to have the National Research Council study this matter was followed up and later cold storages were recommended—a few were established in the thirties and during the past six years four modern cold storages have been built.
>
> The cold storage and the box-pack have played an important part in the rehabilitation of this industry.
>
> Pruning was carried on reasonably well at the time of the report, but there was no thinning. Today thinning of apples on the trees has become a recognized practice.

Dr. Tory's membership in voluntary organizations outside the university had as a major purpose the opportunity it gave him to promote interest in and support for the cause of education and research. As a member of the Federal Conservation Committee, and later as President of the Dominion Fire Prevention Association, he laboured to awaken public opinion regarding the conservation of Canada's natural resources and the protecting of them from exploitation. He was an active member of The Royal Historical Society and The Royal Society of Canada, and was President of the latter organization in 1939-1940.

One of the tasks he accepted which gave him great satisfaction was his Presidency of the Fifth Pacific Science Congress in 1933. He had represented Canada at an earlier congress held in Japan in 1926. The Fifth Congress, held in British Columbia, was in itself an enormous undertaking. In addition to the planning and arrangements for the congress, most of which were handled by Dr. Tory and his associates of The National Research Council, he was responsible for overseeing the preparation of the five volumes of the congress reports.

To one subsidiary of the League of Nations, "The Institute of Intellectual Co-operation," Dr. Tory gave a great deal of time. In 1920 the League Assembly had urged closer co-operation between nations on intellectual matters. A sub-committee was formed to work on university relations, which later gave assistance to European countries where the educational institutions had been in many cases almost destroyed. After 1926 the work of the Institute was that of a clearing house for matters "in the fields of education, science, international artistic life, organization of museums, wireless broadcasting, films, activities in the field of letters, and the scientific study of international relations from the political, economic and juridical standpoints."

Canada did not establish a member committee till 1939. In that year Dr. Tory assumed the chairmanship of the Canadian Committee on Intellectual Co-operation, and the Canadian Department of External Affairs designated the Education Branch of the Dominion Bureau of Statistics as the national centre of educational information for the purpose. In this work Dr. Tory was ably assisted by Dr. John E. Robbins of the

Bureau of Statistics. The Second World War hampered the activity of the committee at first, but soon new opportunities and responsibilities for the committee began to appear. The distress of children in Europe, and the menace of totalitarian educational systems to the future of the world, prompted educationists in many countries to consider, as one remedial effort, the establishment of an International Educational Office, somewhat on a parallel with the International Labor Office. A preliminary conference, held at Harper's Ferry, U.S.A., in 1943, was followed by a succession of conferences with this purpose in view.

Undoubtedly the formation of the Canadian Committee on International Intellectual Co-operation, and the conferences held at Harper's Ferry in 1943 and the following year at Hood College, helped to prepare the way for the establishment of UNESCO and, less directly, for UNICEF. A letter from Dr. John E. Robbins, who was Secretary of the Committee, written June 16, 1953, states:

> In 1946 the Department of External Affairs took the initiative in calling a group together to advise on UNESCO, the delegates to the first annual conference, etc. Dr. Tory and I thought this looked like the beginning of an official committee or "National Commission," and that it would consequently be unnecessary to attempt to revive C.C.I.I.C. The Committee just agreed by correspondence to go out of existence.

Chapter XVII

THE SCIENTIST AS PHILOSOPHER

There was an element of Dr. Tory's character which was not apparent to those who knew him only as a scientist whose compelling interest was in scientific investigation. In his many speeches before service clubs, business men's organizations and scientific societies, as already noted he often appeared to give over-emphasis to the economic values of education.

In an address given before the Alberta School Trustees Association, in 1925, he said:

> A careful investigation of the actual results in wealth production, resulting from education, in the various industrial callings was made some years ago in the United States. By this investigation it was clearly demonstrated, that on the average a man whose education is limited to that given in the public schools increases his earning power only to the age of twenty-five, and henceforth he works through life at the level reached at that age. The man who takes an additional three years of training in some type of high school work increases his earning power until he reaches the age of thirty-five years, at which age his earning power is double that of the one with the more limited education. Further, the man who takes additional higher education necessary to fit him for the greater responsibilities on the average continues to increase his earning power indefinitely, and far beyond that of either of the men in the other two classes.

Similarly, in speaking of the necessity for practical scientific research in agriculture and industry, it was his custom to emphasize strongly the commercial and general economic values in careful investigation. There were several reasons for this. Ever since the days of his youth in Nova Scotia he had been confronted with the prevailing public opinion that while higher education might be useful for ministers, teachers and lawyers, it was of little value in business, industry or agriculture. Education does not prepare youth for practical affairs, they said, and, for that reason, is too costly a luxury. Also the supreme indifference of governments and of the general public toward the scientific development of Canada's great natural resources was to Dr. Tory a source of constant concern. His experiences in the early days of the Alberta Research Council, and later on in the National Research Council, when in 1923 the work and planning of years was casually wiped out by the action of a handful of men in the Senate, convinced him of the need for a prolonged campaign of public enlightenment on the subject. Further, it was obvious that whatever a man's overall philosophy of education might be, the actual money values in solving production problems in agriculture and industry through scientific research could not be over-emphasized. For these reasons he continued to remind his audiences, that the modern university must always be the most practical of all modern institutions, because it aims not only at the development of the intellect but at the solution of every practical problem which requires the trained mind and hand.

In a speech broadcast over the CBC network from Windsor as late as 1936, he said among other things:

> The greatest contribution which the 19th Century made to civilization was the recognition of, and the provision made for, the education of the whole people. It was a tremendous step forward, and no matter how much we may complain about the manner in which the work is done and the taxes associated with it, we all agree as to its utility and necessity. Now, what we do not recognize sufficiently is that the future of our country depends on the use we make in our economic development of the knowledge we have and the degree in which we participate in the discovery of new knowledge.
>
> To show what I mean by that statement, let me sketch briefly what some of the discoveries of the last fifty years have meant to us. Take, for example, the industry which is the foundation economically of the great communities existing in this area—Detroit and Windsor. I refer to the automobile industry. Before this development could take place certain discoveries were necessary. Those we owe to a few men interested in research, first for its own sake, and then, for the use to which its results could be put.
>
> (1) The use of liquid as a fuel. The men who first sensed and

then measured the energy in a drop of liquid fuel were men of genius, even though in their day they were regarded as fools.

(2) Then the technology necessary to give us the internal combustion engine had to be worked out. Who could have foreseen in the beginning that there was sufficient energy in one gallon of gasoline or any other liquid fuel, to move a car weighing three tons for fifteen miles in an almost fool-proof machine? The use of the knowledge acquired in the two directions just mentioned resulted in the greatest industrial development in the history of mankind.

Then take the broadcasting system which I am using to communicate my thoughts to you. The knowledge which made it possible took nearly a hundred years of work and thought by some of the finest minds the world has ever known. First, there was the discovery of the electric dynamo by Faraday; second, the mathematical analysis by which the nature of the energy was understood by Maxwell; third the detection and harnessing of the electric waves by Hertz; and, fourth, the technological development of this equipment with which the names of Sir Oliver Lodge and Marconi and many others will be forever associated. It is estimated today that the value of the industries created by these discoveries is at least five billion dollars, with no limit as to the future. Hundreds of thousands of men and women find employment as a consequence.

May I remind you that a hundred years ago there was not a single industry based on chemistry, as we now know the subject, and that in a recent year there was turned out from the chemical industry of the United States six billion dollars worth of chemical products, and five hundred million dollars worth in Canada, and that the combination of the materials in every product was the result of intensive research in pure science, first carried out on a small scale in some laboratory under the inspiration of a trained mind.

He could not know that, a few years later, a war would boost these figures a hundredfold.

Now it is hardly necessary for me to say that the country first benefits by such activity whose citizens are in the forefront in making such discoveries. Germany led the world at such work in the past and, but for her stupidity in promoting the Great War, would doubtless have the first place in world trade. Other countries are now forging ahead. Japan stands out conspicuously and the Western World has felt the force of her competition. Japan has a thousand scientific experts engaged in her electro-technical laboratories alone. The most conspicuous country at the moment is Russia. She is making unparalleled investment in both men and money for training and research. We dare not be left behind.

These were the truths Dr. Tory had kept emphasizing ever since 1920, and as a result the impression the public formed of him was that of the scientist and administrator with very little interest in or feeling for, literature, music, art, poetry or the finer aspects of education. It would be as absurd a conclusion as to think of Lord Rutherford or Sir William Osler as lacking in an understanding of human nature and in sympathy with its needs.

Great minds—and Dr. Tory's was a great mind—find their motivation and their inspiration in the contemplation of humanity and its search for a better life. These are discovered in the record of man's search for truth and its expression in philosophy, religion, art, music, and the world's great literature. Dr. Tory had taken the regular course in Theology and in addition the Bachelor of Divinity degree. He was a voracious reader of the Greek and Latin classics. He had a photographic memory and quoted widely from Shakespeare, Browning, Matthew Arnold and Tennyson in his speeches.

The University of Alberta celebrated its twenty-fifth anniversary in 1933 with the publication of a booklet called, *These Twenty-Five Years.* In this were learned articles by university professors who had been on the staff since the early days of the institution. Among them were dissertations by his old friends, Dr. R. C. Wallace, Professor E. K. Broadus, Professor John MacEachran, Professor W. H. Alexander, and others. Dr. Tory took the book with him on holiday, and from Guysborough wrote long letters to the authors expressing his delight in each article and pointing out differences of opinion, supported by quotations and suggesting other points of view. These were long, carefully written appraisals of the statements made, and showed an extraordinary understanding and familiarity with literature, philosophy and the classics.

In his letter to Dr. Broadus he says:

> I have read and reread your lecture, each reading increasing my enjoyment of it. I can give no higher praise than to say it is worthy of you at your best; as an analytical presentation of the changing poetic moods of a period—to me, it seems almost ideal.
>
> You may be surprised when I tell you that, from my youth, I have been a constant reader of poetry. In fact when young and

imaginative I used to indulge the hope that one day I might produce something worth reading. I reached the stage after a while when all my efforts went into the waste-basket. Latterly I have sought relief from the intensity of life by reading the Ancients again. Last winter I read *The Glory that Was Greece, The Grandeur that Was Rome,* and *The Tradition of European Literature from Homer to Dante.* Then I turned to Homer and read *The Odyssey;* some plays of Euripides—then I skipped to the Roman period and reread the *Aeneid* and the *Odes of Horace.* Then I jumped to Dante and read sufficient to fix in my mind the scheme and imagery of his poetry. My aim was to get as clear a picture as possible of the extent to which classical ideas still dominate modern writers.

I fear my efforts at appreciation of modern poetry have been limited to trying to judge by Matthew Arnold's criterion—"The substance and matter of the best poetry acquire their special character from possessing in an eminent degree truth and seriousness." I am comforted by the knowledge that the poets themselves often find it difficult to interpret their own writings. Ford Madox Ford's remark about vorticism is a case in point, and is there not a story that someone asked Browning about the meaning of a certain passage in one of his poems, and he replied after reading the passage, that he had not the slightest idea what it meant. Surely if such truth as a poet utters is really worth uttering, it should, both as to form and meaning, be capable of interpretation any time and any place.

I suppose that experimenting with poetic forms, so long as the result is poetry, is as justified as any other experiments in Arts or Science, but I am comforted by the fact that you find some of it silly.

At the same time Dr. Tory wrote to Professor John MacEachran, Professor of Philosophy, and in this letter he outlines, and perhaps for the first time in writing, his thinking about man and his relationship to the unknown and unknowable—the whole field of speculative philosophy.

Let me begin by saying that I read your lecture with the greatest pleasure. It is a fine presentation, beautifully written—an enormous amount of material condensed into a short space, and yet so clear one does not sense the condensing. I am going to comment on some of the topics you treat, not as a technical philosopher but as a layman who has read philosophy and has formed some opinions regarding current thought.

My first difficulty is with the way the philosophers use the word *truth.* I notice you avoid the word somewhat and speak of "philosophical speculation." There seems to be nothing that is final in philosophical speculation. I have read Green and Bradley and

Alexander and I will now read again the *Prolegomena.* I find a tremendous mental stimulation in such reading, and an intellectual enjoyment, but before one gets a settled group of ideas correlated, the outlook is completely changed and nothing remains.

Take the case of Watson.[1] When I was young everyone swore by him. Today he is in the discard with Hegel and Comte and Spencer, and new ideas rather than new truths hold sway. I read, as you know, the honour course in philosophy at McGill, followed by a course in theology. The difference between the two was that one dealt with abstract principles, and the other with concrete doctrine. Intellectually both were unsatisfactory from the point of view of a firm foundation for knowledge. The reason I found such satisfaction in the study of mathematics, and later of physics, was that with a given set of premises you always knew where you were.

This is a paradoxical statement from a man who was never concerned about firm ground, and was always pushing his way into the unknown.

Beginning with a three-dimensional world, you could write down the situation with an exact formula. For four dimensions you could do the same thing. It was only a question of establishing your geometrical basis, and the results follow. Truth from a philosophical stand-point seems such an illusive thing. It does not seem to stay put long enough to christen it as such. Now, I am by nature an idealist. Your own statement of the practical meaning of idealism completely satisfied me: "Not pleasure but self-realization is the idealistic way of life." The effort to practise such a definition is instinctive with me—I accept it as a practical doctrine because it satisfies my mind and it is dialectically defensible.

Then there is another difficulty. I do not quite see why so much is made of disinterestedness in philosophical investigation. I doubt if a *wholly* disinterested mind ever existed. There are some subjects so abstract that they can only be considered in a disinterested way, if at all, because, for the moment at least, they seem to have no relation to life and no concern with practical things. I do not see how subjects like God and religion can be treated merely "with a view to understanding them." They lie so close to life and its activities. They should certainly be considered apart from preconceived notions, unless such notions are based upon substantial foundations. It seems to me that it is all a question of evidence available, and comparison of evidence always leads us into the field of interest. That there have been a few great minds capable of dealing more dispassionately than others with such subjects has

[1]Professor John Watson of Queen's, the greatest living exponent of Kant and Hegel. Dr. MacEachran was a gold medalist under Watson.

meant much in the search for truth, but life and living lie both so near to all our thinking that their action is surely almost automatic.

There is also the fact, even when personal interest does not appear, that racial and national ideas associated with the philosopher's environment enter in as an interest influencing thinking—a sort of mass mind effect expressing itself through representative great minds. This is perhaps the reason why no universally accepted philosophy has yet seen the light of day. I think it cannot be contradicted that even Plato, the most disinterested of all thinkers, was definitely influenced by the political condition of Greece, and his political philosophy coloured by his own difficulties. Your statement that Kant and Hegel "had left the universe under the absolute command of reason" and that "no doubt the absolutism in philosophy served as a very substantial support to the political absolutism which made the Prussian King not only the Emperor of all the German States, but God's chief representative in Central Europe," is doubtless true.

But it can be stated with equal truth, that both Kant and Hegel were influenced in their thinking by the absolutism of the political machinery under which they lived, and that their philosophy was welcomed especially in Germany for that very reason. A similar statement could certainly be made concerning Schopenhauer. His thinking represents the growing national will of Germany—he caught the desire of the ruling classes and made it his own. The same may be said of every philosophy that has arisen in England, France and America—I do not see how it could be otherwise. It would require a mind stored with a universal knowledge to be above the influence of environment, and capable of complete disinterestedness. Could it be that these national moods became necessarily the basis for understanding life as a whole, and that the ultimate harmony of the aspirations of nations would lead to a harmonizing of philosophy?

There is one other phase of the evolution of philosophic ideas that I have not been able to comprehend, and that is the manner in which it seems to me it has been thought necessary to satisfy the demands of reason to put limitations on the absolute. If the absolute "must be self-consistent in the sense that it is completely self-explaining" and be above and *include all relations,* why could relation to the world and man not be included? Why does it render God finite to speak of His relation to us or of our relation to Him, or to speak of His Goodness? Is not this limitation just the limitation of our own minds?

Perhaps after all His Spirit does permeate the whole universe and especially the inner life of man, and that is our greatest claim to superiority and permanence. *If some clue to the nature of God cannot be found in the nature of man, all the speculations of philo-*

sophy will not help us. Viewed scientifically, it seems to me that man's capacity to understand the universe, no matter in how limited a sense, is a definite assurance that he possesses some qualities possessed by the Creative Agency which all admit must be behind the universe, and that Kepler was right when in an emotional moment he said, "My God, I think Thy thoughts after Thee." Perhaps it was a great moment of intuitional activity. I have always, as you know, thought of Bergson as a poet as well as a philosopher. Possibly it is this combination which has made his speculations so penetrating, attractive and satisfying to many thoughtful men. I would say that the mood of science at the moment, as indicated by leading exponents of the scientific position is not materialistic in the old sense, but rather favourable to such view as expressed above.

In my letter to Broadus, I refer in this connection to his quotation from one of Hardy's poems, "Wait"

A star looks down at me
And says: "Here I and you
Stand, each in our degree:
What do you mean to do—
 Mean to do?"

I say: "For all I know
Wait, and let Time go by,
Till my change come"—"Just so,"
The Star says: "So mean I:—
 So mean I."

That seems to me the justified minimum. If I were to follow my own thoughts fully I would be more assertive. Thus (hardly poetry):

What do you mean to do?
Wait and let time go by.
With knowledge as a guide,
And love to point the way,
Faith shall not be in vain.
Hope shall have her reward;
By striving here we shall
The final pageant share,
With the eternal mind.
It may be so: Why Not?

Bertrand Russell of course would not agree with such ideas, but I cannot find any argument from science which justifies his wholly pessimistic attitude. If science has demonstrated anything completely, it is that the universe as we know it is a created universe. I do not think anything is gained by the idea of space-time evolution of the electron. That is only a subterfuge to get the machinery started. Why not say at once that the beginning of matter appears to be a space-time event of which we have no knowledge. The universe however was created at a time which can be roughly calculated. It is also clear that the creative act was completed long ago, and is the basis for all the evolutionary processes which have since followed; life and its associated phenomenon.

The evolutionary process still goes on, for how long in the future we do not know. The picture we have today therefore, is only partial with respect both to the past and the future. The laws of nature as they exist today may not be identical with those of the far-off yesterday or of the far-off tomorrow. They may be part of the evolutionary process. Each age can therefore know the universe in so far as the process is completed and as it exists at the moment, and only so far as the human intellect has itself developed. The evolution of life and mind has been infinitely slower than that of the material universe. We are only getting glimpses now, comprehensive glimpses indeed, just enough to assure us that more, much more, is to come. But these show us an ordered universe of which we can have an understanding.

If God finds expression in this evolutionary process "for the potentialities of His own inner life", and we have been given the power, either through the use of the intellect—or by a subtle intuitional understanding—to follow the steps of the process, it surely cannot be denied that by so doing we are already sharing thought with the eternal source of being, and that our minds are somewhat patterned after His. (I cannot bring myself to say It.) I know that it can be said that this is due to the fact that we are part of nature, but I do not see that that alters the case an iota. I know the same argument can be advanced for the position of intellectual and spiritual activity (e.g. Art and Literature), but in these cases there is no background of ascertained facts to check our ideas against as in the study of the physical universe. If the position is admitted, based on our knowledge, and our power to acquire it, of the physical universe, then the rest follows as a matter of course.

I love your concluding paragraph: "Only that deeper understanding which is born of knowledge and of love will enable us to penetrate the inner secrets of life, to illuminate its true spiritual value, and to give direction in a world of practical affairs." Love and knowledge: a magnificent combination. Intensify these in the lives of men, resting them firmly upon the concept that these two bind us to God in unity of spirit and purpose, and a new and better world of human relations will speedily follow.

I am sure you are tired of this.

Sincerely yours,

P.S. I think you should give me a Ph.D. for this.

In the same little book, *These Twenty-Five Years,* Professor W. H. Alexander had written a provocative article, in which (as was always Doc Alex's custom) he savagely attacked many of the accepted ideas regarding the purpose and values of university education. Dr. Tory had a real affection for Alexander. They had been together from the very beginning of the University of Alberta, and the respect of the two men for each other was based upon their mutual regard for sound learning and skilful teaching. Dr. Alexander was a fine classical scholar and a superb teacher. But the two men were too much alike always to be happy together; both were impulsive, independent, outspoken. It is probable that Dr Tory clashed more frequently with Doc Alex than with any other member of the staff. It is a tribute to the worth of both that they remained good friends.

Dr. Tory also wrote to Alexander, and in his letter he expresses more succinctly than in any of his papers or speeches, his overall philosophy of education:

My Dear Alexander:

First let me say I was delighted with your address. Its form of presentation would of necessity be above reproach because you did it. For the same reason its content would be thought-provoking and so I find it. I hope therefore you will not mind if I give you the results of my own meditation on some aspects of your treatment of your theme.

Now one word with regard to truth for its own sake. If I read aright the history of life in general and mankind in particular, the first and most insistent demand of nature is that life itself should be maintained. The delicate and profoundly mysterious adjustment of nature's processes, through hundreds of millions of years, is without question the greatest argument which science can advance for purpose in nature. The argument becomes infinitely more effective when it is taken in relation to the constant onward movement of life from the lower to higher forms, resulting in the evolution of the intellect. That intelligence in animals, and especially in man, has become an important factor in that selective process which is at work eliminating what is useless and promoting the more useful, no one who studies biological history can possibly deny. The use to which intelligence has been put in every period of the history of life justifies the confidence that to secure continuity is a fundamental process.

Now whether we accept the above as a fair statement or not, the fact remains that the use of the mind to make life secure and more endurable is practised by us all, even by those who most profoundly profess that truth alone is worthwhile. Even those spiritually-minded men who have given their lives for the truth as they saw it did so in the confidence that they were thereby securing a higher life for themselves, as well as making a better life for those who were to come after them.

Dr. Alexander, in his usual trenchant manner, had put forward the idea that the scientist was in fact little more than a plumber.

The fact is, that one can hardly take an abstract idea like truth and separate it out as unrelated to life, and say it is the only thing worthwhile. Now when one comes to think of such an institution as a university, it is easy to idealize it but not so easy to put such idealization into practice. Take your statement from Thomas Aquinas. It has a certain halo about it. First, because of the personality of the man; second, because it is so epigrammatic that it can be completely separated from its context; and third, because it has found a place in the tradition of education. But after all St. Thomas applied the results of his speculative thinking to that one phase of life in which he was especially interested, the religious phase, to the establishment of religious opinion. This speculative thinking in the main could not have a practical application in the ordinary sense, the reason being that it was largely out of the range of human experience. Viewing the whole speculative philosophy of the period of which St. Thomas was the great exponent, I venture to suggest that little of intellectual value has survived, its main value being in that part which had a practical effect upon the lives of men and women who were influenced by it to live better lives. It is interesting as a phase of human thinking—but one would hardly find in it or its methods the foundation on which a university could be reared. The universities as such really did not come into being until the *need* for educated men to do definite tasks was recognized.

Further, I do not hesitate to say that if some of the oft-quoted statements made by Newman had been written by someone less prominent in religious history and less favoured with literary skill, not nearly so much would have been heard about them. In both "What is a University?" and "The Site of a University" he is obsessed with the idea of a centre of learning in which the *unitas intellectus* is the dogma of the Roman Catholic Church, based upon papal authority. Oxford is hardly a university for him because it is not Catholic. In fact he does not approach, except in beautiful phrasing, the ideal of "truth for its own sake."

No better example of Dr. Tory's genius for analysis can be found than here.

To go back a moment to the Greek schools, it seems to me that, in practice at least, Plato's ideal of the importance of truth was nearer "truth for its own sake" than either St. Thomas or Newman. Plato's approach, and certainly that of Socrates, was at least wholly intellectual and not bounded by accepted authority. It was, however, profoundly affected by the political strife of his time. I am convinced that if the start made in the Greek period in the direction of a study of nature had not been interfered with by political strife ending in the fall of Greece, the application of science to life, so characteristic of our own day, would have had its beginnings in Greece. There was no connection between Greek learning and commerce because there could not be; there was no point of contact.

Dr. Tory, as will be seen here did not hesitate to plunge into a field in which Alexander was a great authority.

There is one other aspect of the subject to which I would like to refer. It is true that in the latter part of the 18th Century there were suggestions that the universities might be replaced by professional and technical schools. But was not the real reason the fact that the universities were almost completely out of touch with life, not that they were diligently seeking the "truth for truth's sake?" The modern universities, whatever their faults, have been wiser in this respect. The growth of knowledge and the possibility of its application could not be ignored.

They met the situation in two ways. First, they made provision for the pure sciences as subjects of study and research, and then, through the schools of applied science and medicine, for the application of this new knowledge of life. The effect of this upon speculative thought has been enormous. I am not referring to that type of speculative study which strives to interpret life through literature and poetry, although the influence here has been very great, but to the speculative thought about the universe, its cause, its materials, the forces at work within it, whence it came, and whither it is going.

I agree with you that these questions have not been answered, but neither have they been answered by speculative philosophy, ancient or modern. I do not agree with you that "collection of facts, only, is the work of science." The combining of these into competent theories to explain the facts is now and always has been regarded as the function of the scientist. The truth is, the two things cannot be separated.

The great scientists have all combined the speculative quality of mind with the power and will to observe, but while neither the scientist, nor the philosopher, nor the theologian has yet given us the final answer, science alone has carried us into regions where behind us is a firm basis of acquired knowledge, and before us new fields definitely defined, awaiting the investigating mind. The truth is that progress has been made by the two methods, the extension of speculative ideas and the extension of scientific knowledge.

This was the theme of Dr. Tory's life.

These two methods are bound to be in conflict, but truth is advanced by the conflict and by that way alone. We must use both methods if we are to "prove all things and hold fast that which is good." I have no fear that in the long run the practical sciences will pull down the intellectual life of the university. The world is advancing—the balance has not yet been struck. It will be in due course, and the intellect will still be supreme unless man has reached his zenith and is on the decline, which I for one do not believe.

I think you are rather hard on the student body of the modern university. I know you are not alone in your ideas and I respect the authorities you quote. On the other hand, there is this to be said: the average collegiate institute today is turning out students with much greater knowledge and understanding than the Oxford and Cambridge of the 16th and 17th centuries. I have not the figures before me, but, if my memory serves me, the universities of Oxford and Cambridge, and especially the University of Paris, of the 16th and 17th centuries were as full of students in proportion to teaching power as now, and that the students of that day had no greater love of learning than today. The few then, as now, who became great scholars, were the selected ones from the many. The wastage has always been heavy. Our undergraduate courses of today will be the high school courses of tomorrow. If I were young again I would work for a high school system that would carry students to what is now the second year of study, and let the universities begin at what is now the third year. I cannot bring myself to believe that too many are being educated in a world where the requirements of civilization are based essentially on technology.

I would also suggest to you that, in spite of the material attractions offered to which you refer, the percentage of men seeking advanced study, which is the best evidence that they are seeking knowledge for its own sake, is greater than at any time in the histories of the universities. I know it can be said that even these have their eyes on jobs, and I reply, as in the beginning of this letter, it has always been so, and men must live. It has always been so, in spite of high ideals, and it always will be so.

Please forgive this long screed. You will not agree with much that I have said, but then that is the way of progress.

This preoccupation with literature and philosophy became more and more apparent in Dr. Tory's thinking in the years immediately after his retirement as President of the National Research Council. At the time of his election as President of The Royal Society of Canada in June, 1939, he took advantage of the opportunity provided in his Presidential Address to the Society to present his concept of the essential unity of all knowledge.

Why is it that through the years there has been a cleavage of interest between science and the humanities? The two sources from which man has sought knowledge have been from the material universe around him, and that smaller but equally complicated universe within himself.

The contrast is clear. Science is dealing mainly with the external world of matter; literature with the internal world of the spirit. The point of contact between them is, that both these worlds belong to nature, and each in its own field of activity is constantly using both method and knowledge derived from the other. The two forms of knowledge spring from the same source, the reaction of the mind to the universe. They cannot therefore be really antagonistic. It is only their relation to one another which is misunderstood.

To bring out this contrast, let me quote from a distinguished professor of English Literature:

He does not name his source.

Whereas the business of science is to ascertain, and to set in intelligible and ordered relation, the facts of the physical world, literature takes as her province the life of man in all its aspects and through the feelings quickens that life to a higher consciousness. Of man as a social being science has little to tell us; of his life as an individual, nothing. It may indeed convince his reason that in this vast universe he is but an atom, wholly without significance, yet he remains the centre of his own world, a world greater than that of which science is cognisant, seeing that without it, science would have no meaning.

It is in poetry, however, that rival claims appear most strongly. There is of course a reason for this clash of interest. Poetry is probably the oldest of literary expressions in which man has sought to state his view of his own inner nature in relation to the world in which he lived. The advent of science brought a new approach to knowledge. The external world became the rival subject of study, and in modern times the revolutionary rival. The rivalry started in ancient Greece when Socrates and later Plato began to treat the nature of man as the true subject of philosophy, disdaining the doctrines of the physical philosophers who had preceded them. Let me quote a few short passages from representative writers, to set out the contrast.

There is the oft-quoted passage from Wordsworth: "The man of science seeks truth as a remote and unknown benefactor; he cherishes and loves it in solitude. The poet, singing a song in which all human beings join with him, rejoices in the presence of truth as our visible friend and hourly companion. Poetry is the breath and finer spirit of knowledge; it is the impassioned expression which is in the countenance of all science. The poet binds together by passion and knowledge the vast empire of human society as it spreads over the whole earth and over all time. Poetry is the first and last of all knowledge—it is as immortal as the heart of man."

A briefer definition is that of Dr. Johnson: "Poetry is the art of uniting pleasure with truth by calling imagination to the aid of reason."

Let me also quote from a few representative scientists: Thomas Huxley's statement is well known: "I am the last person to question the value of literary education, or to suppose that intellectual culture can be complete without it."

A more recent writer puts the contrast in these words: "It is for some reasons felt that, if our knowledge of chemistry entitled you to describe water as H_2O, you are incapable of realizing that:

Waters on a starry night
Are beautiful and fair.

and that if you are sufficiently imaginative to liken the Pleiades to a 'swarm of fireflies entangled in a silver braid,' you will necessarily view the nebular hypothesis with indifference."

Sir Richard Gregory puts the contrast thus: "It is commonly assumed that the devotee to science inhibits all sense of pleasure in emotional expression, and familiarity with structure and process of nature breeds indifference to her charms and destroys the aesthetic veil which gives her both mystery and beauty. Science and poetry seem to most people to be poles apart. Yet Coleridge said that he attended Sir Humphrey Davey's lectures in order to improve his stock of metaphors. Though poetry and science represent different attitudes towards nature, they are not mutually destructive and may be complementary to each other. The purpose of poetry is not to present poets, but to express stimulating thoughts in a perfect setting of words. The desire of the scientist is to see things as they are, whereas the poet aims to display the emotional feeling aroused by them."

Science does not want a divorce from literature but closer union with it, and a common understanding of the distinctive qualities by which each can contribute to the fullness of life.

Similarly, in dealing with philosophy and its relation to science, on this occasion, Dr. Tory said:

I need hardly call attention in this gathering to the fact, that in the beginning philosophy and physical science were regarded as a single subject: the first generalizations regarding the nature of the world were deductions from such slight observations of nature as were possible to the state of knowledge of the time—Man had acquired the art of obtaining food, of creating certain forms of wealth, of making tools and weapons and, unfortunately, of fighting for each other's possessions.

Religious systems had been established; substantial astronomical observations had been made and recorded; the stories and legends of the heroes of the past had been committed to writing; travel and trade by land and sea had begun to flourish. The impact of all these activities made possible the beginning of a general study of the universe and man.

For two hundred years, beginning about 650 B.C., philosophy included the physical sciences. They parted company when Socrates declared that the great business of philosophy was not cosmology but "to practise the care and tendence of one's soul." After him philosophy largely confined its attention to the formulation of a rule of life.

Dr. George Sartan, perhaps the greatest living authority on the history of science, defines science as: "Systematized positive knowledge, the acquisition and systematization of which is the only human activity truly cumulative and progressive." On the other hand he says: "Philosophy is a search for a comprehensive view of nature, an attempt at a universal explanation of things. It is both the summary of the sciences and their completion, and like its elder sisters, religion and poetry, forms a separate branch amongst the manifestations of the human mind."

Clearly these two forms of intellectual effort are complementary to each other. This is more apparent when you remember that, in the last few years, the certitude which fifty years ago we attached to the foundations of physics and chemistry has almost disappeared in the light of newer knowledge. Mathematics seems to have the only answers to ultimate questions, and it has become so complicated that only a small number of specialists know what it is all about, when in the higher ranges it is applied to ultimate physical problems.

I turn for a moment to history. If there is a subject to which the scientific sections of The Royal Society should look for sympathy and help, it is history. In Anglo-Saxon countries we have been so absorbed in the progress of science, because of its material benefits, that I fear we have not quite sensed the significance of historical research in the scientific field. Neither have we concerned ourselves much with the relation of scientific history to political and social development.

On the other hand, our historians have concerned themselves with political and social progress, without more than casually relating these changes to the scientific developments which have been largely responsible for them. It is a striking fact that until very recently, apart from courses in philosophy, there has not been in a single one of our universities an organized course in which the relation of science to political and social changes has been presented to students. . . .

After emphasizing the magnitude of the changes in social and economic life brought about by modern knowledge, Dr. Tory then went on to speak of the social sciences and pointed out, among other things, that in this field progress had been slow because the problems to be solved are complicated not only with the materials of civilization but with the social workings of the human mind.

Progress in psychology will be slower still, because it seeks to unravel the more complex problems of the human mind itself, and has taken up the task which the poet, the philosopher and the theologian have each left unfinished.

In the closing periods of this revealing paper, Dr. Tory asked the Fellows of The Royal Society to recognize all new forms of knowledge as a regular part of the work of the Society.

Remember that there was a time when even the Fellows of The Royal Society of London were derided by the intellectuals of their time. Pope wrote of Newton:

> Nature and Nature's laws were hid in night.
> God said, "Let Newton be," and there was light.

Swift in his worst satirical mood could see nothing in the revelations of the microscope, and wrote:

> So naturalists observe a flea
> Has smaller fleas that on him prey,
> And these have smaller fleas to bite 'em
> And so proceed *ad infinitum.*

It was characteristic of Dr. Tory that the shadow of things to come had fallen heavily upon him before many people recognized the shadow was there at all. Seldom had his friends seen him so infuriated as he was over the Munich affair. It was fitting that he should, in June, 1939, close this most memorable of all his public addresses with a reference to the dangers ahead.

Let us never forget that knowledge grows in an atmosphere of freedom. Science, literature and philosophy began their glorious careers in the golden days of the Greek Republics, promoted and cherished by free men. When, after the dark ages, Europe again emerged and began to breathe the breath of freedom, men imbued by the same spirit seized the almost extinguished torch of knowledge and, in spite of political and religious tyrannies, kept it burning down to our own time.

Today a cruel and brutal tyranny is again seeking to bring mankind, body and soul, under the control of a small body of men greedy for power and possession. This struggle is not a dream of something which might occur, it is upon us, stark, deadly, and unremitting. The future of our society as an intellectual force, like all other agencies having a similar aim, is bound up in the struggle. If tyranny succeeds, then liberty, progress and individual freedom will cease to exist in any real sense.

Knowing this to be true, and knowing that no greater calamity could befall the world, this society has placed itself unreservedly at the disposal of the Government of Canada, in the hope that what we collectively possess of knowledge—scientific, literary, historical, economic—might be of assistance in the struggle. In your name I again repeat that offer, knowing as I do, that we are all of one mind in believing that no sacrifice, not even of life itself, would be too great in order that freedom may become the permanent possession of mankind.

Chapter XVIII

CLOSING YEARS

After his retirement as President of the National Research Council in 1935, Dr. Tory and his wife gave a good deal of thought to the possibility of complete withdrawal from all public responsibilities. They both loved to spend their summers at Guysborough, where there was time for reading and quiet hours with old friends. Once, writing from Guysborough to Dr. Lorne Pierce, Editor of the Ryerson Press, Dr. Tory said:

> We will be here for another six weeks. The weather is good, the sailing is fine, the fish are biting, the air is cool, the cream is fresh and the hens are laying. Boy, what a life!

Many of his associates had been urging him to settle down and write for posterity the story of his own life and of the institutions he had founded. But he had served notice in May, 1936, on the occasion when his portrait was unveiled in the National Research Council building, that he did not by any means consider that his work was finished. Shortly after that he wrote to his old friend, Dean Frank D. Adams of McGill University:

> It has always been a matter of concern to me that a man of genius in letters, science or art must of necessity be considered to have finished his effective years at sixty-five, when politicians and men of affairs go on to their eighties in full charge of the destiny of nations. Why should men of sixty-five be considered unfit to continue their work if they show no sign of decadence, while men of seventy or eighty continue as cabinet ministers—or worst of all, sit in power in a country's senate? Many a man in this country and throughout the world who is considered too old at sixty to be a clerk, a professor, or a police-court magistrate is considered just the right age to be Prime Minister of a nation or a province.

The people of Ottawa evidently shared his belief in this regard, for his services were in constant demand by voluntary agencies.

But in 1937 the greatest sorrow of his life-time fell upon him. In that year, after only a short illness, his beloved wife died. She had been his devoted companion for over forty years and her death was a blow from which many of his friends felt Dr. Tory would never recover. Only those who were close personal friends of the Torys could know how much these two people had meant to each other. At the time of Dr. Tory's election as President of The Royal Society of Canada, the *Montreal Standard* carried a long and carefully-written story of his life and achievements and in passing paid eloquent tribute to Mrs. Tory:

> When Mrs. Tory died last year at her home in Rockcliffe Park, Ottawa lost one of the most beloved persons that has ever lived in the Capitol. Across political party lines, in bad times and in good, Mrs. Tory's kindness and warm human affection embraced all sorts and kinds of people, especially women. Husbands might be at daggers drawn in political battles—and the Tory men have been militant Liberals at all times—but the wives all gathered in an atmosphere of direct friendliness that none could resist when they came to sit about, just a comfortable roomful, over a cup of tea with Mrs. Tory. If Dr. Tory's energetic determination to get things done during a long life of great activity has upon occasion ruffled his confrères, Annie Tory quietly smoothed them down again in her drawing room. It made a rare and happy combination.

After her death he must have spent many lonely hours in the Rockcliffe home, living over again the happy years they had spent together, for among his records there are two beautifully-bound volumes in which he had neatly pasted the hundreds of cards, letters and telegrams of condolence he had received from all over the English-speaking world. There could be no thought of retirement now. His very loneliness drove him into action.

That year he completed his report as Chairman of the Royal Commission on Anthracite Coal. On June 2, 1939, he was elected President of The Royal Society of Canada and the following day the *Montreal Standard* in the article referred to above, described him as "One of the most vigorous and aggressively constructive characters ever to enter Canadian public life—a life of advocacy with a constant state of argument describes for Dr. Henry Marshall Tory his own very interesting career."

The same year he became a member of the Board of the Canadian Legion Educational Services. In 1940 he was asked to participate in the work of the Advisory Committee on Rehabilitation which dealt among other things, with the resumption of interrupted education for Canadian service men and women. Writing of this period, Robert England says:

> When I was appointed Overseas Director of the Canadian Legion Educational Services, I spent a couple of days with Dr. Tory in January, 1940, going over the experiences of World War I and trying to chart the future. To his amazing memory of events of twenty-three years before, he joined a keen insight into the difficulties and problems ahead. He delved into a mass of papers and books, all relating to Khaki University, and his enthusiasm burned like a bright flame.
>
> Dr. Tory knew all the handicaps and hazards of an army educational scheme—hesitations of command, difficulties of transport, and the resistance of the troops themselves.
>
> In the library field Dr. Tory and a Maritime Committee developed a regional library project to get books to the troops in the crowded areas along the Atlantic Seaboard. The selflessness and good humour of the man were remarkable.
>
> When the Advisory Committee on Rehabilitation took shape and I became its Executive Secretary in September, 1940, Dr. Tory served on the sub-committee on the "Resumption of Interrupted Education" under the Chairmanship of Walter Woods, Deputy Minister of Veterans' Affairs, and we had the benefit of his advice at every stage of the developing plans.
>
> The idea of inducing the government to back the return on a large scale of veterans to Canadian universities was the sort of project that won his complete sympathy . . .
>
> He did not suffer fools gladly, and could be downright outspoken about "brass hat" obstinacy or bureaucratic arrogance, but he was a genuine humanist and his first love was education.

By that time he had adjusted himself to a new way of life and had recovered his zest for living. The twinkle was back in his eyes again, but he was a quieter man, more relaxed, and his inherent kindness and charity were more evident than ever. Shortly after 1940, he accepted the Presidency of the newly formed Council for Canadian Citizenship (now the Canadian Citizenship Council) of which the writer was a member, and it was good to be associated closely with him again in the work of that organization. He was at his genial best when presiding over a difficult session. His memory of matters discussed at previous meetings, his amazing grasp of detail, and the tolerance and good humour with which he listened to the discussions endeared him to everyone who worked with him. There was no hurry in him now. There was time to move quietly through a disturbed and frightened world; to observe and note, and to decide what were the important things to be done. "Though the vision tarry, wait for it."

Then in 1942 the vision came. It was the dream of a college! He saw it in his mind's eye, just as thirty-five years before he had stood with his back to the Saskatchewan river and had seen rising from his 258 acres of scrub-land, the university that was to be. Professor H. J. MacLeod, one of his early professors at the University of Alberta, and until recently, Dean of Science at the University of British Columbia writes:

> I met Dr. Tory in Ottawa during the time he was just getting started with Carleton College. He invited me to lunch at the Rideau Club and he ran up the middle of the stairs to the dining-room like a youngster—no hand-rails for him even at eighty years of age.

Now he *was* in a hurry again. There wasn't much time and he knew it well. He used all his gifts of persuasion and his infectious enthusiasm to get together the necessary equipment for his classrooms, laboratories, teachers—money to get his new institution started. Who could talk to him now about retiring or taking it easy? The Holy Grail was again in his hands. Time was a thing to spend, not to hoard. If this was borrowed time, he would throw it away like a man who has only a few days to get rid of his riches. So, he gave everything he had to the new college.

It was during his last summer at Guysborough—the summer of 1946—that Dr. Tory became involved in the establishment of the last of his institutions. At his death, in 1944, James Tory, former Lieutenant-Governor of Nova Scotia, had left his Guysborough estate "Belmont Farm" to his younger brother, Henry

Marshall. This is a beautiful property of some fifty acres, with a fine big white house high on a hill overlooking Guysborough Harbour and Chedabucto Bay. Dr. Tory sold the farm but kept the house and the land around it. He had been considering plans for the use of the place after his own death and had considered turning the property into a rest-home for retired ministers of the United Church. But during the winter of 1946 an event occurred which changed his mind.

On February 4th a meeting of Guysborough citizens was held at the home of Mr. L. C. Grant "for the purpose of forming a temporary organization to act in connection with and make all possible progress toward the procuring of a site and the erection of a hospital at Guysborough." The chairman of the meeting, Dr. E. D. Levittan, advised those present that a draft Act of Incorporation had been placed in the hands of the local member of the Nova Scotia Legislature for presentation at its next session. A temporary slate of officers was elected to carry forward the preliminary plans and it was suggested that when a permanent organization was formed Dr. H. M. Tory be appointed Honorary President and the late Professor Ramsey Traquair, former head of the Architectural Faculty at McGill University and then living in Guysborough, the consultant architect. The Chairman further informed the meeting that Dr. H. M. Tory had generously offered to donate a site for the hospital on the Belmont property.

At a subsequent meeting it was decided to write Dr. Tory regarding the possible purchase of his house at Belmont for the hospital. On August 6th, 1946, Dr. Tory who was spending the summer at Guysborough, attended a large meeting of the Guysborough Branch of the Canadian Red Cross and when introduced to the meeting by the chairman, explained his position with regard to the use of his house at "Belmont Farm" as a Red Cross Hospital Building. He was not prepared, he said, to give up possession of his house immediately; it was his intention to give it for use as a Red Cross Hospital as soon as he no longer required it during his visits to Guysborough. He stated that he had already made provision in his will leaving the property to the local hospital organization and suggested that plans be proceeded with at once to make whatever external additions to the building were necessary so that when the time came for him to relinquish occupancy no time would be lost in proceeding with the internal alterations.

Plans were set on foot at once for a financial campaign and after consultation with Dr. Tory who had returned to Ottawa, an architect was chosen to draw up the plans for whatever alterations were required to turn Belmont Farm house into a twenty-bed cottage hospital. Today the beautiful little hospital overlooking Guysborough and its harbour is still another living memorial to a man who never turned his back on any good work.

All that winter of 1946-1947, Miss Erna DesBarres, Secretary of the Guysborough Hospital Board wrote regularly to Dr. Tory, keeping him in touch with the work under way. His letters show that although his health was failing and his duties as President of Carleton College were pressing, he still kept in close touch with the plans for the Guysborough Hospital. He checked the architect's blue-print, made suggestions regarding certain changes he considered desirable, and sent his personal cheque for $500.00 to the Hospital Fund.

On January 11th, 1947, a birthday party was given in his honour by graduates of the University of Alberta resident in Ottawa. One of the features of the banquet held on that occasion was the presentation of a poem by W. S. McDonald, a 1915 graduate of the University of Alberta. After eight verses in which his work in Alberta, with the Khaki University and at the National Research Council are reviewed, the tribute continues:

And still, at eighty-three, he labours on,
Undaunted, unassuming, unafraid.
More genial, perhaps, more at his ease;
So many obstacles in eighty years
He's trampled underfoot,
He cannot recognize them any more.

Far better now than as a callow youth,
I know this man who was but latent then.
Four universities he's brought to life.
What other person ever founded four?

His is a life, not of a world apart,
But of the very fire of earth itself,
Hewing new paths in human history,
Bending the course of history itself,
When shall his country find his like again.

On January 28th, 1947, he wrote his last letter. It was addressed to Miss Erna DesBarres and for the first time there is a break in the firm sweep of his hand-writing.

Dear Erna:

I am returning the plans and letters about an architect: I have been ill for some time and am going into hospital today.

I want the Board to go ahead on their own. Get the architect you please. I would think the Halifax man is the best bet. The only stipulation I make is that strangers be not taken through the house without some responsible person with them as there is valuable material there.

You know, of course, I expect to occupy the house next summer, so no inside construction is to be made until I get to Guysborough.

I am lying on my back writing, hence this scribble.

Sincerely yours,
H. M. Tory

But he was not to see Guysborough again. On February 6th, 1947, Henry Marshall Tory entered that undiscovered country from whose bourne no traveller returns. He would have no fear of such an adventure because he had spent his life in undiscovered countries and it was his custom to walk boldly in new places. The French have a saying that when a good man dies, "He has made the round of his garden." The world he lived in was Dr. Tory's garden; he worked it with his hands, warmed it with his heart and it was fruitful. It is not given to many men to see the work of their hands prosper so fully.

Perhaps in his last moments he would see again the faces of the men and women he had known and loved and like a pageant there would pass before his closing eyes the things he had done, the institutions he had created, and he would know that these would be his monument forever.

The day following his death the newspapers of Canada

from coast to coast carried the story of his life and paid homage to him as one of Canada's greatest sons. On February 10th, the *Ottawa Evening Citizen* said:

The Dominion officially mourned the passing of Dr. Tory at his funeral Saturday afternoon as Prime Minister Mackenzie King, members of his cabinet, and hundreds of educationists, scientists, civic officials and others from both high and lowly stations of life attended the funeral services. All had been his close friends.

Tears of regret at the passing of this unselfish Christian gentleman glistened unashamed in the eyes of many. Theirs was the deep sense of personal loss, which stemmed from the closeness with which they had been associated with the famed educationist-scientist. The service was held in Dominion United Church and was conducted by the Rev. Dr. H. W. Avison. In his eulogy Dr. Avison said, "We are better and richer in character due to the life of this good friend and counsellor, this great scholar, this loyal Canadian, this quiet effective Christian gentleman, who consecrated his attainments to his fellow men and hence to the Glory of God."

Among the tributes quoted in the press across Canada were those of Prime Minister Mackenzie King:

Canada loses in Dr. Tory's passing an outstanding figure in the fields of higher education, of scientific research, and of public service. Illustrious as is the record of Dr. Tory's long and fruitful association with public education in Canada, it does not begin to cover the whole extent of his services. He lent his great abilities on numerous occasions, as chairman or member of important committees and Royal Commissions, both to the Government of Canada and to the provincial governments of his native province of Nova Scotia and his adopted province of Alberta. Through his work on these committees and Royal Commissions and the large part he played in planning the National Research Laboratories at Ottawa he rendered services of incalculable value to Government, to science and to industry throughout our Country.

Dr. Tory's death will be widely mourned by the thousands who knew him and benefited by his great pioneer work in the field of education; by his many co-workers in the field of scientific research, and by all throughout Canada who appreciated his valued services to our Country.

Dr. R. C. Wallace, his successor as President of the University of Alberta from 1928 to 1936, and then Principal of Queen's University, after reviewing his achievements said:

> He was a stalwart in the cause of world peace and intellectual cooperation, an able exponent of science in the modern world and a warm friend to distressed peoples everywhere. There are not many men of Dr. Tory's stature in a generation, for he built the things that will endure.

The Evening Journal, Ottawa, carried an editorial on February 15th, a week after Dr. Tory's funeral entitled "A Great Spirit." Speaking of his courage in embarking upon a campaign for a million dollars for Carleton College in his eighty-third year, it said:

> If Dr. Tory had been given to introspection, the poet's lines might have occurred to him that:
>
> The intent and not the deed
> Is in our power; and, therefore,
> Who dares greatly
> Does greatly
>
> But no more modest man ever lived; and it is certain Dr. Tory never troubled to think that he was doing greatly when he undertook Carleton College—
>
> One reads of faith that moves mountains. The undying spirit of Henry Marshall Tory must have had that sort of faith.

But it remained for Dr. R. W. Boyle, his Dean of Science at the University of Alberta and associated with him for many years in the National Research Council, to provide for Dr. Tory his noblest epitaph. In the closing paragraphs of his memorial prepared for The Royal Society of Canada, Dr. Boyle says:

> It is precisely true that H. M. Tory was a man of his times and exactly suited to his period of Canadian history. Teacher, preacher, philosopher, man of action, he was nevertheless a conspicuous scientist; without leaving treatises or formal scientific contributions on paper or memoirs on specific researches, he was a great missionary and evangelist of research and contributed greatly to

the adaptation of science to his country's needs. Without leaving any formal dissertation of philosophy, he was a philosopher of education and without serving in any legislative hall, he became Canadian Statesman-at-large for both science and education. He was initiator and organiser of institutions designed to last forever; instinctively as it were, he thus pursued his happiness. All his efforts were basic preparations to render fruitful a soil to yield intellectual and spiritual harvests forever.

In front of the Guysborough Academy, high on a hill overlooking the town and the harbour, stands a stone monument erected by the Historic Sites and Monuments Board of Canada to the memory of Henry Marshall Tory. But his name will live in Canadian history as long as time endures and the rivers run into the sea.

INDEX